About the author:

John Donoghue never set out to be to be a
writer... he wanted to be a sailor... and a soldier...
and a policeman.

He has been all of the above and has written
three books covering his escapades so far...

He is still a serving police officer.

Other books by John Donoghue:

Shakespeare My Butt!
*'Marsupial Elvis' to 'No Place' ...ramblings, meanderings,
digressions... and a dog*

Police, Crime & 999
The True Story of a Front Line Officer

For Bethan

ACKNOWLEDGEMENTS

Q. How many proof readers does it take to change a light bulb?
A. Too.

That just goes to show that I have some people to thank... those fantastic individuals who, despite having better things to do, donated their free time and boundless energy to help me out.

Firstly, heartfelt thanks to Sharon, my underpaid and overused editor, who had to buy a new box of red pens just to correct my many errors. I really appreciate your invaluable input, even though you did make me take out that dodgy joke about the party at Spiderman's house.

Thanks to Nancy and Lysa; essential proof reading and medical advice respectively.

Clearly, there is no point having a book out unless people get to hear about it and for that I have Jane to thank for tirelessly promoting my scribblings.

The clever chap that is Rich Endean aka The Creative Agent is responsible for another great cover.

In true Oscar tradition, I'd really like to thank my agent – however, I can't, as I don't have one.

Instead, a big thanks to my friends and colleagues in the police, particularly on E shift – without them, there would be no book. Names and places have been changed to protect the guilty... and if you read this and are offended in any way, please note that I'm a different person than the one you think I am, but just with the same name.

I guess it's here that I say that all the views expressed in the book are my own and not endorsed by any constabulary, living or dead.

If you are a fellow fuzz, I'm sure the incidents and escapades in the book won't come as any surprise to you, as you'll have a million tales of your own to tell. If you are not, I hope this gives you an insight into what the police really get up to – well, this policeman, anyway.

You now hold in your hands the true story of a year in my life as a police response officer, so I guess that the final thank you goes to you, you splendid thing, for taking the time to read it.

So, why not get yourself a cup of tea, and I'll see you back here in five minutes?

I hope you enjoy the book.

John Donoghue

Police, Lies
& Alibis

the true story of a front line officer

John Donoghue

Matador
9 Priory Business Park
Kibworth Beauchamp
Leicestershire LE8 0RX, UK
Tel: (+44) 116 279 2299
Fax: (+44) 116 279 2277
Email: books@troubador.co.uk
Web: www.troubador.co.uk/matador

ISBN 978 1783061 341

British Library Cataloguing in Publication Data.
A catalogue record for this book is available from the British Library.

Typeset in StempelGaramond Roman by Troubador Publishing Ltd
Printed and bound in the UK by TJ International, Padstow, Cornwall

Matador is an imprint of Troubador Publishing Ltd

CHAPTER ONE:

Teaspoons For Arms

"Grab your helmet and get yourself into the town centre."

"I think that may actually be a criminal offence, Sarge... and anyway, it's freezing out there!"

I wasn't exaggerating. There was already a blanket of snow covering the town. It was a bitterly cold morning, and a biting wind straight from the Siberian Steppes was threatening to bring in more snow clouds from the west. It was the type of cold where you trip over the dog turds instead of slipping in them.

It was my first day back since the turn of the year, and I was on early shift. If I was hoping for a gentle introduction back into the job it was clear that I was going to be sorely disappointed.

"I thought I was the town mobile, Sarge." In other words, I was hoping to be able to drive around in a nice warm panda car with the heating set to high.

"Well, Donoghue, you know what thought did?" replied the Sergeant.

"Yes, Sarge, I do." Apparently, he thought he had shat himself, and then found that he actually had. Strange chap.

"Exactly. Now, observe these stripes on my shoulder. Now, note the absence of them on your own. I think you'll find what that means, Donoghue, is that whilst you may be a response driver, when I say you are on foot patrol that is

1

precisely what you shall do. You may find it a bitter pill to swallow, but I'm sure you'd rather take it that way than as a suppository."

It's only a hunch, but I'm guessing that he wasn't really a morning person.

"I'll get my coat."

"Steady on, steady on. We've got a new girl on shift. I want you to take her into town and show her the sights, point out the local Sandford villains, the crime hotspots and so forth. See, Donoghue, I've got your interests at heart. She's up in the canteen making you a cuppa as we speak. Her name is Jessica. She's transferred down from the north of the county."

"What's she like?" I enquired.

"Quirky."

"Quirky good, or quirky bad?"

"Quirky," he repeated, thrusting his hand out towards me. "And Happy New Year, by the way."

"Cheers, Barry," I said, shaking it. He was grinning. I would later learn to recognise this and prepare myself accordingly, but for now I took it at face value. I managed a grimace back although I was still disgruntled at having to brave the elements, even with quirky female company.

"Happy now?" he enquired.

"Nah."

I left the office and went up the stairs to the canteen. A girl in her mid-twenties, with a pony tail and glasses, was standing pouring boiling water into three cups.

"Jessica, I presume?" I enquired.

"John, I presume?" she replied. "I've made you a cup of tea. I'll take mine and the one for the Sarge downstairs. See you there."

After she had left, I searched out my brew; a solitary 'High School Musical' mug stood on the work surface. Oh no, of all the mugs and cups available, why had she used that one! It wasn't even a mug – it looked like something an Easter egg would come in. It didn't even have any handles! I was going to look a right idiot carrying that back into the parade room. In fact, you couldn't even carry it. I was going to have to cup it between both hands, probably making a noise like a hyperactive chimp as it scalded my palms. And it was filled to the brim; I'd never be able to carry it without spilling it all over the place. There was even a meniscus on it! I didn't want to appear ungrateful, but surely it couldn't be that difficult to make a normal cup of tea in a normal mug?

I waited for it to cool, and then started to drink from the top like a dog. What a start to the shift!

Twenty minutes later, and Jessica and I were on our way into town. Wrapped up against the cold in fleece, body armour and with bright yellow fluorescent jackets, we resembled two big lemons on legs... with police hats. As we walked I gave her the lowdown on the area and the shift.

Sandford, known in police radio talk as Kilo 1, was the hub of our area: a dormitory town of about 60,000 people. Kilo 3 was an industrial town to the west, and Kilo 2 was a group of small villages and mining towns to the east.

"There are ten of us on E shift. You've met Barry, our Sergeant – he's a walking encyclopaedia on World War II. At Kilo 3 is George, who is reputed to be older than the internet, along with Ben, our resident rugger bugger. At Kilo 2 we have Geezer, our Londoner, who is always stressing about his weight. We keep telling him to lighten up. Also covering the area is No Nonsense Ron. Finally, at Kilo 1 there's Bob – late of the Zimbabwean police; Lloyd – late for everything; Chad who is the brainy one and Gwen – a lovely lady, and the only one you can hold a sensible conversation with. Oh and last, but not least, there's a new probationer called Andy, who also gets called 'The Boy'. I'll introduce you to them in person when we get back."

"Great," she replied, "And you?"

"I usually cover Sandford town, but on a busy day you can end up anywhere."

"And have you always been in the police?"

I decided against the 'I was born at an early age' introduction, and instead just told her that I'd had a career in the military. After leaving school, I'd run away to sea, or more accurately, caught the train to Dartmouth where I'd enlisted in the Royal Navy. Then, after six years on the high seas, I had transferred to the army, serving Queen and Country throughout the Cold War. When things began to thaw I left, and joined an international security organisation, although it was more budgets and spread-sheets than James Bond and Pussy Galore. Bored, and in search of more fun and excitement, I'd handed back the company car, expense account and keys to the executive toilets, and joined the constabulary.

After I had bared my soul to her I looked over to see her reaction. She was yawning. I guess what she really wanted was for me to ask her what she did. It transpired that she was a keen equestrian.

"Do you fancy being mounted?" I queried.

"I would," she mused, "but the horse sections are slowly being disbanded across the different forces, so response policing was the next best thing for me."

"Well, Jessica," I told her, "I think it's just about the best job I've had. It can be hard sometimes, but there are a lot of laughs to be had too."

"You can call me Jess, if you like," she volunteered. "They sometimes used to call me 'The Owl' at my last station." I checked her warrant number on her epaulettes – 2820. It figured.

"Hang on, if you're joining the shift it must mean someone is leaving." We were never overstaffed. A new starter on the shift could only mean one thing: someone had to be moving on. I hoped it wasn't me. I'd been policing the town for the last year and come to like it. I'd gotten to know the villains and rogues, the trouble spots, the hiding places and even where to go for a decent sausage sandwich in the mornings. Yes, it could be a violent shitty place sometimes, but this was *my* violent shitty place.

As I looked expectantly at Jessica, she responded with a Gallic shrug before giving me a vacant look. It was an expression that seemed to come to her a little too easily.

"Are you cold?" she asked, as we rounded the High Street into the town centre.

"Cold? I'm frozen to the marrow!"

"Are your ears cold?"

"Yes, my ears are bloody freezing.... Hey, hang on! What do you think you're doing, you nutter!"

I found myself having to fend off Jessica's hands from my head. I stared at her in disbelief.

"I was just checking," she replied sheepishly.

"Look, Jessica, I'm a police officer. If I tell you my ears are cold, then they are. Please don't feel as though you have to grab them to ascertain if I'm telling the truth!" I felt it was necessary to add, "You're a bloody fruit loop!" just to make sure I had got my point across sufficiently well.

We walked on in silence. Judging by the gathering clouds, the cold wind and the way the pavement was starting to become slippery underfoot, I'd have wagered that we'd soon have another snowfall that would herald another spate of angry 999 calls. Whenever the snow came, so did the plethora of calls about children throwing snowballs. I think some people forget that they were young once. How dare kids have fun!

Calls to the emergency services about snowballs is one thing, but my friend Nancy in Comms was able to top that. She informed me that just before Christmas someone had dialled 999 or, more precisely, pressed three nines on their phone and asked to be transferred to the police to report the theft... of a snowman.

It wasn't a garden ornament; it wasn't one of those neon light creations; it wasn't a festive gnome... it was a just a snowman... a man made of snow. The operator was at pains to make sure that she had understood the caller correctly.

"A snow man?" her voice was incredulous with disbelief.

She left a pause between 'snow' and 'man' to emphasise the frozen watery consistency of the item being discussed.

"Yes, I hadn't been out to check on him for five hours, but when I went out for a fag he was gone. It ain't a nice road, but you don't expect anybody to nick your snowman."

"Your snowman... your man made of snow?"

"Yes, I made him myself. He had teaspoons for arms," added the caller.

"Well, why didn't you say that in the first place? That makes all the difference! We'll get an officer round there right away."

Actually, I made that last line up. The 'teaspoons for arms' bit is true, but the call handler didn't say we'd get someone straight over. To be honest, I think she was still a little stunned by the whole episode. Instead, I am led to believe that the caller was given 'words of advice'. This is often said by the police when what they really mean is that the complainant was informed that they should stop wasting police time and use their common sense.

I wondered if I should brace myself for a flurry of reports of snowman thefts as soon as a thaw set in? Or perhaps I should steel myself for the inevitable phone call from someone who stumbles on a carrot field, and rings in to report they've found a mass snowman grave?

My musings were disturbed by an urgent call on the radio. "Any units in the vicinity of the town centre. Recent shoplifting from the Red Cross charity shop. Only description is a white female who has stolen a Barbour-style waxed jacket. Believed to be still at large in the town."

"Still at large? Does that mean she's in Evans?" I asked Jessica.

She responded by looking at me whilst making her mouth look like a belly button.

At this stage, if you are thinking: who would steal from a charity shop? The answer is: anyone who thinks they can get away with it. Charity shops don't normally have cameras or security tags, so are considered an easy touch by shoplifters. Don't feel sorry either for the 'poor offender' having to resort to wearing other people's cast-offs – they'll be wearing the latest Nike and Adidas offerings themselves; stolen, no doubt, from their local sports emporium. No, these garments are just to sell on to secure more funds for a quick fix, or beer money. And a Barbour-style sporting or fishing jacket is ideal for any self-respecting thief, with all the hidden poacher pockets for their ill-gotten booty.

As I relayed to Comms that I was already in the town centre, I could hear the sirens in the distance as other units hurried to join in the fun. Catching criminals is what we all join the police for, and now we had one in our midst. The hunt was on!

"All units looking for the shoplifter," Comms were on the radio again. "We've had an update to say she has just left the mini-mart."

It made sense: coffee and bacon are firm favourites for druggies to steal as they can easily sell them on, although I, for one, would rather pay full price for my bacon from a refrigerated counter than get it lukewarm from a sleepy heroin addict, even if it was at a knock-down price.

The radio burst into life again. "Superdrug has just reported a theft at its store."

Toiletries are another target, although judging by the personal hygiene of some of the prisoners I've arrested recently, I don't think it's for their own use. Our shoplifter had certainly been busy, unless we were experiencing thefts from several different criminals – you can never be sure that it isn't a gang hitting the town.

Sandford town centre is pedestrianised, and has seven exits, so even with all available units there still wouldn't be enough of us to block them all *and* have officers on the ground to flush out the thieves. With my colleagues hurtling towards the town centre, I radioed ahead to ask Lloyd to block off the main north exit, Bob the southern exit, and asked Barry to cover the multi-storey car park. Jessica and I would search the shops.

"I'll leg it to the other side of the town centre," volunteered Jessica, "and we'll work our way in." She then ran off to get into position.

No doubt our thief would also have heard the sirens, and might already have made off. We sometimes try a silent approach, without our two-tones blaring, for that very reason. However, on a busy weekend, it is far better to lose a thief than incur an accident because an innocent driver or unsuspecting pedestrian crossing the road is unaware that a police car on an urgent call is about to come speeding by.

Returning to the hunt for our felon, the question now was: how long could they hold their nerve? Chances were that they were still in the town complex. If they had already abandoned the stolen jacket and pilfered gear, they would easily blend in with the hundreds of other shoppers going about their daily business. In actual fact, the description we had for our suspect wasn't that good, but was our offender aware of that? It would be very easy for them to slip into a changing room to avoid detection.

Jessica and I began searching each shop in turn, asking staff if they had seen any suspicious activity – the more eyes looking for the criminal the better – whilst we simultaneously kept a look out in the main shopping area for any likely looking suspect.

"I saw your colleague running," enquired one shopkeeper. "Is there something wrong?"

"I think she always runs like that," I replied, "but there are some thieves about in the town."

After ten minutes of searching, and just as I was beginning to think that our suspect had slipped the net, Barry gave a shout over the airways. From his vantage point on the multi-storey, he had seen a flick of the curtains in the photo booth just inside the entrance to the post office. It was enough to give him reason to believe that was where our villain could be hiding. Jessica was directed into the shop to check it out by eagle-eyed Barry, and as soon as she entered, he reported that someone matching the suspect's description was making a run for it out of the other door.

"She's heading in your direction, John." I could see a rotund figure waddling fast towards me, chased by a noisy Jessica shouting at her to stop. Our thief hadn't seen me as all her attention was directed towards her pursuer. I tucked myself into a shop doorway, ready to grab her as she waddled past. However, just before she reached me, she slipped on a patch of black ice, her legs shooting out in front of her.

There was something almost beguiling and balletic about the way she left the ground; slowly spinning in the air, body perfectly straight, feet moving ever further from the earth, head moving towards the concrete. At one beautiful moment, her frame was parallel with the ground, moving slowly forward as if being propelled on some kind of space-age hover board. When gravity finally caught up with her, she landed unceremoniously on her back with a sickening thud.

I was now in the horns of a professional dilemma: head says no, belly says laugh. Belly won.

"Hello, Mariana, you're nicked." I said, as I walked over to her prostrate form.

Mariana Trench was a regular shoplifter in the town. I've ceased to be surprised to discover that I lock up the same miscreants over and over again. They always seem to have an excuse for the courts and, as a result, seem to get the everlasting 'one last chance'.

Under the current judicial system, being a drug addict appears to be a winning card to play – you'll simply get enrolled on yet another rehabilitation course; being an alcoholic is also advantageous as you'll even be entitled to an increase in your benefits to buy more booze.

The last time Mariana was in court, she said she was 'seeking help for her shoplifting'. Indeed, she was true to her word, and didn't come to our attention for a period of at least two months. The 'help' in question, however, was bringing her little brother along to keep a look out for the security guard. She was eventually caught, and once more brought in front of the judge. "I thought I said I never wanted to see you before me again!" he scolded. "I didn't want to come," was her reply, "but PC Donoghue made me!"

She was currently on bail – the term which some newspapers would have us believe is the convenient arrangement between magistrates and offenders that allows the accused to continue with their crime spree right up until their sentencing date.

I hadn't recognised her initially as normally she was a gaunt, bony specimen. She now looked like a well fed school dinner lady. I appreciate she was wearing an oversized jacket, but she still appeared bigger than usual. Then, before my very eyes, she slowly started to deflate. A creamy goo oozed from her coat, and a wonderful aroma filled the air as various cosmetics and a lipstick floated out into the sticky mess.

"I think I've broken something, PC Donoghue," she intoned.

"I think you are right – about a dozen bottles of L'Oreal shampoo and conditioner, if I'm not mistaken. Why do you do it, Mariana?"

"Because I'm worth it," she groaned, trying to manage a smile. "Seriously, though, I think I've broken something."

"Just lay still, and I'll call an ambulance."

A heavily panting Jessica had now arrived on scene.

"Did you ring me around about midnight, Jess?" I enquired.

"You what?" she replied.

"Doesn't matter."

I decided that at this juncture that it was best to leave Jessica with our patient whilst I checked the town for any other errant wrongdoers. Once we had established that it was just the one rogue felon we were dealing with, we set about getting statements from all the victims. I explained to Barry that the charity shop usually didn't want to prosecute shoplifters, hoping that he would take the hint and use his gift of the gab to help get our witness onside. Whilst I understand that the charities perhaps don't want their volunteers bothered with having to make statements or attend court cases, I am, however, convinced that those of us who give items to the charity would want to see any thief brought to justice. I give my items to be sold on to help those less fortunate, not to assist a drug addict in the procurement of their next fix.

"Leave it to me," commanded Barry in an authoritative tone.

Result! I was looking forward to a master class in charm. As we entered the charity shop, I noticed that the volunteer was an elderly woman who, clearly, must have been shaken by the earlier events.

"Excuse me, Madam, are you sure you're old enough to work here?"

"Oh, young man!" she giggled, as Barry instantly put her at ease with his effortless charm.

"Does your mother know you're out working?" I enquired, keen to join in.

"She's dead," came the flat response, accompanied by the immediate cessation of goodwill. Everything seemed to go quiet. I shuffled my feet, looking down at them before mumbling an almost inaudible, "Sorry."

Barry shot me a withering glance as he tried to get her back on side. "It's just you look so radiant today."

"Do you know how old I am?" she enquired, smiling once again as she fished for the obvious compliment.

I immediately went into a panic. There are a couple of questions women ask that are fraught with danger. One is when they ask if you notice anything different about them, and the other is when you are asked to guess their age. It's like deciding whether to cut the blue, red or green wire to diffuse a bomb. I looked her up and down and gave her my best guesstimate, hoping to win her back onside.

"Seventy?" I queried.

An Arctic blast suddenly swept the room. Barry grabbed my shoulder and took me to one side. "Unless you work at a fun fair, keep your age guesses to yourself," he hissed. "But if you have to guess, always go under!"

"I thought I had."

"I'm sixty-three," she clarified in a flat monotone, interrupting today's lesson in decorum.

After my obvious faux pas, I was deemed 'surplus to requirements' by a vote of two to one, and was told to seek pastures new in the form of taking a statement from the lovely ladies in Superdrug.

Several pages later, I was back at the station, preparing the file for the job. I radioed through to Jessica to ascertain how Mariana was. Her condition was, she informed me, officially diagnosed by the nurses at the hospital as 'hilarious'.

All in all, it had been a successful operation. One felon in police custody, and comprehensive statements from all concerned. In a buoyant mood, I bounded up the stairs to the canteen. As I entered, I noticed Gwen carrying a tray of sausage rolls. They were carefully deposited in the middle of a table that was already brimming with assorted party foods and numerous balloons.

"What's up?" I enquired.

"The mystery of Jessica's arrival has been solved. I know who is leaving the shift."

A shiver went through my body again. It was a good shift. We all worked hard, but had a good laugh too. Nobody wanted to leave. This was our little family now. I prepared myself for the worst.

"So, come on, who is it?" I looked at her, asking the question but also not really wanting to know the answer.

She left a pregnant pause as if she was trying to find the right words. I swallowed hard. I had already started concocting my mental list of reasons why I shouldn't be moved from the station that I loved when she broke the silence.

"It's Bob," she finally revealed.

"YES!" I said, punching the air. "Thank God for that!"

It was only then that I saw Bob sitting despondently in the corner.

"I should have probably rephrased that," I began to explain.

"I'm being transferred up north," he moaned.

"We'll all miss him," explained Gwen, "so I thought I'd treat him to a little spread."

"That's a very nice gesture," I commented, "but I'm sure the buffet would have been sufficient."

Gwen smiled before the implications of my suggestion slowly dawned on her.

"No! No! Oh my goodness!" she stammered. "I didn't mean that! I only…"

Before a flame-faced Gwen could fire back a concerted riposte in defence of her good character I quickly darted out of the door, narrowly dodging a cocktail sausage hurled by the irate party planner.

CHAPTER TWO:

Terror, Like Charity, Begins At Home

Laughing and joking, we all filed in for the nightshift briefing. This was our first duty of the week, and according to the newspapers, today was 'Blue Monday'. Apparently, this was not a reference to bongo films, rather this was meant to be the most depressing day of the year. Statisticians use a complex formula involving post-Christmas debt, early failure to keep New Year's resolutions, bleak weather and low motivational levels to calculate when Blue Monday will fall. Theoretically speaking, this last Monday in January was the day we should all have been at out lowest ebb. However, we were all in a pretty buoyant mood until it was abruptly deflated by the radio signalling one of the scariest incidents I've ever faced.

"Reports of a disturbance at 194 Peel Way. Shouting, swearing, crying and smashing heard from within by a passer-by."

"That's Oxley's address," we chorused, and immediately began throwing on our body armour and strapping on our weapons – as much as a small tin of pepper spray and short metal baton can be classed as weapons. We ran to the vehicles, a series of broken whoops and wails from our sirens heralding our departure from the sanctuary of the station and into the dark and deserted streets. 'Blue Monday' now seemed very apt as we all suddenly became deadly serious. We knew we were in for a fight, and a hard one at that.

Ray Oxley had first been introduced to us at a briefing just before Christmas. Barry had taken us through the pages of his many previous convictions, which had clearly escalated in violence as the years progressed. Oxley was a local 'hard man' who had been jailed three years ago for a series of vicious woundings, but was now out on early release. Far too early for my liking.

A shaven head, emotionless grey eyes, the obligatory broken boxer's nose, and a face that appeared blue black through want of a shave, had stared ominously down at us from the briefing screen. This was a face that looked a decade older than its thirty-three years. At six foot four, and weighing in at eighteen stone, Oxley could be described as the proverbial man mountain. Evidently he had been a body-builder; his arms alone were the size of thighs, and his head seemed to simply emerge from his body. In prison, someone had once called him 'No Neck Oxley'; the inmate in question was called 'No Teeth Tony'. Previously he was just called Tony.

"He looks scary!" we had chorused.

"You have nothing to fear but fear itself," Barry quoted, as he sought to reassure us, rather spoiling it by adding, "And, of course, Ray Oxley running at you with a claw hammer!"

Oh, how we laughed... and oh how we were shitting ourselves now.

I had encountered Oxley a few days after that initial briefing, although I hadn't realised it at the time. I had pulled up outside Tesco in my panda car when a male, wrapped up in a thick coat with a scarf drawn across his face against the cold, had thrust his hand out towards me. "Happy Christmas, Officer."

Instinctively, I responded politely, and proffered my hand back, assuming it was nothing more than a well-intentioned festive greeting. "Happy Christmas," I replied, as I smiled back, shaking his hand.

"Now I know your strong side," he said in a slow, deliberate manner that sent chills up my spine. "I'll remember that when we meet again and, believe me, we will meet again."

I barely had time to mutter, "I'd rather not," before he had slipped back into the crowds of shoppers. It is said that Albert Pierrepoint, one of the last official hangmen in England, used to shake hands with the condemned man in order to estimate his weight, and therefore calculate the length of rope needed for the drop. It needed to be long enough so the spine would snap, but not so long that the head would be severed. Just thinking about Oxley's words made my blood run cold.

Over the next couple of days, nearly all my colleagues experienced similar encounters.

Upon his release, Oxley had moved back in with his girlfriend, Marie, and her four-year-old son, Jamie. According to the domestic violence records, he had physically abused her numerous times in the past, putting her in hospital on more than one occasion. It is said that time heals all wounds, but in Marie's case, it didn't apply as she still walked with a slight limp – a souvenir from all those years ago when he had thrown her down the stairs and broken her leg. Oxley would also have us believe that time wounds all heels, as he had told Marie he was wracked with grief, and full of remorse for all his previous transgressions. He had had time to dwell upon his past he claimed, and if she would only take him back, he would be a different man. She had relented, and the pair had reconciled.

Marie had been warned not to have him back several times, but it was too late. Everyone had warned her: family, friends and even the authorities, but to no avail. She was convinced he had changed. Sadly, she was the only one who believed him. It's a grim fact, but according to a UN study, 75% of women are killed by someone they know – a staggering 35% murdered by their current or ex-partner.

Furthermore, women are much more likely to be killed where they think they are safest: in their own home.

Therefore, when a woman is found murdered in her house, three out of four times the police can reliably assume that she knew her killer, and once out of those three times the murderer will be her husband or ex. Given the sobering statistics, is it really surprising that the partner is usually a prime suspect? Perhaps we ought to spend less time warning women of the danger of strangers and dark alleys, and more about the threat they face closer to home.

This disturbing picture deepens when you learn that over half of ex-cons re-offend within a year of being released from prison.

An alert had been put on the computer system which would immediately flag up if an incident came in for Oxley's address, stating that any call to that location should be treated as urgent. We all knew that something was going to happen there, the only question was when. The instruction also advised that at least two double crews were to attend, and to expect extreme violence. On this occasion, Oxley would have the company of the entire shift.

We rendezvoused at the end of the street while Barry quickly briefed us: two units round the back, two at the front. A quick call to Comms secured a dog unit travelling from the other side of the county as back-up. We then quickly moved into position.

I was in one of the teams at the front. We made a silent approach, and jogged in the darkness towards the address. Once a quick call from the units at the rear confirmed that containment of the address was complete, I banged on the door, and then withdrew a few yards before getting out my pepper spray. I could hear the others behind me, racking their extendable batons.

There was no answer. I tried the door. It was locked. I bent down, lifting the flap of the letter box, listening intently. Then I remembered who we were dealing with, and moved my head to the right so it wasn't directly in front of the opening – I didn't relish the thought of being skewered by a knife thrust through the gap. Still nothing. All was silent.

I shouted through the opening, stating that the police were outside, and demanded that we were let in. Still no response.

The house was in darkness. Perhaps it was a false call or the passer-by had been mistaken. Whilst we checked the details with Comms, Lloyd climbed over the side gate into the garden, and peered through the patio windows. The curtains were drawn. So were our battle lines. However, those lines were soon depleted: an anonymous caller had reported a fight over in Kilo 3 which took away Ben and George; soon after a report of an on-going burglary on the industrial estate meant the departure of Chad and Jess.

Those of us remaining turned our radios right down, peering up at the windows for any signs of movement, straining for the slightest sound, but it was eerily quiet. Gwen and I started to call on the neighbouring houses to find out if anyone had seen or heard anything. They had all been peeking out through the gaps in the blinds earlier, but when we knocked on their doors, the blinds closed tightly and no-one answered. It seemed as though nobody wanted to get involved. Instinct told us something wasn't right.

Another call went up for silence. It was as if we were rescue workers at an earthquake site, listening out for the faintest cry. We stood stock still for a full minute, listening for the slightest sound. Then we heard it: a raised voice. That was just the excuse we needed.

"Boot the door in!" Barry ordered. Geezer and Ron set to work, kicking at the door in turn. Four, five, six kicks, until the bottom panel was smashed through, followed by the whole door slamming open. They barged into the house, batons drawn, quickly followed by Barry and myself. At the rear, I could hear the garden gate being kicked off its hinges as Lloyd and Gwen swarmed into the yard.

The house was pitch black inside. The initial rush was halted as we stood for a second, trying to orientate ourselves. We tried the lights but it seemed that Oxley had cut the fuses. Clearly, he too, had been prepared for the inevitable fight. All the internal doors were closed, and we had no idea what was behind each one. Glass crunched below our boots as we made our way to the first room. Ron tried the handle, instinctively jerking his hand back, informing us loudly that it was covered in some form of grease. Thereafter, all doors would be kicked in. A snarling dog was heard behind the kitchen door – that one could wait.

As we started to slowly inch our way up the stairs, shoulder to shoulder, we felt a rush of cold liquid being poured over us from above. I had no idea what it was, but my thudding heart knew I didn't want to be in that house any longer than was absolutely necessary. Suddenly, and with a roar, Oxley appeared at the top of the stairs, stark naked, holding a flaming sconce of rolled up newspaper, providing just enough light to illuminate his bulging eyes and pock-marked face. A handsome man Oxley was not.

An undignified scramble saw us disappear down the stairs and out of the house. I had no idea what had been thrown over me, but I didn't like the thought of it one bit. Despite the freezing weather, both Geezer and I quickly shrugged off our body armour and soaked fleeces, throwing them onto the ground as far away from us as possible.

"Petrol!" exclaimed Geezer. "My missus is going to go ballistic! That fleece was clean on today!"

For the first time in my policing career, I began to wonder what I had signed up for.

Then commenced a bizarre stand-off: Barry and the rest of us standing outside, whilst a naked Ray Oxley stood at the top of the stairs.

Warrior Celts often used to go naked into battle, shrieking viscerally, bragging and defiant, displaying an outrageous contempt for their own life. It gave them a certain psychological 'edge'. Perhaps Oxley wanted to intimidate us with his unconventional appearance; I can't really speak for my fellow officers, but in my particular case, he was succeeding very well.

Shaka Zulu, the most influential leader of the Zulu nation, had his own reasons for stripping down to a bare minimum what his troops wore in battle. Warriors had previously fought wearing crude leather sandals, but when Shaka took command, he realised that going barefoot would give the advantage of speed and manoeuvrability over their opponents in the cut and thrust of conflict. To harden his soldiers up, he made them dance on fearsomely sharp thorn bushes. Should they flinch one iota, they would be killed instantly.

He also possessed a troop of female warriors whom he would order to strip naked and dance provocatively in front of arrayed lines of equally naked male soldiers. If a male displayed any form of arousal, he would be clubbed to death on the spot. I'm not sure why Shaka Zulu did that. Maybe he didn't want his warriors to be *too* hard.

As Geezer and I stood contemplating our narrow escape, Barry attempted to initiate a dialogue with Oxley: "Where's Marie and the child?"

Oxley reappeared, holding Marie by the hair with one hand, and holding a large shard of glass in the other. She was clearly terrified, shaking uncontrollably as mascara streamed down her pallid face. He threw her out of sight, and turned back to face us.

"Come on, Ray," shouted Barry, "Let Marie go. And where's the kid? Where's Jamie?"

"No one is leaving here," he snarled back, "unless they're in a fucking body bag. And that means you too, copper. I've been expecting you, and now, boys and girls, it's show time."

I don't think it was his intention to invite us in for a pleasant game of cards, unless it was strip poker, but even if it was, it looked like he had started without us.

"I'm going to kill cop tonight!" he roared.

"Does he mean us?" I asked Gwen.

She responded by placing a reassuring hand on my arm. "No, dear," she whispered. "Just you."

I had attended an incident the previous week when a drunken man had phoned 999 for the express purpose of luring an officer to his home so he could fight him. That officer was me. I realised Gwen was trying to ease the tension by joking with me now (at least I hoped she was), but there remains a serious undertone: it would appear that whenever we don the uniform, to those people who wish to vent their spleen of all their nasty, small-minded, vitriolic hatred, we are considered legitimate targets – more so than any other group in society... with the possible exception of gingers.

Repeated attempts to persuade Oxley to release his hostage, and further questions to try and establish the exact whereabouts of Jamie, had proved fruitless. This was a stand-off where time was not on our side. At this stage, all that we knew for sure was that Oxley was upstairs with Marie. Uncertainly abounded: where had all the broken glass come from? Had Oxley booby-trapped the house? Where was Jamie – was he injured? How was Marie coping, and what was her current mental state? Comms had contacted the on-call negotiator, and both he and the Inspector were on their way over, but all this would take time – time that we didn't have. Oxley was a volatile and unstable man who could erupt at any moment.

"Barry, they're false calls." George was on the line to the Sergeant. "There is nothing happening over here. I've been in touch with Comms, and it's the same number that was used to call in the job on the industrial estate. Looks like Oxley made the calls to reduce our numbers at the address. We're on our way back."

Oxley, sensing that his plan had been foiled, screamed that he was going to 'cut Marie up', and that we wouldn't be able to stop him.

It was now that the dog handler, who had arrived during the brief tête-à-tête, slipped the leash off his snarling German Shepherd which raced up the stairs towards the violent thug. Oxley stood his ground and punched the dog hard in the face, sending the animal tumbling back down to land in a heap at the bottom. Our protagonist then sent another bucket of petrol down the stairs, soaking the creature.

"Do you want me to make your doggie go woof?" he taunted, as he grabbed the lighted paper. The handler quickly ran in, and dragged the dazed canine out of the danger area. The ruse had worked though, in that it took Oxley's attention away from Marie, and back to us. Then the most bittersweet of bittersweet moments: before Barry could decide on a Plan B, Oxley let out a thunderous yell, and began bounding down the stairs – three at a time. I could hear the booming as his heavy frame hit each step. A man mountain thundering towards us, hell bent on his killing spree. In his frenzied state he was oblivious to the broken glass underfoot. I knew that this meant he'd also be immune to the pain from our baton strikes.

As he emerged from the house and into the light from the street lamp, I could see that he was clutching an object in his right hand – a claw hammer raised above his head ready to be brought crashing down on an officer's skull. How ironic: Barry must have been psychic. When the petrol had been poured over the dog, we had all retreated, and were a good fifteen yards from the front door, giving Oxley ground to cover to reach us. As he ran towards our line I shone my powerful torch directly into his face, attempting to momentarily blind him, but I probably only succeeded in giving him a clearer idea of where I was standing.

As the psychopath charged towards us, Barry, Lloyd, Ron, Geezer, Gwen and I instinctively fanned out, giving ourselves enough space to wield our batons as we braced ourselves for the onslaught. My life flashed before me in those seconds as he hurtled towards us.

Suddenly, there was a shout from behind, and I heard a crack next to my right ear as a Taser was fired, hitting Oxley directly in the chest. He dropped the hammer, but, unbelievably, he grabbed at the barbs embedded in his torso, tearing them out. Another crack, and a second Taser hit him full on.

"More, more! Give me more, you fuckers!" he thundered, as he dropped to his knees, 50,000 volts surging through his body. He knelt, head bowed as though in prayer, but still snarling contemptuously at the firearms officers, who must have arrived as we were preparing for Custer's Last Stand.

"Give me more! More, or I'll come and kill the lot of you!" Not wishing to be accused of failing to give the customer what he wants, the first officer reloaded. Injuries to police officers are estimated to reduce by over 75% when Taser is deployed. I am certain that their timely use here helped push those statistics just a little higher.

There is an obvious danger when petrol and electrical charges are in such close proximity, so we rushed forward and, for his own safety, dragged a still kneeling, but now very subdued Oxley away from the pools of petrol. An offender going up in flames would have just been *too* much paperwork. Despite his earlier attempts to kill us, we still had a duty of care. Due to the thickness of his biceps, we struggled to get his arms behind his back, and even then we had to resort to joining together two pairs of handcuffs in order to restrain him. Meanwhile, Ron, Lloyd and Geezer made their way upstairs, still wary of potential booby traps, to ascertain the safety of Marie, and to locate Jamie.

Gwen and I were left in charge of Oxley. It appeared that the strong, involuntary muscle contractions caused by the Tasers also had an unexpected side-effect on our prisoner: suffice to say that if he was in Shaka Zulu's army, he'd be having his head stoved in at this very moment.

"Oh, erm… ummm… oh my gosh," was Gwen's restrained response before she decided that her talents were better put to use inside the house.

Oxley then looked up and stared at me, his eyes meeting mine. He didn't shout, but instead spoke clearly and calmly. "I'm going to find you, and when I do, I'm going to tear your windpipe out. Then I'm going to rip you a new arsehole..."

As I was quite happy with the arsehole I had, I decided that a conversation with the firearms officer would be far preferable than listening to Oxley's biologically-themed threats. I caught my colleague's eye, hoping for some light-hearted banter in lieu of listening to Oxley's plans for my various body parts.

"Oxley looks like a steroid abuser," he volunteered. "A guy I knew took too much of one type of steroid and it shrivelled his penis."

"Anabolic?" I asked.

"No, just his penis."

After all the excitement, my adrenalin levels began to fall, and I shivered as I felt the cold night air. I looked back down at Oxley; either he, too, was now feeling the effects of the cold, or the steroids had kicked in.

"I'll get you some clothes from the house," I informed him.

"Fuck off, soft shite," came the retort.

Oxley was led away struggling, and, with some difficulty and much swearing, was placed in a reinforced cage in the back of a police wagon. As he was driven away he was last seen snarling through the bars, much like the animal he was.

Inside the house, Gwen was comforting Marie who, miraculously, appeared to have suffered only relatively minor injuries: superficial cuts from the glass that Oxley had held to her throat, two suspected broken ribs from the sheer force with which he had thrown her to the floor, and a possible fractured cheekbone from where he had punched her full in the face. Jamie was found cowering in his bedroom, physically unharmed, but, no doubt, scarred by the mental and emotional trauma that only the passage of time would unveil. Once paramedics had provided Marie with first aid, and were preparing to take her to hospital, Gwen began outlining the on-going support that was available to her.

Our statements alone would be enough to guarantee Oxley's recall to prison, but her testament regarding her false imprisonment and the events prior to our arrival, would, ideally, ensure he faced a far longer sentence. However, despite the fact that Oxley had tried to murder her and her child, Marie was unwilling to make any statement against him. In all likelihood she needed a cast iron assurance that if she did testify against this maniac he would be sent down for a very long time, and not simply appear at her door in six months' time seeking retribution. It's a difficult dilemma: one can never predict the courts, and then there is always the prospect of early release, promoted by a government intent on reducing prison numbers and costs.

Marie was an intelligent, articulate, decent, hard-working woman – not one you would automatically class as a stereotypical victim. I think she knew deep down that Oxley had to be put away again, but was just paralysed by fear of him. Oxley was a callous, manipulative and vicious bully, who had no qualms in intimidating anyone. It wasn't just physical abuse that she had suffered: it was years of mental subjugation too.

We made no promises, but tried to encourage her to cooperate with us. In situations like this, the actual crime is one matter, but a heartfelt account of how the incident has truly affected the victim can significantly influence the judge when he hands down the sentence. It took days of support and reassurance, but in the end, Marie did testify against her attacker.

We later learnt that Oxley had meticulously planned the entire attack. He had made the anonymous call about the initial disturbance that had dispatched us to Marie's address, he had cut the fuses in the house and scattered broken glass so he would hear us if we tried to creep up on him in the dark.

He had also made the other hoax calls to draw resources away from the scene. Each room was rigged with a variety of booby-traps, and he had a small arsenal of weapons at his disposal at the top of the stairs to use against us. His downfall had been his uncontrolled anger following the dog attack. His unbridled rage had caused him to deviate from his carefully considered tactics. As they say, the best laid plans…

Back at the station, we slumped down into the seats in the canteen, exhausted from the stand-off, and put the kettle on to make a cup of tea which, apparently, would make everything better.

Barry strode in clutching a batch of statement forms, telling us he wanted our own version of events by the end of the shift. "I know your adrenalin is still pumping, but make sure you get your facts straight and spelling correct. Jessica, I'm looking at you."

Last week she had assisted the RSPCA in rescuing horses who had allegedly been given the vote – or so it read in her report. There is a big difference between being 'emancipated' and 'emaciated'. She hung her head in shame.

Lloyd had started to laugh, but quickly curbed his mirth when Barry pointed an accusing finger at him, too. He had been on his way to an incident on the Black Estate where a local troublemaker had blocked the road. Lloyd had told him to move, but the lout had become abusive. A smashed police car windscreen and foot chase had ensued, but the main reason for Barry's glare had been Lloyd's subsequent statement:

I saw Smith standing in the middle of the road and said to him, "Would you please get out of the way?"

He replied, "What the fuck has it got to do with you?"

I told him for a second time to get out of the road and said, "Fuck off, daft cunt!"

Cue broken windscreen and Benny Hill style chase.

"I'm not surprised that Smith got irate if you were speaking to him like that!" Barry had commented. It was then that Lloyd had realised the major impact that a mere solitary word could have if it was missed out. Ten minutes later, and Lloyd had corrected his initial report.

I told him for a second time to get out of the road, and HE said, "Fuck off, daft cunt!"

I was also eager to get things right following the unfortunate incident at my local amateur dramatics society. Shamed, I was asked to leave because I had apparently 'misinterpreted' the stage directions. My script had clearly said 'Enter Juliet from the rear'.

CHAPTER THREE:

Hooray For Boobies!

"Your postman will think you're a slapper," I informed her.

It was Valentine's Day, and Jessica had just revealed to me that today was also her birthday. It wasn't only Jess that had mixed feelings about the day; I did too. It was three years ago today that I had asked my ex-wife to marry me again. She had refused, saying that I was only after her for my money.

February 14th is a strange date to say the least: what kind of perverted saint would want people to fornicate in his memory, for goodness sake!

As we sat contemplating our individual predicaments, I navigated the police car around the big roundabout and onto Dominion Road. I was still introducing Jess to the joys of the different Kilo sections, but this time we were warm and cosy inside a panda car, heading towards the industrial estate.

"Look! There's Steve and Lysa!" I exclaimed, instantly cheering up, and pointing at the ambulance advancing towards us. "We always get on well with the paramedics."

I smiled as I prepared for the traditional friendly exchange of waves. We see our medical counterparts on a regular basis, and close friendships develop through a mutual experience of shared adversity... or so I thought.

What happened next shocked me to the core. As the ambulance drew closer, I saw Steve – my old buddy, Steve –

let go of the steering wheel with his right hand and proceed to give me the universal 'dickhead' sign. Looking straight at me, he raised his hand to his forehead and tugged at the imaginary penis that was stuck there, even staring straight at me as our vehicles passed each other. What the...?

What on earth was going on? I wasn't putting up with this, and especially not in front of my new colleague!

I quickly spun the car around and followed the ambulance, indicating for it to pull over in a lay-by. I was out of my vehicle like a shot and at Steve's window before he'd even fully lowered it.

"What do you think you're playing at – calling me a dickhead?"

"Well, you called me a wanker!"

I was completely taken aback. Mentally I repeated my actions in that preceding minute: I was driving; I looked; I saw; I pointed; I warned him about... then it dawned on me.

"I was telling you to put your seat belt on, you loon!"

I mimed the actions again as I spoke... rapidly pulling an imaginary seat belt across my body several times. Actually, even I had to concede that it did look like I was masturbating a large male appendage, or, indeed, as Steve so eloquently put it, calling him a massive wanker.

"To be fair, John, he's not in the best of moods after that last job we went to," volunteered Lysa, who was now leaning forward to talk to me. "It was another one of those emergency calls that should never have been put through in the first place."

It's not only the police who receive bizarre 999 calls – the NHS also receive more than their fair share of strange requests. Most are weeded out by the call handlers before they get through to the paramedics on the ground, but there are always those that slip through the net.

As it was a good opportunity to show Jessica where the ambulance station was, and with the promise of a cup of tea and some 'tales of the unexpected', we all drove the short distance to their depot. In the rest room, while Steve put the kettle on, Lysa took centre stage and began regaling us with her stories.

Enthralled, we heard the unfortunate story of the woman who rang 999 because she had hiccups, another who contacted paramedics because her rabbit was injured, another who wanted a dead pigeon removed from her loft, and the young couple who had contacted the emergency services because their washing machine had broken.

"And then there are the 'I just sat on it by accident' calls," she added. We all leaned forward in our chairs – these are the A&E highlights that everybody secretly loves. There is nothing like hearing about someone else's misfortune to make you feel better. It appears that it's not just onions that can bring tears to your eyes.

Drug dealers often secrete their stash in various hiding places in an attempt to avoid detection by the forces of law and order. In fact, just the very use of the word 'secrete' makes me feel dirty and desperate to wash my hands. Furthermore, when the word 'secrete' is used, you instinctively know that it will almost certainly lead to one of the most unpleasant tasks that a police officer can undertake in their career: the strip search. Usual procedure is as follows:

A drug dealer, or, indeed, user, is arrested and taken into police custody. Unfortunately for all concerned, he cannot be placed in his cell until the custody sergeant is confident that the detainee hasn't any drugs hidden on or, indeed, inside him.

Protocol dictates that two (unlucky) officers accompany the suspect to the cell where he then strips naked. Clothes are discarded in a heap on the floor, or invariably thrown in the faces of the officers tasked with the duty from hell. The garments are then meticulously searched for anything that the felon is not allowed to take into his cell. When it comes to hiding their drugs, criminals can be quite inventive, and contraband has been found sewn into linings, hidden in folds, or at the bottom of a sock. Every single garment has to be turned inside out, and laboriously examined. In my experience, what makes this such a singularly unsavoury undertaking, is the fact that it seems most druggies are forgetful folk, therefore, washing themselves, and changing their clothes on a regular basis seems to be low on their list of priorities. I have often found myself gagging on the stench from their abandoned attire that has clearly been worn for weeks on end. Layers of socks are peeled off, taking flakes of damp, clammy skin with them, but there is something particularly offensive about checking still warm boxer shorts stained with urine, faeces, blood and other assorted DNA that I'd rather not think about. Sometimes the owner gives them a shake as he takes them off, and a fine mist of unknown particles fills the air. Hands are quickly placed over mouths to avoid breathing any of them in.

However, just when you believe you've reached the lowest point of your day, it gets worse. The suspect is required to squat and cough, whilst you look to see if anything is shaken free, or peeks out from the Black Hole of Calcutta. I've always liked *Star Trek*, but after several searches like this I've seen enough Klingons to last me a lifetime. Moving to the front, it's also alarming what can be hidden under a foreskin: cigarettes, lighters and drugs have been found, and so a roll back is also required. Personal hygiene is no better around the front than it is at the back. Based on the standards of hygiene we have encountered here, I am sure they could do a remake of the 70s private investigator TV show and call it *The Roquefort Files*.

Consequently, when Lysa told us that someone had been found with coke up his rectum, I wasn't particularly impressed (maybe impressed isn't the right adjective to be using here). Reading our expressions, she quickly clarified that she actually meant a bottle of 'The Real Thing' up there. Well, I guess you haven't always got a bottle opener to hand…

One man, she told us, had shoved a vibrator up his anus… and lost it. He was too ashamed to go to A&E because he was human. Instead, he tried to fish out the sex toy with salad tongs. He was later admitted to hospital needing both the sex toy AND the salad tongs removed (and hopefully washed... in bleach).

Another chap lost a mobile phone that he had unfortunately sat on after getting out of the bath... or so his story went. It was still taking calls even as he underwent surgery. Let's hope he didn't have a cheesy ringtone, otherwise the whole incident could have been very embarrassing indeed.

A small model car, she informed us, had also recently made an appearance on the list. I made a mental note that if I got another person complaining that 'a police car was right up my arse', I'd just tell them they needed to find a more suitable toy box.

"It may give us all a laugh, guys," Lysa continued, her tone becoming more serious, "but it doesn't half waste our time." It seems it isn't just English teachers who are upset about improper use of the colon.

Today's abortive mission had been altogether virgin territory for them. A female had phoned in reporting she had a light bulb stuck up her front bottom. The patient wasn't able to give any reasonable explanation as to how it got there and, according to Lysa, she wasn't the brightest. I assume from that, it was a 40 watt.

Was this sort of bizarre experimentation a modern phenomenon I wondered? A product of a society with too much time on its hands, constantly having to push the limits to achieve the next thrill? Or had this sort of thing been going on for centuries? Certainly, if it had happened a hundred years ago, Steve and Lysa would have instead been faced with the dilemma of how to safely extract a Davy Lamp and a canary from a womb with a view.

As for us, recent 999 calls that week had included a couple wanting to know the exchange rate before they caught the plane to Turkey, an elderly incontinent woman who thought her son was trying to electrocute her because he had bought her an electric blanket, a man 'testing' his new mobile, someone reporting a fight on *EastEnders*, and a woman who rang to say she had just watched *The Wicker Man*, and was scared. I tried to get Nancy in Comms to give me the address for that last one so I could go round and make spooky noises outside her house, but she refused. Spoilsport.

I was about to go and apologise to Steve once more for the seat belt/wanker debacle, when I saw Lysa signalling to Jess, enquiring if she wanted to come outside and suck on a midget's pee-pee. Well, either that or she was doing the old 'do you want to come outside for a smoke' sign.

"I've given them up for Lent," replied Jess. Midgets or cigarettes? I was still no further forward.

Then, just as Steve arrived with the tea, our radios burst into life: "Kilo 1 mobile, are you free for a Sierra Delta?"

I'm sure Comms have a special radar that lets them know when you are having a break. Last week, Andy and I had popped to the Sandford Chippy to collect our dinner, and just as we were served an emergency call came in about a fight on the other side of town. We dashed out to our vehicle, jumped in and raced up the street, sirens blazing and lights flashing.

The fact that we weren't going to be getting our food was bad enough, but what was worse was seeing the knowing looks on the faces of the people in the street. Everyone was now convinced, beyond any doubt, that the police only ever use their blues and twos to get back to the station before their chips get cold.

A 'Sierra Delta' is a sudden death... give it to us straight Comms, we can take it!

The sudden death didn't necessitate an immediate response; the body was in the local nursing home, but we had to get there sooner rather than later. I had the choice of getting a furry tongue from a cup of boiling liquid, or forgoing the pleasure of a brew.

Steve had a little giggle as we got up to go to the job, only to be hoisted by his own petard as the same call came through from ambulance control to their radio sets. A minute later, we drove in a sedate convoy to the address.

Sudden deaths are never a bundle of laughs, but I was thankful for small mercies. The paramedics would confirm death, and I could probably persuade one of them to attach the identity tag onto the deceased's wrist on my behalf. I didn't mind being in the presence of a cadaver, but I just didn't relish touching their damp, clammy skin. Physically checking the body all over for signs of trauma or anything suspicious would be up to me and Jess though; there was no avoiding that.

When we arrived, the family were already in attendance. Our victim was a poor old dear in her nineties, who had been in ill health for some time. It didn't take long for Steve and Lysa to do their checks and confirm that she was dead. Frantic whispered negotiations then took place, where the promise of a chocolate orange eventually secured Lysa applying the ID bracelet. I followed the ambulance staff outside as they left, waving them off, and also reminding Steve to wear his seatbelt. This was purely for the sake of his safety and wellbeing, and not connected in any way with his refusal to help out with the wristband, or his subsequent ridicule of my squeamish nature.

I walked in from the cold, and back into the stiflingly hot bedroom. A hushed reverence appeared to have descended. The three relatives, who all looked to be in their sixties, were either sitting in quiet contemplation, or gently sobbing to themselves. I nodded at Jess. It was time for the body check – it could be put off no longer.

"You couldn't give us a few minutes alone with your mother, please?" I was reluctant to perform this task with a distressed audience looking on. However, my request hit a stonewall of silence. Nobody moved and nobody spoke. A second request was met with the same response. It was evident that they wanted to stay with their relative until the bitter end. Then so be it. We would have an audience after all.

I asked Jessica to help roll the dearly departed while I checked for anything unusual. It was quite awkward to manoeuvre the body in the confined space, but as we began to turn her I heard a familiar rumbling noise building up, followed by a rancid smell which suddenly filled the room. Oh, no! The Death Fart!

The flora and fauna of the bowels normally produce gases, but after death the process of decomposition also begins. Additional noxious gases are a bi-product of that process, and that is why after death (amongst other things), bodies become bloated. Pressure builds up from within, and when they reach a certain level, these stale and fusty vapours are expelled via a suitable orifice. The anus is one such convenient and, indeed, tailor-made vent. It's the sulphurous content that makes the expelled gas stink, and stink they certainly do! Granted, it's not a very scientific explanation, and I doubt very much that they are actually called 'Death Farts' in the official text books on the subject, but you get the general idea.

It was Lloyd who actually coined the term after a memorable experience at the turn of the year. He had been helping a funeral director move a body which had farted out loud as they had lifted it. They had all collapsed in fits of hysterical laughter, which is what I wanted to do now, but a glance at the distraught relatives told me that it could be a very bad career move.

The relatives were clearly mortified by the situation: the fact that their beloved mum would forever be remembered in this way. I felt terrible for them. I was a maelstrom of different emotions: I wanted to giggle; I wanted to find a hole to hide in; I wanted to make things better; I wanted to give the family back their dignity. Instead, I just looked down at my boots.

Then, after a few awkward seconds, Jessica broke the uncomfortable silence.

"I'm awfully sorry. That was me."

Bless her! She had just confessed to a serious social faux pas just to save the reputation of a dead woman. What a beautiful, selfless thing to do. It almost brought tears to my eyes, and I don't just mean because of the smell. To sacrifice herself to save the relatives' blushes – she was a better person than I could even aspire to be.

"You didn't need to do that," I whispered. "I would have explained everything to them. That was a lovely thing you did, though." I couldn't help putting my arm around her, and giving her shoulders a gentle squeeze. I'm not usually a 'touchy feely' person, or prone to any outward displays of affection, but she deserved it. She had a heart of gold.

"No, really, it was me. I think I strained too hard."

I quickly pushed her away again.

A very uncomfortable wait with the tearful mourners then ensued until the funeral directors eventually arrived, and we could leave.

Darkness had already descended by the time we got back into our car. The shops in the town were starting to close, and the pubs were beginning to open up. We patrolled the streets for a couple of hours to discourage the criminal element, and to reassure the law abiding citizens. Gradually, men scurrying home with their petrol station flowers were replaced by couples strolling hand in hand to the bars and restaurants.

At around ten-thirty a call came in from the town's nightclub: a male was harassing females. Harassment is a run of the mill job, but what made this more challenging than usual was that the club had reported that he was 'deaf and dumb' – hastily re-worded by a nervous Comms operator to read 'hearing impaired and mute' before it was broadcast over the airwaves.

The average police officer may be prepared to take on knife wielding maniacs and drunken brawlers, but however brave and fearless we may appear on the outside, we all are terrified of the politically correct police... and I feel more vulnerable than most.

When I was seven we went on a family holiday to France. In my absence, and, unbeknownst to me, they changed the currency in the UK from old, mathematically difficult, oversized coinage to new, easy to calculate, decimal money. I accept there must have been plenty of publicity about it at the time, but, at age seven, I wasn't really a big news aficionado, and neither *Scooby Doo* nor the *Clangers* had said sod all about it!

Upon my return to Britannia, I was deeply shame-faced and embarrassed when my thruppence was refused at the sweet shop (and no doubt the owners, Mr and Mrs Whitehead, laughed at my stupidity at not keeping abreast of the important matters of the day). As a direct result, I boycotted the establishment for the next twenty minutes; well, until I could prise the shiny decimal ten pence piece out of the presentation frame my nana had given me.

I say that I feel more vulnerable than most because, like the conversion to the new currency, I seem to have missed out on the 'new Politically Correct expressions' conversion course. Many of the 'pre-decimal' expressions that I grew up with are now outlawed as grossly insensitive, and carry with them a horrified stare, along with the immediate attachment of an 'ist' label. Attach 'ist' to anything, and suddenly that person becomes an abominable pariah, or to put it bluntly, a nasty shit.

My colleagues, however, are always on hand to assist, and if I happen to err they are only too quick to feign having the Dark Ages on the phone, demanding the return of their expressions. Even I have to reluctantly admit that I'm no longer hip, cool and up with all the latest terms, as proved by my ownership of an Ikea club card.

What was once black became 'coloured', and then, as Amy Winehouse said, went 'Back to Black'. Apparently, a dirty old man is a dirty old man no more, but rather a 'dirty old person'.

Even my bank treads carefully in case I indulge in a little cross-dressing at the weekend, addressing me as 'Dear Sir/Madam' in their letters. The same bank who I believe are also branching out into making porn movies, as whenever I contact them they always ask what my first pet was called, and for my mother's maiden name.

My musings had left me no further forward as to how to deal with our deaf and mute suspect, and as we arrived on scene I looked over at Jessica for inspiration. She just sat there with a blank expression on her face.

"Any ideas?" I asked.

She responded by making her mouth look like a cat's bum.

Outside the entrance to the club I could see the door supervisor (bouncer) and a male in his twenties, while the owner (purveyor of cheap booze, and strippers on Wednesdays) stood with a female. Whilst Jessica spoke to the girl, I went over to the guy with the doorman.

It seems that the male, Walter, was loath to let Valentine's Day end without a romantic encounter of his very own. As he was unable to speak and, therefore, use cheesy chat up lines and fail dismally like the rest of us, he had invented his own unique style. His novel approach was to write down on a notepad what he thought of a particular girl, and then hand over his scribbling for her to reply. In some cases, the correspondence back and forth had almost become a novel in itself, so to expedite the process he had opted to draw pictures of how he envisioned the evening unfolding.

I indicated that I wanted to see these drawings, and he handed the pad over to me. It was no more than a picture of two people sharing a candle-lit dinner. I felt quite sorry for our hapless romantic. This didn't really seem like a police matter at all.

Just as I was preparing to leave, Jessica walked over to update me on her findings. "Turn the pad over and flick the corners," she suggested.

As I did so, the two innocent-looking stick people drawn on the corner of the pad leapt into life. Stick person one suddenly was transformed into a stick lady with the appearance of grandiose boobies; stick lady then appeared to drop something on the floor and proceeded to bend over to pick it up. Stick person two used this opportunity to reveal himself as a stick man with the sudden acquisition of an additional half-sized leg. Instead of assisting her with her search, stick man appeared to kick her in the bottom with his new leg... and, oh dear!

In the event of any confusion regarding the animated adventure, Walter had also written a caption. I wrote a message to our Casanova in my police note book, and showed it to him: "You are either being very rude to the girl, or threatening to kill her cat. Either way, you can't say you would like to 'destroy her pussy'."

He read it, and then looked down in shame, as if he had tried to buy something with an old sixpence.

Apparently, I was informed by Jessica, he had been working his way through the whole bar, initially attempting his question and answer technique, but as he became increasingly desperate, he adopted his porno flick book approach.

"He's just annoying everyone, and keeps pestering the girls," explained the bouncer.

A few more messages were swapped between Walter and I before I was convinced he had fully understood that his pestering could be perceived as harassment. 'Just be nice,' I wrote, 'and remember no means no, or we will have to take more serious action.'

'Take my pencil away?' came the written reply.

I didn't have time to draw a series of stick police leading away a stick Walter, so I just pointed to my handcuffs.

When I felt my warning had finally sunk in, I approached the manager and informed him that I had spoken to the male about his behaviour.

"I'll let him know that he's not welcome back after his behaviour towards your female clientele," I informed him.

"Are you saying I shouldn't let him in because of his disability?" replied the owner indignantly. "We don't discriminate against people here. That's deafist."

I don't think 'deafist' is a word, but it's that 'ist' again.

"No, I'm not saying that at all!" I was taken aback by his sudden conversion to pc world. This wasn't the nightclub owner I knew. "What I'm saying is that if someone has usually been accused of harassing females in your establishment in the past you've said they are no longer welcome. Are you saying that's not the case now?"

"Come on, fella." The manager had now wandered over to our mute friend and was shepherding him back into the club. As I looked over to the bouncer he rubbed his fingers and thumb together. I think I had my answer: it transpired the owner had discovered our Casanova was loaded.

We returned to the victim, who seemed to have been ignored in all this as our opportunistic capitalist pampered to our suspect. She was clearly shaken by the incident, and was debating going home after her intimidating experience.

"Well, you shouldn't be drinking when you are pregnant, anyway," joked Jessica, trying to lighten the mood.

"Who's pregnant?" The girl was now standing, hand on hip. At least she wasn't upset anymore – angry I'd say.

"Certainly not you," Jess squeaked.

The girl was pretty, but did have a bit of surplus weight on her... and I could see where my colleague was coming from, and I could also see where she wanted to be headed – back to the car and as far away as possible. I touched my ear piece and leant my head to one side as if listening intently before announcing that there was a job across town that we had to attend immediately. In actual fact, there was no job, but I thought it best we removed ourselves from our current awkward situation. Instead, I drove to the 24 hour Tesco and bought a chocolate orange for Lysa as payment for the wristband application. It was almost home time, and, so far, St Valentine's Day had passed off relatively quietly.

"Kilo 1 mobile. Free for a quick detail?" It was Comms again with another incident to attend. "Just a quick job on your way back to the station. Female wants her partner removed from the house."

When we arrived, it looked like there had been a St Valentine's Day massacre: red stains adorned the lounge walls as well as the clothes of the couple in question. However, it was quickly clarified by the female caller that this had been a case of mutual red wine throwing after an argument, and she just wanted her partner to leave the house. In any domestic, the parties involved tend to need separating to allow tensions to calm. As it was her house, he would have to leave. Whilst Jessica took details from the woman, I tried to ascertain from the male if there was an alternative address he could spend the night.

He began to grumble, protesting about how he had 'bought her a card and everything', flinging it in my direction. I picked it up and placed it on the mantelpiece, reading it as I did so. Fair play; he had made an effort – it's not easy to find a word that rhymes with 'minge'.

He then spent the next ten minutes telling me that there was nowhere that he could go, citing a multitude of reasons why she should leave her house, and let him stay instead. He was drunk, swearing and peppering his justification with abuse; alternating between shouting insults through to his partner, and enlightening me as to why he hated the police. I was indifferent to his drunken tirade – I just wanted him out of the house so the woman could feel safe again. There are over 13 million separate incidents of domestic violence every year in the UK, and I didn't want to be responsible for allowing another woman to become a statistic.

Offering him a lift to wherever he intended to go was met with yet another belligerent response before he went on to inform me, in no uncertain terms, that he would never accept a lift from a pig. Eventually, after it became evident that he wasn't going to go of his own accord, I gave him the option of coming with us in a non-voluntary capacity in order to prevent a breach of the peace, or one last chance to find alternative accommodation for the night. Amazingly, he suddenly remembered a mate in the next street who could put him up.

After a show of putting his shoes on, he was ready to leave. I thought it best that Jess and I accompanied him to this friend's house to verify that he did actually go there. We walked through the deserted Sandford streets in the early hours of the morning, escorting our package to its destination. Our package, meanwhile, swore, taunted, threatened and staggered his way to the front door where we left him, bidding him goodnight.

As we arrived back at the station, the rest of the shift were already preparing to go home. We quickly changed out of our uniform and put on our civilian jackets.

"Look, this is for you," I told Jessica, giving her the chocolate orange I had bought for Lysa.

"It's for your birthday, Jessica. It's nothing to do with Valentine's Day… and don't leave it in the sun, or it'll coagulate into a hard, chocolate cricket ball."

"I'm touched," she replied.

"Well, just don't go around saying that you were touched in return for a chocolate orange, otherwise the Professional Standards Department will be asking questions."

"Well, at least I got something. I almost feel a bit sorry for Walter and that last guy," Jessica told me as we headed out to our respective cars. "Valentine's Day and no treat for either of them."

She had a point. This was the day for overpriced flowers and under-sexed lovers, although, I've often thought that as an alternative to buying extortionately priced bouquets and boxes of chocolates, why not liquor?

"I wouldn't worry about them too much," I told her. "They've both got their own special day coming up soon."

"What's that then?" she enquired.

"Palm Sunday."

CHAPTER FOUR:

The Sandford Two

"All I can think of are Jessica's boobs," I told the sergeant.

"And John handled them very well," chirped Jess, leaving a short pause before sighing, rolling her eyes heavenwards, and adding in a resigned monotone voice, "and I really enjoyed his cock up."

Barry frowned, and left the room.

As we had arrived for duty, he had called us into his office, and asked if anything had gone awry during the previous shift. We had wracked our brains, but all we could think of was Jessica's death fart, telling the woman at the nightclub that she looked pregnant, and me inadvertently calling a paramedic a wanker – not that I would necessarily class that as a cock up anyway.

I had told Jessica not to worry about it, and to just play along with Barry. Whenever he had to break bad news to us, more often than not, he would adopt the 'shit sandwich' technique whereby he would say something positive before and after the negative, so we didn't leave the office feeling too despondent. This was obviously just a shit sandwich in reverse. No doubt something good had come to light; perhaps someone had written in to thank us for a job well done and he just wanted to caveat it with a minor indiscretion so we wouldn't get too big headed.

Barry re-entered the room. He looked stressed and serious. He shook his head at me before turning his attention to Jess. "I think from your response, young lady, that John has been rubbing off on you."

"Sergeant!" exclaimed a clearly affronted Jessica, "That is so rude!"

As his face flushed crimson, Barry deliberately looked down, and pretended to tidy his desk before muttering the order for us to go down to custody straight away to see Inspector Soaper.

"Who's Inspector Soaper?" enquired Jess as we walked down the corridor.

I was about to tell her that Inspector Dick Soaper was my nemesis – nay, my arch-nemesis, but I think it's only superheroes that have one of those. Instead, I told her that for some unknown reason the Inspector had taken a dislike to me. The feeling was mutual. I thought he had left for pastures new, but clearly he was back like the proverbial bad smell.

I informed her that Soaper used to cycle to work in the mornings before showering and changing into his uniform. Rumour had it that on his last day, an anonymous person had secreted a boiled sweet into one of the shower heads. On such an occasion, if all goes according to plan, the unsuspecting shower user is unaware that as he scrubs himself clean, the boiled sweet overhead is slowly dissolving as the water flows over it. Indeed, it's diluted to such an extent that the user is unable to detect any discernible difference in the water. However, when he gets out, and begins to towel himself dry, there is a slight stickiness to the touch. So, of course, he gets back in the shower to wash the stickiness off, and the whole episode starts over again. As all the best shampoo bottles say, rinse and repeat…

Just as I was telling Jess that Soaper was one of those characters determined to rise through the ranks at all costs, and someone who didn't seem to care who he upset on the journey, we turned a corner to find him standing right in front of us.

"Hello, Inspector."

"Donoghue, we meet again." Soaper sounded like he should have been stroking a white cat as he addressed me. I couldn't be certain, but I think he may well have sharpened his teeth since our last encounter. "And you must be Jessica," he said, turning to my colleague.

He was flanked by Daisy, our regular custody sergeant, and Sgt Ingarfield from the previous shift. Behind them I could see the force doctor and one of the crime scene investigators flicking through some paperwork. Everyone looked serious, but that didn't really surprise me now that Soaper was back on the scene.

Jess and I were taken into an interview room by Daisy and Sgt Ingarfield where we were enlightened as to why our presence was required.

"There's been a complaint about something that happened last night," Sgt Ingarfield informed us.

"The doctor will be taking swabs of your hands, and scrapings from under your finger nails," added Daisy.

I hoped they weren't referring to Jessica's comments about me handling her boobs, and I shuddered to think what scrapings would be required if they took her cock-up line seriously.

"The CSI is then going to photograph your hands," clarified Ingarfield.

Jess and I exchanged glances. A complaint? I read from her expression that she was as confused as I was.

"We are going to need your uniform, too," continued the sergeant.

I was confident that this was some sort of mix-up. A fart, a wanker sign, and a non-pregnant female – not our finest hour, I admit, but nothing to warrant this. Something serious must have happened that involved another crew, or even another shift, but certainly not us.

"Sarge, a complaint about what?" I asked.

"An assault that occurred near the end of the shift."

Things were now beginning to make more sense. In the cases of serious assaults or sexual offences, there is always the chance of cross contamination of evidence. For example, DNA from the victim might be found on the suspect's clothing. If the same officer had attended to the victim as well as eventually arresting that suspect, a defence lawyer might claim that the vital forensic evidence was inadvertently transferred via the mutual contact with the police officer. This is why it is always best practice to have different officers dealing with the victim, the crime scene, and the suspect to avoid any such contamination issues.

Deoxyribonucleic acid, or DNA, contains the genetic instructions for all known living organisms, or to put it another way, is an individual's unique genetic blueprint. Everybody's DNA profile is different, with the exception of identical twins (who still have different fingerprints). Despite it being a staple of police investigations nowadays, the technology for a comprehensive DNA database wasn't established in the UK until 1995.

It's now standard procedure to take DNA samples from anyone who is arrested. This is then checked against records held on a national police database to ascertain if the prisoner is wanted for any other outstanding offences. As a direct result, a number of high profile cold case crimes have been solved decades after the initial investigation stalled.

The DNA result doesn't even have to be an exact match to get the investigation reopened. In June 2008, a 19-year-old man was arrested for careless and inconsiderate driving. His DNA was taken as per standard police protocol, and uploaded to the database where it flagged up as a close, but not perfect match, for the probable killer of a young hairdresser. She had been abducted, raped and strangled back in October 1983 – five years before our careless driver was even born. Still, the DNA hit was so close that the cold case team investigated further. Recent advances in DNA profiling indicated that the killer could actually be a member of the driver's family. Further re-testing and analysis eventually resulted in the young driver's father being arrested for the crime. In interview, when presented with the compelling forensic evidence, he subsequently admitted to the murder, nearly 25 years after he had committed it. Furthermore, and equally important, after more than two decades of anguish, the victim's family finally had closure on their daughter's death.

Waking the Dead, the fictional cold case series that was only one letter from being the most controversial TV show ever made, contained lots of story-lines that weren't so very far removed from the truth. Yet having said all that, some campaigners are still trying to reduce the length of time a DNA sample can be kept.

Despite public perception, the taking of DNA is a relatively straightforward process, and to ensure samples are not corrupted, surgical gloves are worn. I'm not sure what exactly goes through the prisoner's mind as I approach, gloved up, but some have instantly backed themselves into a corner, stating that they know their rights, and demand to know where the lube is. In reality, swabs are simply taken from the inside of their mouth. However, judging by some of the people I've arrested recently, it's a wonder that the DNA hits don't all come back to Colonel Sanders, or Ronald McDonald.

As my fingerprints and samples had been taken when I joined the police, I had to speculate that the hand swabs and scrapings that were about to be taken from me now were needed as an extension of my forensic profile. If it was believed that Jessica and I had compromised a crime scene, then they would have to ensure that records were up to date in order to differentiate between police DNA and that of the suspect or victim.

The need for our uniform was easier to explain. Last year, I had been first on scene at a murder. It had been pouring with rain, so I had taken my jacket off and placed it over the victim who was lying in the street. This wasn't done just to preserve the deceased's dignity, but also to ensure that vital forensic evidence wasn't washed away by the rain. Subsequently, my coat had been seized as evidence, never to return. Today, however, I could offer no explanation as to why my fellow officer and I needed to be photographed.

"You should have said at the beginning, Sarge," I said as I finished my musings. "I can see why you need the samples, but I think you've got us mixed up. We didn't attend any assault yesterday. I'll call Barry and find out who did, if you want?" I started to get up, and had my hand on the door before Daisy spoke up.

"No, John. You don't understand. The complaint of assault is in relation to you. *You* have been accused of committing the assault."

Jess and I again exchanged bemused looks. I sat back down.

"You've lost me, Sarge. I've no idea what you're talking about."

Step by step, I was taken through the allegation.

It transpired that it was the most insignificant job we had attended the night before that was at the root of this complaint. The routine domestic which had ended in us escorting the drunken male to a friend's house; the same routine domestic where we had endeavoured to diffuse the situation instead of just arresting him for a breach of the peace, and locking him in the cells overnight.

Later that morning, police had once again been called to the female's house due to the sounds of another domestic emanating from the address. When officers gained access, the drunken, foul mouthed male was back at the property – his conduct as rude and offensive as before. It was almost a re-run of last night's incident; however, this time his face was badly swollen and bruised. He was still drunk and uncooperative, telling the police, in no uncertain terms, that they weren't welcome. When the attending officers asked how he had come by the injuries, he suddenly went silent. His partner closed ranks, too. Unable to obtain any further information, the officers informed him that he would have to be removed from the house again in order to prevent the risk of any further domestic disturbances; that's when he dropped his bombshell. Taking one of the constables aside, he told him that he had been beaten up; beaten up, he clarified, by the male officer who had attended the previous call out. The female officer, he alleged, had simply looked on.

I was dumbstruck.

I tried to think of what could have happened to my accuser to explain away his injuries. When we had left him he was drunk and abusive, but physically unharmed. We hadn't actually seen him enter his friend's house, therefore, had he begun wandering the streets after we had departed? Had he set his lip up against a group of chavs, and taken a beating as a result? Maybe he had gone to his friend's address after all, and had been as abusive to him as he was to us, receiving a few punches to the face as a consequence? Alternatively, was it possible that he had returned to his girlfriend's house, and she had assaulted him? Had her brothers heard how badly she was being treated, and decided to teach him a lesson in civility? Or, had he self-inflicted the injuries to frame me?

This, however, was pure conjecture. So far there were only two facts that I knew:

1. I didn't assault him.
2. He had injuries consistent with having been assaulted.

The constabulary, so far, only knew for certain one of those facts:

1. He had injuries consistent with having been assaulted.

Apparently, he had refused to formalise his complaint when he was visited by the duty Inspector later in the day. Clearly, the hierarchy also had reservations concerning his accusations due to his reluctance to commit the allegation to paper. As such, I wasn't under arrest.

In the meantime, I was left wondering if I was seriously in the frame for the assault, or were the constabulary just at pains to demonstrate that should a formal complaint eventually come in, they could show that they had taken prompt and effective action to capture any evidence, should it exist. If I had beaten him, I would have bruising to my hands, perhaps his skin under my nails, and in all probability, blood or other DNA on my uniform.

With these thoughts racing through my mind, I accompanied Sgt Ingarfield into the medical room. My details were recorded before the doctor carefully examined my hands, swabbing them both, and finally taking scrapings from under my fingernails. Everything was sealed into exhibit tubes and bags, and all of it completed in relative silence. My hands certainly didn't bear the marks of having beaten anyone. In theory, I could have cleaned my nails during my time off duty, but you can't heal bruises to your knuckles in a twelve hour period between shifts. The doctor tried to engage me in light hearted banter afterwards but I wasn't really in the mood.

Next, I was escorted to the small photographic studio, exchanging stunned looks with Jess as we passed in the corridor. The crime scene investigator then took photographs of the front and back of my hands. It was the same CSI who had taken the photographs of my injuries when I had been hospitalised by a violent criminal last year. We exchanged small talk about my stay in the police treatment centre before he apologised for having to take the pictures in such circumstances. I appreciated the sentiment, but accepted that he was only doing his job.

"Sorry, John, I've been told to seize everything for forensic examination. Have you a change of clothing in your locker room?" enquired Sergeant Ingarfield. It was unusual for him to be so pleasant; normally he was an abrupt sort of guy.

I hadn't, so I was accompanied home instead. Throughout the journey neither of us spoke. In the silence I mulled the situation over and over in my head. My dog,

Barney, came to greet me as I walked in the door, wagging his tail, excited that I had come back mid-shift to see him. He then turned his attention to the custody sergeant, running to pick up a toy to present to him, and then rolling over for a belly rub. It wasn't his fault: he was oblivious to the Machiavellian dealings of the human species, and the stress and anxiety I was feeling. I went and got Barney a biscuit, gave him a pat on the head, and then went and got changed. I carefully folded my clothing which was then placed into evidence bags and labelled in front of me.

I got a brand new pair of uniform trousers out of the wardrobe as all my others were in the laundry basket. They were too short. I then ventured into the garage, and got a pair of my old army boots to put on, shaking them vigorously to make sure there weren't any spiders hiding inside. I didn't have any replacement body armour, though. However, it seems that had already been thought of, and a spare set was retrieved from the panda car by the sergeant. I tried it on. "It's tiny, Sarge. It's like a bloody crop top!" I looked like a clown.

I should have known it was going to be a bad day when I had found my first grey pubic hair that morning. It was in a ham sandwich.

I had got up early to take my car in for a service, and had bought the offending snack from a shop at the petrol station next door to the garage. I had contemplated working around the curly hair as I was starving, but in the end I had binned it; not even Bear Grylls would have eaten that. Instead, I decided to walk into town and purchase something from one of the fancy delicatessen shops there. However, things didn't really improve when I found myself in the queue behind a man dithering over what fillings to choose. For God's sake, it's a sandwich. You're not studying the small print before signing an agreement on a bloody worldwide peace treaty!

To darken my mood even further, it had started to rain by the time I'd left the shop, so I opted to catch the bus back to collect my car. As I took my seat a little girl came and sat next to me, cradling a large white cardboard box on her knees – her mother taking the seat across the aisle from her. Every few seconds, the mother chided her daughter in an annoyingly high-pitched voice, telling her to be careful with the box of cream cakes as they were for her grandmother's birthday party, and they needed to be kept perfectly level. If she told her once she told her a dozen times, in a voice loud enough for the whole bus to hear.

I was becoming increasingly irritated, and was seriously considering getting off and walking the last few stops in the rain to avoid this verbal assault on my senses, when a rather large lady boarded and made her way down the bus, stopping to pause for breath right beside us. At that precise moment, the bus jerked as it pulled away. The woman frantically grabbed at the pole for support, and as the bus accelerated, she promptly swung around it, her ample behind landing slap bang on the little girl's lap. In a violent instant, the box was flattened, and cream spurted in all directions. I almost chewed my knuckle off as I tried not to laugh.

I was still chuckling as I reached the garage, paid for the service and drove home. If only I had known what events were to befall me later in the day, I'd have tried to make that moment of mirth last just that little bit longer.

Just as Sergeant Ingarfield and I arrived back at the station, Jess was being dropped off by Daisy, having had her uniform seized too. Blood and gore could have feasibly splashed onto her as she took a ringside seat at this imaginary beating.

As we entered the parade room in Sandford, I realised just how a wounded gazelle on the plains of the Serengeti feels. I'm sure that on a one to one basis, my colleagues would be full of concern and sympathy for my predicament, but when a group of police officers are together, the pack instinct tends to kick in.

"Here comes Krusty the Clown, and Sideshow Bob," shouted George, as Jess and I walked through the door.

"I heard about what's happened," added Ron, patting me

on the back before adding, "Don't worry; things will get a lot worse before they get any worse." Cheers.

"I remember Barry once telling me," began Gwen, "that you only get complaints if you are doing your job properly." Very true. We are paid to get in the villain's faces, and prevent them from carrying out their criminal activities. They are hardly going to write a thank you letter afterwards. Finally, someone with a bit of empathy. However, this was short lived when Geezer added his own interpretation of Barry's quote. "Of course, it's also true that you only get complaints if you are doing your job badly, too."

"If you get banged up, you can always see Ray Oxley again; I'm sure he'd be delighted to see you." Ben's contribution made me wince. I recalled only too well what he had threatened to do to my rear end last time he and I had met. Laughing and joking aside, the stark reality was that if a member of the public was convicted of an assault like this, they would most likely get a community sentence. As a police officer, on the other hand, if I was convicted, I'd lose my job, and almost certainly go to jail. And I certainly did not want to be an ex-police officer in jail.

I knew I was innocent, but it didn't stop those thoughts racing through my mind. I felt helpless, too. So many questions remained unanswered. If I was conducting the investigation, I'd be seriously questioning why the alleged victim didn't want to put pen to paper. Was it because if he did, and it was subsequently proved that he had been lying, he could be prosecuted for perverting the course of justice? Had door to door enquiries been conducted yet? Where was this alleged assault supposed to have taken place? Surely there would be blood found at the scene? At what time did the assault occur? Had CCTV been checked?

I knew I couldn't interfere, or question how comprehensively the investigation was being conducted, for fear that I would be seen to be meddling in the case. There was nothing I could do except wait.

"Why do people do this?" I asked. "I might be just a uniform to him, but this could rip my life apart. What makes these people think they can make these random accusations?"

"When they invent flip flops that don't make a sound, and when the chicken is able to cross the road without everyone quizzing him as to his motives, then you'll have your answer," commented Chad. He could always be relied upon to take the non-emotive stance.

"It looks like we're the Sandford Two," I informed Jess.

"Hang on a second." She took a step back to physically distance herself from me before continuing with her response. "The Inspector informed me that I apparently looked on as you did the fighting. It looks like the Sandford One from where I'm standing."

I could see the beginnings of a smile at the corners of her mouth. Well, at least she found it funny. From the laughs erupting behind me, so did the rest of the shift.

"Anyway," she added, "The Inspector has said that I can't team up with you until the allegation is sorted. I've been teamed up with you, Gwen, for the next couple of weeks."

"You've palmed John off already, have you?" laughed Gwen.

"Gwen!" exclaimed Jess, clearly affronted for the second time that evening. "That's disgusting!"

"No, no... I didn't mean..."

We quickly exited the parade room, leaving behind a highly embarrassed Gwen.

Outside in the car park, dusk had fallen. I got in my patrol car, and slowly made my way to a quiet spot on the outskirts of town. I needed time to just sit and take stock. I had taken comfort in my colleagues' jibes back in the parade room. It was all good natured, and just their own particular way of showing that they cared. I knew that I could pick up the phone to any single one of them if needed, and receive a sensible, sympathetic response regarding my predicament.

The fact remained, however, that, in reality, I was on my own. Realistically, no one could help me. Potentially, the allegation could destroy my reputation, my career, my life. I hadn't even been given a finite time scale – "It'll take as long as it takes," I had been informed.

I was angry, frustrated, confused, but more than that, I felt as though every ounce of energy had been sapped from me. My colleagues must have known how I was feeling, as they responded first to every job that came in that night. At the end of the shift I drove home to be greeted by an over-enthusiastic Barney, and opened a bottle of beer. There was no point going to bed – I knew I wouldn't sleep.

CHAPTER FIVE:

Dear Diary...

The afternoon sun had been playing on the dashboard for the last ten minutes as I sat in the car, looking out of the window... waiting.

It was one of those early March days when the sun shone, turning the inside of the vehicle into a stuffy greenhouse, yet outside it remained cold, windy and miserable. When I was a boy, my dad would drive us to the beach on days just like this. There was always something soporific about the long journey, and when we finally arrived, all I ever wanted to do was to stay warm and cosy in the car, and day dream. Unfortunately, my wish never came true, and instead, I would be ejected, along with my brothers, and forced to march along the beach, buffeted by the freezing cold winds gusting in from the sea. We would walk into the prevailing gale at a virtual forty-five degree angle just to stay upright, and when we turned around to go back, we were carried along at a veritable run. I'd return to the car, my face glowing red from the sand blasting I'd just received.

I wanted to stay in the warm now, but no such luck. The clock on the dashboard indicated that it was two o'clock. It was time to brave the elements, and see what other treasures Pandora had in her box for me today.

Three weeks had passed since the allegation had been made against me, yet there was still no resolution in sight. I had spent two unhappy weeks on leave, thinking of little else other than the possible consequences of the accusation, and now to add insult to injury, I was on the dreaded diary car.

"It's not a punishment," Barry had reassured me, as he allocated the duties.

"Well, it's not exactly a prize either," I had replied.

From the point of view of the constabulary hierarchy, the diary car was a noble concept: for non-urgent matters, members of the public would be given the option of a specific time slot when, by hook or by crook, a police officer would visit them at their home to discuss whatever crime related issue they might have.

In the days before the diary car, complainants would be obliged to wait at home until a response officer became available. However, Sod's Law usually dictated that just as the officer was en route to their address, a fight would break out on the other side of town, or a shoplifter would be reported at Tesco. Needless to say, the officer would be diverted to the on-going incident, leaving the member of the public sitting fuming at home, wondering why nobody had turned up, and concluding that the police didn't care about them, or their woes.

Therefore, in theory, the diary system was also great news for the public. It allowed the police to do what British Gas and Ikea couldn't do: set a specific appointment time and stick to it!

Every single day, members of the public experience a whole plethora of incidents that they feel require advice: from emails from the scam artist formerly known as *Nigerian Prince*, through to incidents of harassment, theft, slander and stalking; calling at all points in between. Sadly, this virtuous new police initiative appears to have been hijacked from the outset, as it quickly became the vehicle of choice used by every yob in town to score points against one another. Until I began my week of diary car duties, I never realised Facebook could be a verb. I have also discovered that text messages have opened up a whole new world of opportunities for cyber bullying between former friends and ex-lovers.

"I'll get the police onto you," has now become a familiar cry on the estates. If you're angry, or upset with someone, why count to ten when you can instant message them with your spiteful thoughts? Why try to rise above it when you can text back a vindictive, hot-headed response?

More to the point, now that the diary car was in operation, as far as the Chavs and Chavettes in the town were concerned, why try and resolve your own issues in a civilised manner when you can get the police involved, and have your adversary served with a harassment warning into the bargain?

After reading a series of acrimonious and bitter messages on social media sites, as part of my innovative solution I usually advise the caller to take a radical course of action, and simply delete the other party off their friends list. "You won't see the likes of them again," I tell them. It's a Facebook joke; don't worry, they don't laugh either. And to think I waste my time on this valuable social platform by just using it to post rude pictures of vegetables and of dogs making funny faces.

When we enter the fray, the exchange of venomous text messages has usually been going on for days. Of course, the person who rings in to complain about the latest malicious message they have received doesn't always seem to appreciate that, as police, we will thoroughly investigate their concern. At the very least, this will involve scrolling down to see what correspondence they've previously, or, indeed, subsequently sent. I have often had to resort to explaining that two wrongs don't make a right.

"You what?"

"She might have texted, calling you a name, but you shouldn't have sent her a message insulting her back."

"Eh?"

I then recount my poo flinging monkey analogy. If you fling poo at the monkey you will still get thrown out of the zoo, even if the monkey started it. I believe it's called an analogy because they are both behaving like arses.

Sometimes, however, poor spelling can dilute the brooding darkness of a threat; indeed I would be inclined to think I was in for a treat if an ex-girlfriend sent me a text saying: 'You will face my furry'. Not too furry, though; that's so 1970's.

Of course, there was a reason for this (misspelt) threat. The reason being that our protagonist had sent his former partner a text, informing her she was 'a lying, useless, skanker retard' – Lord Byron he was not.

"How very charming of you," I had informed him.

"Really?" he replied, seeming pleased that I had taken his side.

"No, I was being ironic," I told him. When he gave me a blank look, I thought I ought to clarify what I meant. "Irony: the opposite of wrinkly." He seemed satisfied with that explanation.

Nevertheless, not wishing to make light of it, I warned him to stop sending insulting, hurtful messages to her. Perhaps to him it was simple name calling, but things can escalate. Nobody likes being called names. Name calling can get people into trouble; name calling can cause diplomatic rows.

If you don't know the story, some years ago a British primary school teacher working in the Sudan asked the children in her class to think of a name for a teddy bear. The excited boys and girls chose the name Mohammed for their new mascot. Astonishingly, the teacher was promptly arrested and imprisoned by the Sudanese authorities for insulting the holy prophet. Eventually, after significant and delicate diplomatic intervention, common sense prevailed, and the teacher was released. Clearly it was never her intention to offend anyone, let alone insult the Islamic faith. She was just naming a toy. Who would have thought an innocuous teddy could cause so much unintended offence?

Let's all be thankful that she didn't adopt AA Milne's approach to naming bears, otherwise she really would have had to face the furry!

Another bizarre fact I have discovered about Generation Text is that despite all their menace and hatred channelled into their war of words, it is almost guaranteed that before the week is out most of the sparring exes will be back together – until their next round of fighting that is.

Don't get me wrong: I'm not perfect, and I've made more than my fair share of mistakes in relationships, but, hopefully, I've learnt from my experiences. If I could impart just one piece of advice to all the venomous Facebook users and texters it would probably simply be this: don't play silly games in a relationship (unless it's naked Twister).

Neighbour disputes are another set of calls that I dread mainly because there is usually never any resolution other than telling people to be more tolerant, and nobody it seems, ever wants to hear that. Invariably, it's the complaint, and then the inevitable counter complaint about noisy neighbours, street parking, and even the odd call about the woman over the road who 'looks at me funny'.

The one constant in all these types of jobs is that the initial complainant steadfastly maintains that they are the voice of reason, and it is the other party involved who is the intransigent rapscallion. Tony Benn used to wryly observe that the government always reported that unions demand and management offer. Of course, the same story is repeated in reverse when you talk to the other party.

Time and time again I try to advise neighbours to just ignore each other, and concentrate on getting on with their own lives. For every sixty seconds you spend seething with anger, you lose a minute of happiness. Keeping your nose out of someone else's business was good advice at Crufts, and is good advice now, but of course no one wants to hear that.

Sadly, these issues often start from an innocent misunderstanding – as I told the police officer all those years ago. I can recall it as though it was yesterday. I was a young sailor wandering back to my ship through the deserted streets of Portsmouth; my mind miles away when I saw a woman walking about twenty yards in front of me in the darkness. She turned and looked back at something, and then quickened her pace, so I did, too. She then began running, so I did, too. She screamed, so I did, too. I never did see what we were running from.

The real tragedy is that there are genuine people in need of our help, but it is often very hard to pick out the deserving cases from all the white noise.

It's not just celebrities that have their obsessive followers: over 1.2 million women, and 900,000 men are being stalked every year in the UK thus a vehicle dedicated to identifying, and addressing these potentially serious crimes can only be a good thing. It's such a shame that the people who really need our time and assistance are in danger of being lost in this sea of tit for tat accusations and petty arguments. Sometimes I feel that due to the mountain of spurious complaints the diary car is driving with the brakes on.

But I have digressed long enough. I got out of my warm car, and shivered in the cold as I walked towards my appointment. If 'every day is a gift', as the desk calendar said, today was socks, and sock day had started on a low, and had gone steadily downhill.

My first diary call had been to a female who had reported a series of silent phone calls: "At least he could have talked dirty to me, and made it worth my while," she complained.

The next case for PC Donoghue had been a stolen wheelie bin.

"But there *is* a wheelie bin outside," I had informed the caller after I had taken a look in his rear yard.

"Yes, but mine had 43 written on it. This one has 41 on the side."

"Have you checked at number 41 to see if they have your bin?"

"Yes, I have. That's the crime I want to report!"

I highly suspect that the refuse collectors (not rubbish men – I'm learning!) had probably put back the bins at the wrong address. I swapped them around myself.

My third appointment of the day had turned out to be a disturbing case of Skillage.

The elderly gent had reported that a few of the local kids had been having a kick about with a football at the bottom of the street. As he had gone to his car the ball had rolled over so he had kicked it back. The children had seemed pretty impressed with his foot work, enquiring if he had skillage. He had been delighted with their obvious appreciation of his skills – or skillage as they had charmingly called it. He had told the lads that he had a lot of skillage, and had a bit more of a kick around with them. Each time his ego was massaged, as they encouraged him to tell them how much skillage he had. Eventually, really getting into the spirit of things, and, at their suggestion, he had agreed that he was, indeed, the king of skillage. At this proclamation, the children had run off, laughing uncontrollably, before turning and shouting back that skillage was a disease of the anus in African cattle.

"Now I'm plagued with shouts of 'skillage' whenever I go outside my front door," he had complained bitterly. I had told him it wasn't really a police matter whilst writing furiously in my notebook. I hadn't made notes regarding the mischievous children; I just hadn't wanted to forget how the scam worked so I could play it on Ron when I got back to the station.

At high noon it had been 'two nurses in a custardy battle'. Had someone been accessing my dreams? At last, something that had looked like it could be an interesting, if not messy job. Sadly, it had all been rather lost in translation due to a tragic misspelling. There had been two nurses involved, but two male nurses, and it was a custody dispute over an animal. As I had wandered up the driveway to the property, a small black cat had padded towards me, meowing. I had meowed back, and it had scampered off. I had then been a bit worried as to what we might have agreed to.

Inside the house, I had met the joint owners of the aforementioned puss. In essence, following the end of their relationship, each of them had wanted to keep the pet cat, both citing evidence as proof that the animal was theirs. My attempt at shocking them into common sense with my own version of the Judgement of Solomon which suggested that they cut the cat in half, failed dismally when they had eagerly agreed to my suggestion. It hadn't been a case of them both wanting Mr Tiddles, but rather they both were determined that the other party didn't get their hands on the feline – even if that meant neither of them did. I had informed them it was a civil matter, even if they clearly couldn't act in a civil manner themselves. I then suggested that maybe they should have the cat alternate weeks, made my excuses, and left.

At one o'clock I had attended an office, where the manager had wanted to report a case of criminal damage due to a phantom toilet user. It was a unisex facility in a communal office block. The sign that had been stuck on the wall said it all:

To whom it may concern. Stop pissing all over the lavatory like a chimpanzee. What is wrong with your penis? Is it a corkscrew? Does it flick around like a hosepipe? Here's an idea – try pointing it even vaguely towards the water. You might even enjoy the tinkling sound. Give it a shot. Go on, you fucking animal!!!!

I had told the manager that it was a better solution than anything I could suggest. It wasn't really criminal damage, but perhaps he ought to consider using industrial strength bleach.

My current job – the one that I had left the warm car for, was in relation to 'the pig next door'. I had visited a house earlier in the week where the proprietor had phoned the police to complain about 'little animals' running around outside, spoiling her quality of life. Initially, I thought it was an environmental health matter, but after speaking to the woman in person, I soon realised that the 'little animals' were actually the neighbour's children playing in their garden – as children do. Armed with my newly acquired knowledge of the emotive language used to express their discontent with their lot in life, I fully expected to walk into another neighbour dispute over kids; instead, I actually met the pig next door.

It was a small, pink, four legged piglet to be precise. I've come across a pony living in a kitchen, and ducks sharing the house with the owners, but I have never encountered a porker living in someone's front room before. The owner was at pains to explain to me that pigs are intelligent creatures, supposedly, after man, the fourth most intelligent creatures on the planet (although, sometimes I think we only hold that position because we sent the survey back first). Consequently, our four-legged, cloven-hoofed friends need a lot of stimulation. By the way her owner waxed lyrical about the animal's mental dexterity, I half expected the piglet to be sitting crossed legged on an armchair, wearing a smoking jacket and perusing *The Times*. Instead, she just snuffled around my feet. I'm not sure this pig intelligence theory isn't just a myth – pottering around in their pigsty, the oinkers have never seemed that clever to me, well except for *Babe: Pig in the City*; now she was bright.

Pinky here, was unhappy at her lack of exercise, and was consequently expressing her frustration in a bountiful supply of grunts and squeals that were clearly annoying the neighbours. When I asked the owner why she didn't just take Pinky for her much needed walks, which would surely alleviate this problem, I was subsequently enlightened to the strict criteria that had to be adhered to when keeping such a beast at home. I knew you needed a licence to go fishing, to drive a car, to own a gun and get married. My American friends are always amused, if not slightly bemused, to also learn that you need a licence to watch TV in the UK. I had learned something new today: you also need a licence to walk a pig. You also have to notify the authorities in advance the route you and your porker will take. Feeding it scraps from the table is also prohibited – so much for greedy pigs! So, until the licence was granted, the owner explained, Pinky was living a life of pampered luxury in a house twice as big as the one I lived in. Perhaps pigs weren't as stupid as I had previously thought.

When finding a pig in the front room of a residential house is the highlight of your day, personally speaking, it's an indication that your days aren't that wonderful.

The final case of the day had been a call from a dog walker. Everyone knows that people should pick their dog's poop up, but why oh why do people leave their bagged up poop on the roadside or tucked in a bush instead of putting it in a bin?

Our unfortunate dog walker had been out walking her dog when she had been hit in the face by a bag of dog faeces hanging from a tree branch. What upset her most was that it was still warm. No, I informed her, I wouldn't be conducting DNA tests on the contents, no matter how many episodes of *CSI* she'd seen.

Between jobs, I tried to remind myself that these calls *were* important to the individual who rang in. They deserved my attention, but my heart just wasn't in it. It didn't help that I seemed to have developed a recurring cold. It was just like an old girlfriend I once had. Just as I thought I was getting over her, she would return to suck the life out of me again.

When I eventually returned home that evening, I realised how heartily sick of my life I was. I still had the assault charge hanging over me, I was wasting my days away on the diary car, and, to top it all, my chin still ached from the night before when I'd climbed into bed, pulled the duvet up too fast and ended up punching myself in the face. It had been gusty outside, too; the neighbour's wind chimes sounding like a demented xylophone player, which had kept me awake half the night. I was both mentally and physically exhausted. To add insult to injury, my eye was beginning to twitch uncontrollably. I felt like a cyborg with faulty wiring.

I was alone and miserable. I turned on the glowing box in the corner that tells me stories to see if there was anything on that could take my mind off my situation.

On BBC 1 was a film about a young girl who is transported to a surreal land, kills the first person she meets, and then teams up with three strangers to kill again. I'd seen *The Wizard of Oz* before, though, so looked to see what was on Channel 4 instead. It looked like there was a good film on at ten. The write up included the phrase: 'may contain nudity'; well, either it does or it doesn't – stop wasting my time! I turned the telly off. It would only detract from my drinking.

Although I felt like these were very dark days, I at least took comfort in the knowledge that my problems paled into insignificance in comparison with Charlie Seller's plight. Charlie Sellers was a Geordie who had apparently been run out of his native Newcastle after he was seen wearing a jumper. He was also a drugs dealer – but a feckless one. (Incidentally, there is a theory called nominative determinism that suggests that a person's name can have a significant role in determining their character, or profession. It was a commonly held notion in the ancient world, and some believe that it is still relevant today. I recently was introduced to a gynaecologist called Dr Khunti, and whilst I appreciate that it doesn't prove the theory totally, it's an opening that makes you want to explore further.)

All business men and women appreciate the intricacies of the relationship between supply and demand. It's one of the most fundamental concepts of economics, and is the backbone of a market economy. Drug dealing is a business just like any other; illegal, but still a business. When you run out of stock it can have a detrimental effect on your operation.

Sellers had run out of his stock of heroin at a crucial time. It was crucial because it was the time when 'Big Vince' wanted to score. Big Vince was another of the town's 'hard men', and also a steroid abuser. He had recently been introduced to smack by the Geordie who, initially, had given him some free hits to get him hooked. Sellers had thought he had secured himself a nice new source of income, but what he hadn't accounted for was how quickly Vince had become desperate for his new high. On the day in question, he had turned up at Sellers' home, and demanded a fix. Sellers tried to explain that he had run out, but Big Vince was having none of it, believing that the Geordie was holding back on him. Sellers then said those fateful words that he will live to regret to his dying day: "If you don't believe me, search me!"

Challenging a desperate Big Vince would turn out to be the worst mistake Charlie had ever made. Vince forcibly bent Sellers over the kitchen table, ripped his trousers and underpants down, grabbed a bottle of Fairy Liquid, jammed it into the Geordie's anus, and violently squeezed the contents into his rectum. He then donned a pair of Marigolds, and stuck his hand up Sellers' bottom, executing his own improvised cavity search. It wouldn't have been a gentle operation, either; I doubt there was any foreplay, and a reckless Vince would have been grasping away frantically for any bags of drugs that may have been hidden away up in Nature's Purse.

I'm sure that Charlie Sellers thought he'd probably escape with just a quick pat down at the most.

Sellers thought he was the tough guy of the town, but then along came Big Vince; bigger, tougher and a man with no fear. Let's face it: a man's rectum is no place for a chicken. Sellers was later found by his girlfriend, curled up in a foetal position on the kitchen floor, shaking uncontrollably. By all accounts, her attempt to comfort him wasn't well received: "You should be thanking me. Good job I went to Asda for washing up liquid yesterday, otherwise he would have gone in dry!"

Poor unfortunate Charlie – he'll be farting bubbles for a week... or possibly up to 30% longer if the leading brand adverts are anything to go by.

CHAPTER SIX:

Single Shot Espresso

"Spread your legs."

It wasn't the return of Charlie Sellers' Fairy Godfather; it was me talking to a suspect, as I prepared to search him. I was standing in a supermarket car park in the dark, getting soaked to the skin in a thunderstorm... but I wasn't complaining.

At the start of the shift, Barry had called me into the Sergeant's office, telling me that he had something that I would want to see. Initially disappointed that it wasn't a mechanical monkey playing the cymbals, I was, however, delighted to discover that it was a letter from Inspector Soaper. It stated that no action would be taken in relation to the assault allegation, and that I was free to collect my confiscated uniform and end my run of diary car duties. In essence, the letter implied that I should crack on as if nothing had happened. I read it several times, turning it over, shaking it upside down, and even holding it against the light, but I still couldn't find any hint of what was going to happen to the man who had set all this in motion.

"What's going to happen to the person who made the accusation?" I asked.

"Nothing," came the reply. I was informed that my accuser had made the verbal complaint on the morning, but despite several visitations from senior officers since that date, he hadn't committed to anything in writing, and refused to comment any further on the issue.

"So are you saying the matter is dropped because he's not pushing it, or am I in the clear because the bosses know I didn't do it?"

"Does it matter?" asked Barry.

"It does to me!" I told him indignantly. "If it's just over with because he's not put pen to paper, then there's still a finger of doubt hanging over me. If I have another complaint against me in the future, they'll drag all this up again. I'd much rather it was put to bed properly, and be formally exonerated of any wrongdoing."

Statistically, it was highly likely that a complaint would be made against me in the future. There are over 600 complaints made against police officers every week, which gives the impression that we aren't doing our job very well at all. It's only when you appreciate that many of those complaints are made by criminals that we have locked up, that the figures can be taken into context. After all, they're never going to thank us for spoiling their nefarious schemes, and depriving them of their liberty. And if someone doesn't get the answer they want to hear when we visit them, then, potentially, it is yet another complaint heading our way.

"Is there nothing the Crown Prosecution Service can do to make sure he doesn't do it again?" I asked again, labouring the point.

"Not a thing," came the reply.

"That's not justice," I protested.

"It might not be justice, but it's the law."

I understood his point, but couldn't help feeling that things didn't seem fair. Actually, that's a bit of an understatement: I was furious. I had endured weeks of sleepless nights, my stress levels were through the roof, my very integrity had been called into question, and I had faced the real prospect of jail time if I had been convicted, and all because of a small man with a big grudge. All those repercussions for me, yet no consequences for my accuser.

Still, I was off the diary car, and back on normal duties.

The big grey cloud that had been hanging over me had moved on, and even though I stood in the rain outside Tesco with the storm clouds thundering overhead, doing their worst, I felt like a weight had been lifted off my shoulders. I was back doing the job I loved, so I wasn't complaining.

The call had initially come in from the supermarket, stating that a couple were acting suspiciously in one of the clothing aisles. According to the security staff, they appeared to be exchanging the labels on different priced products. It's an old scam with a simple concept: swap the price labels over, and at the checkout pay for the lower priced item and swan off with the more expensive one.

Crooks are becoming more ingenious by the day; Lloyd had recently arrested a man whose modus operandi was to take his selection of meat to the self-service checkout, and after placing it on the weighing platform, instead of choosing beef or pork from the price menu, he would select carrots. Obviously, as carrots are cheaper than meat, he pays a much lower price, and so another scam is born.

Just as I had arrived at the supermarket that evening, there was a loud clap of thunder, the heavens opened and the downpour began. Despite the dark and rain I could see the security officer motioning frantically towards a car where two people had just finished loading their shopping into the boot. As they slammed it shut, I quickly drove up alongside, and gave a quick squawk on the siren to grab their attention, hoping to catch them before they got into the vehicle – I didn't want a car chase in this weather.

They both jolted, startled at the noise, and then whipped round, their gaze meeting mine. A pregnant pause descended whilst they appeared to weigh up the situation. He wasn't a particularly large man, but had a self-assured aura about him akin to a London gangster. The woman was much thinner, with a pale complexion, and straggly auburn hair. He indicated towards her, telling her to get into the vehicle, and looked like he was about to do the same until he realised that I was on my own.

As I stepped out of the police car and into the rain, I looked around to see if they had any accomplices waiting nearby but it was late, and there were only a handful of cars in the whole car park. Anyone with sense wouldn't venture out on a night like this.

Our mockney Cockney made it clear that he wasn't even going to try and evade my attention; quite the contrary. He made a deliberate show of clicking his door shut, and facing me square on, puffing his chest out, and flexing his arms back to push it out even further. He flicked his cigarette butt onto the ground, and stamped it out.

I swiftly glanced at the shop exit where the few people who had started to make the return journey to their cars now retreated inside after seeing me and my suspect poised as though we were about to start a wild west gunfight. I reached down and felt for my baton and spray, not wanting to break eye contact with him for one second.

The rain was now dripping down both our faces as we faced each other. He snarled under his breath as he started to make his way towards me, stretching his neck muscles first to one side then the other, cracking his knuckles as he did so. Every movement was done slowly and deliberately, in an exaggerated manner.

He reminded me of a hardened criminal who had been on the run in Sandford last year. We had searched for him for weeks, but he wasn't holed up in any of his usual haunts. It so happens that he had just been turning up at random pensioners' houses, and informing them that he was living with them for a few days. There were no choices or options. The message had been clear: accommodate him, and keep silent about it, or face a beating. Most had been too intimidated by the thug to refuse, and he had secured a run of safe houses for a couple of weeks as a result. However, even desperados have to sleep and he was eventually captured when an unhappy host had smashed him in the face with a frying pan as he lay in bed. She had then calmly phoned us to report her unwelcome guest.

It looked like our gangster was trying to intimidate me now.

"That's not nice," he drawled as he walked towards me. "Not nice at all, is it? Giving us a shock like that? Just one lone copper all on his own, are you? I don't think you've weighed this situation up very well at all, have you? Now maybe you'd better get back into your nice police car and drive off, there's a good boy. You don't want your daddy to give you a slap now, do you?"

"You're going to tell my dad?"

Clearly, he didn't like my answer as things suddenly intensified, and he lunged at me, arms raised in front of him like a mummy from a B movie horror film.

Instinctively, I drew my incapacitant, and directed a stream of pepper spray straight into his eyes. He reeled back, and then dropped to his knees, clutching his face as he roared with pain.

To be honest, if this had been a movie, I'd have probably made the action sequence last a bit longer, and made myself out to be some sort of hero; maybe dodged a few punches and danced around him for a bit as he became dazed and confused, before diving over the bonnet, spraying him as I flew through the air. I'd have also probably said something clever like: "I'm not alone, big man, I've brought my friend, Doctor Pepper, with me." But it isn't, so I didn't. I'm sorry.

My musings on who should play me in the feature length blockbuster were rudely interrupted by the sound of a car door opening, followed by the voice of the woman shouting as she ran round and squatted next to her partner. The third Kray twin was still on his knees, crouched over, and slapping at the wet tarmac with his palm as if that would somehow alleviate the pain. I could hear the exchange of frantic whispers between them before she looked up and stared at me, narrowing her eyes as she did so. I had read that the ancient Greeks believed that redheads turned into vampires when they died. With her wet hair now matted against her face, and her vampiric countenance twisted into an evil scowl, I could readily believe it. Another clap of thunder added to the brooding atmosphere. I didn't wait for her to start speaking in tongues, but instead got onto the radio to request back-up.

"Things are looking a bit ugly here," I told Comms before feeling that I needed to clarify my comments to the woman on the floor – "Nothing personal."

I kept my pepper spray levelled at her in case she, too, decided to lunge at me, but she just maintained direct eye contact. I think this was her own attempt to intimidate me, but I wasn't fazed. I've made eye contact with women on the first day of the January sales – a manic woman is a mere stroll in the park in comparison.

In witnessing the fate of her companion, I hoped that she, too, had learned respect for the pepper spray. I didn't want the effect of it to wear off and then have to face a two pronged attack on my own from my angry human bull and his faithful cow. An uncomfortable stand-off in the rain ensued before I was joined by Jess and Chad, and the balance of power was once again restored in my favour.

Finally, before setting off for custody, I handcuffed the male, and quickly searched him to ensure that he didn't have any items on him that could present a danger to him or us. It was left to Jess to search the vampire.

On arrival at the nick, the filibustering immediately began. First they wanted a solicitor then they didn't then they did again. He refused to speak to anyone until a medic had come to check his eyes; she wouldn't talk until she'd been allowed a cigarette.

"You can't smoke in here," I told her. "We don't just put up the 'No Smoking' signs for the good of our health!"

The pair then demanded to be fed and watered. I could

only smell the food as it circled in the microwave, and look longingly at the hot drinks, whilst my stomach rumbled away. I'd left my sandwiches back at the station, and a recent edict said we weren't allowed any of the prisoners' drinks, so I went without while they tucked in. It's not unusual to go home with your sandwiches still in the plastic box after a ten hour shift; my dog would be pleased.

Then, even after the medic had assessed him and declared him fit and well, our gangster wouldn't speak. His partner was just as awkward and obstructive when the custody sergeant tried to get details from her.

"Do you have a job?" he asked.

"Of course I do," she sneered, "I'm not just a trophy wife."

The Sarge, Jess, Chad and I were taken aback at her rebuke. If she did consider herself a trophy, it certainly wasn't first prize. Despite the sergeant's continued questioning, she remained deliberately evasive, and point blank refused to state what she did for a living.

"It's difficult to say," was all she would reply, so it is quite possible, although highly unlikely, that she sells seashells on the seashore.

The sergeant wasn't alone in having problems eliciting such information from people: I've also had some interesting answers whenever I've asked that question. One 'customer' said he was an airline executive, but it turned out he just was in charge of the hose used to pump up the tyres at the garage; another said he was a mother tester, whereupon a string of bizarre images ran through my head – most of them unprintable, but I'm sure I've seen a video about it. In actual fact, it transpired that he worked in an electronics factory. However, my most embarrassing experience to date was when I asked a German lady what she did for a living. She had been the victim of a bag theft, and after taking the statement, I needed to get some basic details for the crime report. Her English wasn't great, and my German was non-existent.

We had managed surprisingly well, despite the language barrier, and had had a few laughs along the way. We were nearing the end, and we chuckled over my difficulty in mastering the spelling of her hometown. Almost there – just a few final questions left: date of birth, place of birth and what she did for a living. That's when we hit the stumbling block: I just couldn't get through to her that I needed to know what her job was. Eventually, I thought I'd try and establish if she was over here for work; that might prove to be the key. I talked to her slowly, deliberately and, obviously, loudly, so she would understand.

"What. Have. You. Come. Over. Here. From. Germany. For?"

I left sufficient time for the question to sink in before I added, "Occupation?"

Her mood suddenly changed, and all the friendly bonhomie disappeared as she glared at me with disdain.

"Nein!" she barked. "I am on holiday!"

My friend, Sharon, had a similar issue when her German friend came to visit. It was Poppy Day, and as they stood watching the soldiers and veterans march by, my friend asked what they did in Germany to commemorate the Armistice.

"Nozeeng," came the reply. "Vee did not vin."

Back in custody, the couple's solicitor eventually arrived, looking as sweet as dolly mixture, carrying her briefcase like a gunslinger, and trailing perfume in her wake. I couldn't be sure, but she seemed to be quite flirty with me; talking in a voice like tinted glass, looking at me with her eyes of aquamarine as I outlined the details of the incident with her. She was an attractive woman, and I had been single for a while. I tend to find that girlfriends are like buses; you wait around for ages and I like the bendy ones best.

"Don't be stupid, Donoghue," the custody sergeant told me when I mentioned it to him later. "She's only being flirty with you to try and elicit more information from you. Anyway, she's much too good looking for you. You should choose a wife like you choose patio furniture – you want it attractive enough that passers-by admire your good taste, but not too attractive that they want to steal it." He had a point, but it also probably explained why he was still single.

"There are plenty of fish in the sea," were his parting words. "Go out and start dating lots of women; I'm sure you'll catch something."

Eventually, after much delay, our fraudsters were interviewed and dealt with. After advice from their solicitor, they admitted the offence, and as the couple didn't have any previous convictions for fraud, they received a caution; effectively a slap on the wrist.

The couple looked at each other and smirked. I was sure that this was just the tip of the iceberg. They must have got away with their scam time after time, and were just unlucky to have been caught on this occasion. They couldn't believe they were virtually getting away with their crime.

It didn't really seem enough of a punishment, in my opinion, but I thought back to what Barry had told me about the difference between justice and the law, and resigned myself to the outcome. I had spent more time than enough in custody due to their delaying tactics, and all I wanted to do now was get back to the station, but before I could do that, however, the custody sergeant told me to give the pair a lift back to their car which was still in Tesco's car park.

The police service are deemed responsible if anything serious happens to a suspect up to seventy-two hours after being released from custody. If they were to unfortunately drop down dead, for whatever reason, during that period, it would be termed as 'death following police contact', and major investigations would result with the world and his wife becoming involved. As a consequence of this, I'm routinely expected to forget what shenanigans have occurred prior to and during an arrest – the violence, threats and abuse – and act as chauffeur to deliver them safely back home.

Reluctantly, I directed them into the panda. My mood

didn't improve during the short drive through the dark and lashing rain back to their car. I was tired, hungry, and I still believed that they had got off lightly. To rub salt into the wound, throughout the journey they had sat sniggering in the back of the vehicle. As I dropped them off, they got out of the car laughing and joking, which irked me even more. Then, just as I was about to drive off, I heard the male shout out. As I turned, I could see him rip something off his windscreen. I wound down my window to get a better view.

"What the fuck is this?" he shouted at me, shaking a wet piece of paper in my direction.

I studied it, and then grinned widely.

"Oh dear, it looks like you've been parked in the car park for more than the stipulated three hours. Looks like the supermarket have hit you with an £80 parking fine."

"This isn't the law!" he roared.

"You're quite right," I replied, "This is justice." I smiled to myself, waved and honked my horn as I drove off, leaving a furious fraudster standing in the rain. I wasn't sure if it was a moral thing to do – to laugh at his misfortune, but then I remembered what Ernest Hemingway had said about morality: 'I only know what is moral is what you feel good after, and what is immoral is what you feel bad after.' On that basis, it was very moral to laugh.

Back in the parade room, Ben, Gwen, George and Geezer were sitting typing away. I told them I had a tale to tell, and they eagerly pulled their chairs around. This is what I had missed during those dreary diary days; the camaraderie as we all sat around and swapped our stories. I felt I was home again. Gwen volunteered to make the brews before we began.

"I take my coffee like I take my women," crowed George as he leant back in his seat, hands behind his head, awaiting the inevitable question.

"I've told you before George, we don't do single shot espresso," sighed a world weary Gwen as our lothario quickly sat back up in his chair. Five minutes later, we were all gathered around with our brews cradled in our hands, relaxed for the first time that night.

Ben began proceedings by informing us about an insurance scam that had backfired. A car owner, in an attempt to get a pay-out, had left his car in the town centre overnight with the doors unlocked, and the keys in the ignition. He had obviously hoped that someone would steal it. No doubt, he would then invent some fairy story to explain how it had gone missing. Unfortunately, instead of grand theft auto, an old tramp had just climbed into the backseat and defecated. Justice indeed.

Gwen then informed us of a 'missing from home' she had recently dealt with. Following a family argument, a fifteen-year-old boy had decided to punish his parents by staying out all night, and not telling them where he was. Distraught, the family had contacted the police, and Gwen had been the officer who had been allocated with following up all the leads throughout the night in an attempt to locate him. She had visited his friends' houses, gone around to all the usual haunts where kids hung out, searched the streets, and rung him on his mobile several times. He had initially answered the calls, but had then proceeded to give her the run around; arranging to meet her at different locations but never showing up. Eventually, he didn't even bother answering. As is often the case, in the morning, when he'd eventually had enough, he rang us to arrange a lift home.

A missing person is reported to the police every two minutes, and frustratingly, many follow a similar pattern, tying up police resources in the process. In fact, 14% of police time is spent looking for missing people.

"He thought it was one big joke," Gwen informed us. "When we got back, he just stood smirking as his mother tried to get through to him the amount of worry and stress he had caused her, let alone the amount of police time wasted. They were clearly a decent family, and were mortified that the police had had to get involved, and even more embarrassed that her son was treating the matter so contemptuously." However, there appears to be a finite limit to how much dumb insolence a beleaguered mother can take.

"As I explained how he had taken us on a wild goose chase – arranging to meet me and then not showing up, the mother took her son's phone off him, and placed it in the middle of the kitchen table. She then quietly went over to a drawer and retrieved a marble rolling pin. As her horrified son looked on, she then rained blow after blow onto the handset, smashing it into a thousand pieces. When she had finished, she flicked away the hair that had fallen across her face during her rampage, and calmly asked if I wanted a cup of tea."

"It's like living in a prison here!" the boy bellowed before stamping his feet, kicking the kitchen bin over, running upstairs and slamming his bedroom door.

The mild mannered mother had then slowly walked to the bottom of the stairs, before enunciating calmly, yet in a loud voice: "Spare me the hard luck story, Adam. Like a prison here? I hardly think you are going to get bummed relentlessly by a gang of hard men up in your room."

She had then strolled back into the kitchen, and filled the kettle. "Well," she told Gwen in mitigation as she dropped the teabags into the cups, "I read about it in *Bella* magazine."

Everybody likes to hear tales about scammers, villains, and spoiled children getting their comeuppance, and now it was Geezer's turn to add his two-penneth worth. It all revolved around a scam turned on its head. Hard pressed for manpower, but keen to get results, one force decided that instead of hunting down the crooks, for once they would get the crooks to come to them. They simply sent out scratch cards to all the wanted criminals, and, surprisingly enough, they were all winners. To collect their £1,000 prize and to be in with the chance of winning a big screen TV, all they had to do was turn up at the address given... and scores of them did, where officers were waiting for them and justice was well and truly served.

The one big lesson I had learnt that day is that the law didn't always provide you with justice, but when justice is served, it can be a sweet, sweet thing.

We looked over towards George, waiting for his contribution, but I could see that the cogs in his brain were still working overtime, trying to think up a witty comeback to Gwen's earlier put-down. He had had his chance and missed it. We finished our brews, stood up and slid our chairs back under the table before preparing for a final patrol of the town before the end of the shift.

"I like my women like I like my coffee..." piped up George, only to be drowned out with a chorus of "Too late!" by the rest of us as we left the room and disappeared into the night.

"From Aldi," he muttered to himself as he stood all alone in the parade room.

CHAPTER SEVEN:

New Shit Has Come To Light

Self-service checkouts: making shoplifting a 'mistake' since 1998.

I had popped into Tesco to buy a sandwich before work, just as I had done every day for the past week. In fact, I'd been through the self-service checkout so often over the last few days (payment in full, I hasten to add), that I fully expected my photo to be posted behind the customer service counter labelled 'employee of the month'.

As I collected my receipt from the machine, pondering on what I would say in my acceptance speech, I noticed a woman standing by the exit, desperately trying to attract my attention. Instinctively, I checked over my shoulder to make sure that it was definitely me she was waving at before I responded. There is nothing more embarrassing than getting over excited, grinning back, mouthing an over exaggerated 'Hellooooo' and waving enthusiastically, only to find out that she is motioning to her friend who is stood behind you.

Well, perhaps there is; creeping up in a supermarket behind an off-duty colleague, jabbing your fingers in her waist to make her jump as you growl, 'Got you!' in her ear, only for her to then turn around and be someone you've never seen in your life. Fortunately, security were very understanding.

"It is PC Donoghue, isn't it?" she asked as I approached. I hadn't started my shift yet, and was on my way to the station. It was probably quite easy, however, to recognise that I was an officer of the law. It was a warm day, and whilst the men were walking around in t-shirts and shorts, and the women were giving their summer dresses an early outing in the late April sunshine, I was the only one in store wearing a jacket over my white shirt, black trousers and shiny black boots. I don't know why I bothered: I might as well have had 'ECILOP' written on my back as I'm sure everyone knew I was a police officer en route to work.

I confirmed that I was indeed PC Donoghue, but then a silence descended as several shoppers walked past. As we stood there awkwardly, I racked my brains trying to think where I had seen her before. I recognised her face, but I wasn't sure from where. Had she been a victim at an incident? Had I arrested her before? Had I met her socially somewhere? If I could place her, then I could say something relevant and to the point. It was either that or resort to the old stock phrase that gets dug up whenever a conversation runs dry: 'Soooo, what's in the bag?'

However, I was saved such embarrassment when her true intentions became clear. As the last of the shoppers faded into the distance, she looked around conspiratorially before she positioned herself at a forty-five degree angle to me, and began whispering in my ear.

"You know that Mr Wallace in the town?" she began, "Well, I don't know for sure, but someone told me he was up to his old tricks. I think he is, well, you know, doing that stuff he used to do. I haven't seen him do it myself, but my friend Betty said he was wearing that old coat, and goes out early in the mornings..."

As I felt her warm breath on my ear, and felt her touch on my arm as she emphasised certain parts of her monologue, my thoughts drifted to the Greek philosopher, Socrates. He had his own opinion on rumour, gossip and slander, and there is a tale of how he was approached by one of his students...

The story goes that one day a pupil ran up to him excitedly. "Socrates," he panted, "do you know what I've just heard about Diomedes?"

Before he could utter another word, Socrates stopped him, and told him that before he'd listen any further, he wanted to know if the information he was about to hear would pass his triple filter test. The student looked perplexed.

"Firstly," asked Socrates sagely, "have you made absolutely sure that what you are about to tell me is absolutely true?"

"Well, no," replied his pupil, "I just heard about it."

"So, you don't know if what you are about to tell me is true or not? After the filter of truth, there is the filter of goodness. Is what you are about to tell me about Diomedes something good?"

"Well, no, on the contrary," came the reply.

"So, you want to tell me something bad about Diomedes, even though you are not certain if it's true or not?"

The pupil looked down at his sandals, feeling more than a little embarrassed.

"The third filter is the filter of usefulness. Is what you are going to tell me about Diomedes going to be useful?"

"No, not really."

"Well," concluded Socrates, "if what you have to tell me is neither true nor good, or even useful, why tell it to me or, indeed, to anyone else?"

His pupil was deeply ashamed, and took heed of his wise teacher's words. Socrates' quest for pure knowledge, and his refusal to be tainted with anything other than pure knowledge, was the reason why he was such a great philosopher and held in such high esteem.

It also explains why Socrates never found out that Diomedes was shagging his wife.

In police circles, however, every bit of information needs to be considered; whatever source it comes from. Some may be irrelevant and useless, some may be malicious, some may be wrong, but sometimes just one scrap of seemingly innocuous detail could be the final piece in the jigsaw.

I listened intently to what the woman was telling me, opening the appropriate files in my mind as she spoke, dropping the information into the different folders, hoping I didn't look too Faustian as I encouraged her to pour forth her worldly knowledge – or more precisely, her updates of the comings and goings in Sandford.

When I got to work I would disseminate the information to the intelligence officer, CID and Barry accordingly. It's the collation of this vital intelligence that allows the police to track, solve, and, ultimately, predict a criminal's activities. The aim is to move from a reactionary to a pro-active investigation of crime, or 'intelligence led policing' as they like to call it.

I was already aware of some of the information that I was being told about Mr Wallace aka The Sandford Flasher. As well as being an exhibitionist, he also seemed to get a bizarre sexual gratification from the whole police and court process. He had been arrested last year, and had got off on a legal technicality. I thought he had hung up his raincoat for good, but from the information I was hearing, it was clear that he was intent on sticking it out for one more year.

Arriving at work I bounded up the stairs to pass on the information before returning downstairs to take up my seat in the parade room. As Barry commenced the briefing, I was eager to share my findings with the shift, but as the ensuing banter proved, the term 'criminal intelligence' can sometimes be an oxymoron.

Gwen chimed in first with her tale of two local hoodlums who had taken a car for a joyride before abandoning it on the outskirts of town. When the car was recovered, the owner of the vehicle was relieved to find that her digital camera hadn't been stolen, and was even more delighted when she discovered that the joyriders had been stupid enough to snap photos of each other driving the car. It didn't take long before the notorious Skinner brothers were back behind bars.

Playing dead can be a good tactic when attacked by a grizzly bear, but not so good when hiding from the police. Andy told us about an intruder who, after breaking into a funeral home in Kilo 2, had decided to blend in with the other residents when the police arrived on scene; he simply lay in a coffin and pretended to be dead. He was, however, quite easy to spot as he was the only one breathing, and wearing dirty tracksuit bottoms and a hoodie, as opposed to being dead and dressed in a suit.

After a hard night's graft stealing metal from an electricity sub-station, one criminal, no doubt ecstatic with his haul, decided to answer the call of nature before he left, and urinated at the scene. Unfortunately, he directed his stream onto the station's transformer, causing a power cut to over 2,000 homes in Sandford, and 'permanently disfiguring' himself in the process. He was very easy to locate, explained Chad, as he was the only person in A&E with smoke coming from his head and a penis that looked like an overdone sausage on a barbeque. He was arrested and charged for the second time that night.

I had dealt with one particular Sandford villain who had passed off counterfeit notes at a betting shop – an offence otherwise known as 'uttering'. So convinced was he that he had backed the winner at the two-thirty at Ascot, the rogue had left his contact details so the shop could ring him to tell him when he could come and collect his winnings. Needless to say, I didn't even have to go looking for the crook – I just waited in the shop for him to arrive, and then uttered my own winning words: 'You're nicked'.

Intelligence about the illicit activity of a group of disillusioned college students allowed Ron and Geezer to foil a plot to bring panic and mayhem to Sandford town centre on a busy Saturday afternoon. We listened intently as with those two there was always a twist in the tale. It appeared that an unusual level of interest in the new batch of piglets at the local farmer's market in Kilo 2 had triggered suspicion.

Word got back to the duo, and they investigated further. A student was brought in, lightly grilled, and eventually cracked, revealing the details of the operation. The concept was inspired and its application was meticulously planned. It's such a shame that I didn't get to see the intended result.

In brief, their plan was to acquire four piglets, paint the numbers 1,2,3 and 5 on their backs, let them loose in the high street, and then watch everyone frantically search for number 4. Genius.

Finally, George and Ben took full credit for discovering a cannabis factory in a house in the Kilo 3 area. Again, it didn't take a lot of detective work. It transpired that the resident, feeling paranoid and nervy after partaking in some of his own produce, had rung the police in the early hours of the morning, insisting that he had heard a burglar in his house. George and Ben had attended, conducted a full search of the property, but found no intruder; instead, though, they did discover a large amount of cannabis growing in the back bedroom. When the house owner was asked how it got there, he said someone must have planted it.

I waited until the general banter and laughter had died down again before I revealed my pièce de résistance: the intelligence that I had just received from the woman at the supermarket. In addition to the update on Mr Wallace, she had also told me that two of Sandford police's regular customers, Mot and Clint Skinner, had called at her house, trying to sell her a widescreen TV. To all of us sitting around the briefing table, this information was intelligence gold.

There are 24 million instances of anti-social behaviour in the UK each year. That equates to 26 every minute. It's a huge problem for the police, and society. These figures are inflated, I'm sure, by the Skinner family who also list fraud, theft, intimidation, harassment, drugs, violence, criminal damage and prostitution on their CV of shame.

The father of the clan, Brett Skinner, was a particularly unpleasant character. A weasel of a man, with soap opera villain hair, he had chiefly occupied his time over the last few years writing to football clubs, telling them about his young son, a big fan of the team, who was dying of leukaemia. He asked them, if it wasn't too much trouble, if they could send a strip signed by all the players. Who could refuse such a request? Certainly not the kind-hearted clubs who promptly dispatched a signed shirt and accompanying merchandise to cheer up the unfortunate child. However, none of his children actually had leukaemia. Instead, the shirts were immediately auctioned on ebay, whilst Skinner looked for other generous benefactors to scam.

When he was exposed and brought to trial, he managed to avoid a custodial sentence due to his disability. It was what we would term a 'DSS disability' as opposed to an actual disability. Whenever he was at court, he would be leaning on his walking stick, gasping for breath, or slumped pathetically in his wheelchair, yet whenever we called round, he'd be on his feet, jumping from foot to foot, spouting abuse and spoiling for a fight.

The matriarch of the family was Ruby Skinner. It takes a special type of woman to carry off a glass eye, but she managed it with aplomb. She had the names of all her former boyfriends tattooed on her arms, making her look like a mobile school register. I'm not sure if they had been added in chronological order, or whether it was some kind of leader board. She was loud and hostile, with short, dyed, plum coloured hair, and a set of teeth that looked like they were doing a Mexican wave. I wouldn't like to comment on her size; suffice to say that she was no stranger to a pie.

Her two sons, Mot and Clint, had inherited her propensity for ink. Mot's actual name was Tom, but he acquired his particular moniker after he tattooed his name on his forehead whilst looking in the mirror. Clint also had a nickname, although his particular appellation arose after he let Ruby tattoo his name in block capitals on the back of his neck. Either she was ham-fisted with the needle, or he had upset her that day as the 'L' and 'I' of CLINT seemed to be co-joined. It did, however, describe his personality to a T.

Both boys possessed large ears, pasty complexions and a lazy eye to accompany their lazy, lanky bodies. Despite being in their early twenties, neither had ever done an honest day's work in their entire lives. It was difficult to believe that they were the result of the sperm that won.

They were often to be found wandering the streets late at night. They had started off just trying the handles of parked cars, but with a fair degree of success: it's surprising how many people leave their vehicles unlocked with all sorts of electrical items inside. They would specifically target cars with the tell-tale sucker mark on the windscreen as it was probably a good bet that there would be a satnav stowed inside the glove box, waiting to be stolen. Later, they started on a spate of 'letterbox' or 'two-in-one' burglaries. Even when people do lock their vehicles, they often just leave the keys on the hall table. Mot and Clint carried an extendable aerial with a hook on the end; they would feed the pole through the letterbox, hook the keys and the vehicle was then theirs to drive away.

Whilst her brothers had an ugly streak about them, their sister, Angel, was a real head-turner. By that, I mean that whilst the others were nasty social misfits without a shred of decency between them, Angel was actually possessed by the devil. She was convicted of stealing the toys from the children's graves at the cemetery to sell down the local pub. There is a special place in hell for people like her... and the person who decides what time breakfast ends at McDonalds.

It was Angel who, in her early twenties, had dabbled as a low-class escort for a number of years. Her Facebook page showed this self-styled businesswoman offering 'oral favours' for £3 a go, or at the knockdown price of a fiver for two. I had considered reporting her to Trading Standards as a 'favour' is classified as 'an act performed out of goodwill or generosity', not for money. However, I was afraid that they might have wanted a blow-by-blow account of her activity, and there is a limit to what I'll do, even for the job. In the end, to put paid to her enterprise, I arranged for the council to plant thorn bushes behind the garages where she did her entertaining.

The final member of the Skinner household, Dean, was a good foot taller than his brothers and sister, even though he was almost ten years younger than them, prompting speculation that Ruby had had her four children by at least five different fathers. It would be wrong to call Dean ill-favoured – he was just 'unfortunate' looking.

I had first encountered the Skinners shortly after I had started at Sandford. The house was due to be raided after it was discovered that the family were supplying drugs to children on the estate. I had been delayed with another job, and so arrived late, unsure as to whether the operation had already started. All I could see were a number of officers wandering around outside, rubbing their hands together as if they were hatching some sort of cunning plan. It turned out that they were using their anti-bacterial hand gel in a desperate bid to delay the onset of cholera.

It all became clear when I entered the house. Whilst the front garden looked like someone had been playing battleships with dog turds, it was inside where it was really squalid. The whole place was jumping with fleas; it stunk to high heaven, and everything was coated with a layer of grease and filth. Imagine not vacuuming, cleaning or dusting your house for a month, then a year, then three years, then five years. Every room was littered with discarded cans and takeaway boxes, piles of unwashed clothes, plates with congealed food, carpets thick with dog hair, while an overpowering smell of urine prevailed throughout. Windows that had never been cleaned inside or out gave the impression of looking through heavy net curtains. Cobwebs hung thick with dust, and boxes of unidentified 'stuff' were balanced precariously on top of one another, crammed into every corner. In the bathroom, the toilet was so blocked up with faeces that they had started to urinate and defecate in the bathtub.

As I quickly made my way out, I could hear banging coming from the two police vehicles, indicating that some of the family members had already been arrested, and were now kicking at their cages in protest. A caged vehicle is exactly that: a police van has a metal cage in the back, consisting of bare metal seats and metal bars to keep violent prisoners from assaulting officers as they are transported to custody. Usually, perspex sheets have been added later to prevent offenders from spitting at officers through the bars. Obviously, the designers didn't fully comprehend the foulness of some of the people that we deal with. Hopefully, one day they'll also soundproof the cages so we won't have to listen to their threats about how they will rape our wives and girlfriends, how they hope our mothers will die of cancer, and that they know where our families live and how they are going to come round and torch the house in the middle of the night.

The banging inside the van had also attracted the attention of the neighbours, who now peered like meerkats over garden walls and through gaps in blinds and curtains, curious as to what the police were here for this time. They didn't want to attract the attention of the Skinner family, but it was too late.

"What the fuck are you all staring at?" yelled Ruby aggressively. Nothing else was said, but it didn't need to be; the tacit implication was there, and all the heads immediately shot back inside, just leaving the broken glass topping nervous looking garden walls. It wasn't just people they terrorised; perhaps one of the most unpleasant things I've seen is Clint holding one of his dogs up to a neighbour's window so it could bark, intimidate and bully the poor dog inside.

I had encountered the Skinner men several times since in relation to various offences. They were nasty, unpleasant individuals whose favoured modus operandi was to spit in your face if you ended up fighting with them, which was particularly unpleasant when you knew the squalor in which they chose to live.

Angel's M.O. was quite the opposite, but just as disagreeable. I had stopped her a month ago wandering through the deserted industrial estate in the early hours one Sunday morning. She was dressed like she was returning from a party: revealing top, leather skirt and fishnet stockings that looked like they were a size too small, giving the impression that she was trying to mince herself. I asked her what she was up to.

"I'd tell you, but then I'd have to thrill you," she informed me, cupping her ample bosoms as she did so.

"Don't point those at me," I told her as I recoiled in horror.

She gave an evil cackle before wandering off into the darkness.

A few weeks later, a number of plasma televisions were stolen from a unit on the industrial estate. I remember the night vividly. It was the same night that I'd found a single stick from a table football game with three lone blue players on it. I'd waved it about a bit, and did the usual 'I've got an away game,' joke for the rest of the shift to no discernible laughter. So, instead, I'd attached a label to it reading: 'As requested', and left it on Inspector Soaper's desk. That would keep him guessing for a while when he got in the next day.

With the new information my supermarket informant had told me, it all added up. I'd no doubt Angel had been surveying the area when I had stopped her, and as regular burglars on the estate, Mot and Clint had already been in the frame as potential suspects. Now we had more than mere suspicion. It was decided that there was enough credible intelligence to justify us searching their house. I was certain we would definitely find the rest of the stolen television sets there – but only if we moved fast.

I quickly planned a mini operation, and lined up the necessary resources. First, though, we would need a warrant.

Since the courts had already closed their doors for the day, I contacted a local magistrate, and visited her at home. After swearing on the Bible that the information I was presenting was the truth, the whole truth, and nothing but the truth, I outlined why I wanted to raid the house, what I was looking for, what legal legislation I was acting on, what the intelligence was based on, who would be at the property, and, if necessary, what provisions I had made if children were present. Only when the magistrate had studied the report I had prepared, and questioned me in detail on every aspect of the plan, did she approve my request, and I was given the green light. I was now heading back to the Skinner residence armed with a warrant.

As I headed to the address, my biggest worry was that Angel would think that I was turning up because I wanted to take her up on her offer of being thrilled by her weapons of mass distraction, or that by arriving mob handed with Chad, Lloyd, Jess, Gwen, Ron, Geezer and Andy in tow, she might think that I was trying to negotiate a group discount for her favours.

It was almost midnight by the time we arrived at the address. It was a clear, still night. I just hoped that Mot and Clint hadn't thought it was a good night to go out stealing cars. I wanted the full pack – not just a couple of jokers left at home.

A dog unit was on standby around the corner in case things kicked off, while we walked in silence to the front of the address, leaving Gwen and Lloyd watching the back and side windows in case they made an attempt to ditch anything when they got the knock. In one hand I clutched the search warrant, but, more importantly, in the other I had a pair of rubber gloves.

Just as we arrived, Dean was returning home on his bike. "It's the coppers!" he yelled at the top of his voice as soon as he saw us, hammering at the door, waking the dogs in the yard who were now straining on their chains, barking furiously, adding to the cacophony of noise. Bang went our element of surprise.

Meanwhile, lights went on in every room inside the property, and I could hear the sound of frantic activity from within. I could hear a key in the lock, but they seemed to be playing for time as they kept shouting that they had the wrong one, and were going to try another. They must have known that we couldn't break the door down when someone was standing right behind it. My operation was falling apart before my very eyes.

"Empty out your pockets," I told Dean. It was an unusual time to be returning home, and I told him he was going to be searched. I suspected that he had been out looking for potential targets, or he might even have had some stolen gear on him. At least we could salvage something from the job. If we could find anything that he could use in the course of a burglary or theft, he could be arrested for 'going equipped'. I was on slightly dodgy ground trying to prove any criminal intent when he was actually 'returning equipped'.

Heinz tomato ketchup exits the bottle at 0.28 miles per hour – any faster than that and the batch is rejected. However, I'm sure that even a bottle of sauce would have been faster at opening the door in these circumstances. I shouted out my own personal brand of encouragement, which, although not strictly taught in training school, seemed to work as eventually the door was opened and we gained entry. Ruby Skinner was there to greet us, standing in the doorway, blocking our entrance.

"You're not coming in," she declared emphatically.

"Well, I am. I've got a warrant to search the property," I explained, waving it in front of her.

"I'll deal with this," shouted Brett from the lounge, "I'm the one who brings in the benefits in this house!"

"Shut the fuck up, I'm dealing with it!" shouted back an angry Ruby. Brett immediately complied. It was clear to see who actually wore the jogging pants in their relationship.

"You've already questioned us," jeered Mot and Clint, who had now joined us from the kitchen. I wouldn't say questioned – they had been asked where they were on the date the burglary occurred, not exactly given the third degree. How did they know what we had come about anyway?

"Information has been received that implicates ..."

"Yer what?" interrupted Ruby. "You've talked to them already. Fuck off!"

"Intelligence suggests..."

"Yeah and...? Whaddya mean?" she interjected again. I was getting a tad exasperated with their delaying tactics. I just wanted to get in, and start searching the house before we lost any more time.

"New shit has come to light," I clarified in terms they'd understand, "and we're coming in regardless." I pushed past her, and my colleagues followed.

"Why are there so many of you?" demanded an irate Mrs Skinner.

"We've come to clean the place," replied an unidentified voice from over my shoulder.

The family skulked back into the lounge, and carefully sat down on their sofas and armchairs, the greasy marks at differing head heights indicating who sat where in the household.

"So, PC Donoghue, what are you looking for today?" voiced a smug Angel, before sucking on her middle finger provocatively.

"I have reason to believe that stolen television sets are in this property."

I heard a popping noise as she pulled her finger out sharply, changing from provocative to abusive as she jerked her erect digit in my general direction.

"We ain't even got a telly!" replied Brett as he motioned around the room, where, indeed, there was no television set to be seen. The family began laughing raucously at his obvious comic talent aimed at embarrassing the bumbling constabulary of Sandford.

"Well, what's all your furniture pointed at then?" queried

Chad. The laughter abruptly ceased. Both sofas and the two armchairs were all angled towards the same empty space.

Whilst Lloyd and Gwen came into the lounge to watch the family, the rest of us searched the house, room by filthy room. We looked through hallways jammed with pushbikes, into bedrooms with mattresses on the floor covered in sheets stained with blood and assorted DNA, in bathrooms that looked as if they were the stunt doubles for the 'before' photos in cleaning product adverts, and in airing cupboards rammed with dirty, stinking clothes.

We had drawn a blank upstairs, and the only space left to check was the attic. It was where I suspected the televisions had been hidden all along. Whilst they were using their delaying tactics downstairs, this was where they must have been hiding the gear. We just had to get in there now. Andy was volunteered on the basis that he was younger and thinner than the rest of us. Even so, he still had to take his body armour and belt equipment off so it wouldn't get stuck climbing through the opening. We pushed open the loft hatch cover and hoisted him up. There is always a danger when popping your head into a felon's loft: they usually don't want you up there, and, occasionally, as you peep into the void, any person still up there can take a swing at your unprotected face with a golf club, plank of wood or size ten boot. Andy seemed quite excited about the task in hand, so we decided not to elaborate too much on why we were all patting him on the back and wishing him luck.

The entire family were accounted for downstairs so, hopefully, it would be a safe ascent into the unknown for our intrepid boy. One good shove, and he shot into the darkness. I could hear him banging and crashing away as he got himself onto his feet. As I shone the torch up, I could see him making rapid Kung Fu moves; perhaps there was an accomplice up there who had been lurking in the dark recesses. As Andy didn't have his equipment with him, I hurriedly got out my ASP baton to throw up to him.

"Someone up there?" I shouted urgently.

"Cobwebs!" came the unhappy reply. Other than that, apart from a water tank, rolls of insulation and a dead pigeon, the place was empty. Andy even climbed through to the wall of the adjoining property to see if they had knocked through into next door's loft to secrete the goods there, but the wall was solid. It was hard not to hide my disappointment as he relayed the information.

As Kung Fu Panda dropped down, we considered our situation. There must be some place we still hadn't looked. I'd been convinced that the contraband was in the house. Lloyd and Gwen had confirmed that nothing had come out the back of the house when all the fiasco at the front had been going on, so I was happy that we hadn't missed anything being thrown out of the windows or through the back door.

I told Andy to clean himself up. Meanwhile, we all proceeded back down the stairs and into the lounge. Maybe I would have to reluctantly accept that I had got it wrong; that I had acted in haste on the information I had received; put two and two together and made five. Perhaps I really wanted the TVs to be in the house so much that I had made everything fit together in my mind.

Yet, the fact that we hadn't even found the telly that the Skinners had so clearly hidden when we were at the door prompted me to think again. Chad was right: the furniture had to be pointed at something. It was most bizarre; unless they were worshipping the only clean square of carpet in the whole house. If we couldn't find the telly they had been watching, there must be other items we hadn't found.

The family remained seated as I entered the room, but stared intently at me. There were none of the usual attempts to intimidate and deride. This wasn't normal. I stood in quiet contemplation for a few seconds before I addressed my suspects.

"Up you get, let's see under the cushions."

The amount of swearing and general discontent that erupted indicated that I had hit the jackpot. Our checks revealed that the sofas and chairs were all hollowed out. No wonder they had all sat down so carefully. Inside were the plasma TVs and other assorted stolen items. A victory for the long arm of the law snatched from the jaws of defeat.

"Someone's grassed us up!" declared a seething Brett.

"Someone is going to get their ass wiped out!" spat out Mot, obviously thinking he was in LA as opposed to Sandford.

"Yeah! There is going to be a lot of ass wiping done!" contributed Clint. I'm not sure if he was subtly trying to tell me that he had just got a job as a carer in an old people's home. Anyway, he was going to have to wait; we were off to custody.

They were all arrested, and led out to the awaiting transport – extra vehicles being requested from the neighbouring towns to accommodate our extended human haul. Mot and Clint were compliant enough when they were led out, but started to bang, kick and shout abuse and threats as soon as they were ensconced in the cages. A lot of prisoners do it. They make a big fuss while they are in the wagon, but as soon as you open the door when you get to your destination, they quieten down again. They're known as 'perspex heroes'. They will be as brave as they like from behind the perspex confines of the cage, when there is no opportunity of retribution, but as soon as the door is open again and there is a real risk of confrontation, they'll magically start to behave.

They are closely related to the '100 yard hero' – a breed of lout that shouts obscenities at the police from the end of the street, but when approached, runs away. These are gradually being replaced by 100 metre heroes.

As Brett, Mot, Clint, Dean and the head turner were driven away in their respective vans, I was left standing with Ruby Skinner and Jess, awaiting the final transport vehicle.

"Any chance of a smoke before I go?" she queried.

"Sure, if you've got the doings," I replied.

She pulled a tobacco pouch out of her once white, but now greying bra, and started to deftly roll a cigarette with her nicotine-stained fingers.

"Got a light?" she enquired of Jess.

After a negative answer, she turned her attention to me. "You look like someone who'd have a light."

I wasn't sure if that was meant to imply that I looked like a smoker, or that I was the sort to keep a lighter in my pocket just in case I heard a power ballad on the radio. She was wrong on both counts.

"Well," she said, throwing her half-rolled cigarette down in disgust, "you've ruined my day for the second time! Happy now?" she intoned.

"Well, I'm not sad, if that's what you mean." I thought it best not to sound too upbeat in my reply, but I didn't want to lie.

There is a movement called 'Radical Honesty' which takes that approach to the extreme. Their basic premise is that the world would be a better place if we all stopped lying and told the truth. It all seems very laudable until you have Anne Frank living in your attic and the Nazis come knocking at your door.

My dad instilled in me that honesty is always the best policy, although that's a bit rich coming from the man who told me about Father Christmas, the Easter Bunny and the Tooth Fairy. Without lies, marriages would fail, egos would be shattered, workers would be fired, and politicians would be out of business. I consider myself an honest person, but I lie. They are mainly little ones to help maintain the harmony in a relationship:

"Does my bum look big in this?"

The only way to answer without lying is to perhaps play for time by seeking further clarification.

"In this room?"

However, I don't think such deviation or hesitation is allowed within the official rules of Radical Honesty.

I think white lies should be allowed, and perhaps even encouraged. I don't really want to be told I'm not looking good, or that my jokes aren't funny – even worse still, that they were funny the *first* time I told them. According to a survey, men tell twice as many lies as women, although I guess we're assuming here that the women didn't lie when they were asked the question.

Regardless of gender, a criminal's best asset is also their lie ability. Some have had decades of practise at it, too. Therefore, in my quest to improve my interviewing techniques, and to get to the truth, over the years I have invested in a veritable library of books on body language to help alert me to the tell-tale signs a liar inadvertently shows, rather than just listening to what they say.

The three wise monkeys: hear no evil; see no evil; speak no evil cover some of the basic gestures with regard to deceit. Children will often cover their mouths with their hands to literally stop their lies coming out, or cover up their ears if they don't want to receive a reprimand. If there is something they don't want to see, they'll simply cover their eyes. As we get older, these gestures become less obvious and more refined, but they usually still occur to some degree when someone is being deceitful.

The nose rub is a sophisticated refinement of the mouth covering gesture. The hand goes to cover the mouth, but at the last moment, to make it less obvious, the brain subconsciously changes it to a nose rub. The eye rub is the adult version of 'see no evil'. The ear rub is the grown up 'hear no evil'.

I needn't have bothered with all the amateur psychology. With Mot, Clint and the rest of the Skinner family it was back to basics. I could easily tell when they were lying – it was usually when their lips were moving.

All the Skinners gave differing alibis and accounts of how the television sets came into their possession. The trouble with lying is that you generally have to have a good memory. I usually opt for asking as many questions as I can, probing any response further, drilling deeper into their version of events, looking for any conflicts or anomalies. If someone is telling the truth, however improbable their story may be, they will stick to it. Liars, on the other hand, always tend to eventually trip themselves up.

I put my file together with my report and interview transcripts, and rang the all night CPS hotline. I was put through to a solicitor at the other end of the country, and scanned my paperwork to her. I waited on the line for an hour as she worked through it all, and asked me questions about the case. Eventually, at five-thirty in the morning, I got my reply. Charges were authorised. I was delighted. Not a bad result following an off-duty conversation with a helpful member of the public.

As I wandered happily back into the parade room, I toyed with the idea of giving the radical honesty approach one more go. I faced my first real test when Gwen approached me and asked me what position I wanted her in.

"I'm flattered," I replied, "but you're a married woman Gwen…"

"No, no," she spluttered, as the rest of the shift looked up at her in astonishment. "I meant in the charity football game you were arranging…"

I gave her a blank look as though I had no idea what she was talking about.

"Jess said you were arranging a football game! You *were* arranging a football game, weren't you?"

As the rest of the shift murmured that they didn't know what she was on about, she blushed as red as a beetroot, and quickly made her exit. When I was sure she was far enough down the corridor, I spread out the sheet of paper on the table with everyone's name on.

"We'll play Gwen in goal on Saturday I think."

CHAPTER EIGHT:

Too Much Scooby Doo

It was the May Bank Holiday weekend, and the weather was glorious. After a timid start, the buds on the trees and hedgerows had finally decided it was safe to venture out, and the countryside was now awash with fifty shades of green, interspersed with fields of golden barley.

A young couple from the town had decided that this was the ideal opportunity to give their new tent its first outing of the year, and had set off for a few days under canvas in the beautiful countryside, away from the hustle and bustle of Sandford.

After a day hiking in the late spring sunshine, they had stopped for a picnic next to a gently gurgling stream before finally setting up camp next to Todd's Plantation, an ancient copse of lush deciduous woodland. Swathes of delicate spring bluebells carpeted the forest floor, the hues of the flowers changing as they slowly morphed from rich dark blue at their youngest and freshest, to a soft pale blue as the summer months drew closer. The scene was highlighted by the soft, dappled sunshine as it peeked through the rich canopy above. The gentle scent of the flowers wafted through the warm air, adding to the serene, dreamy feel of this heavenly place. No one ventured here now, and so the woods had become a tranquil haven solely for the birds and local wildlife to enjoy; a laudable enough role in itself.

After cooking a meal of beans and sausages on a campfire,

the couple had swapped stories under the stars whilst becoming quietly merry from a couple of bottles of wine before retiring for the night. Exhausted by a day spent in the fresh air, they had quickly succumbed to sleep accompanied by the soundtrack of owls gently hooting in the distance.

Suddenly, they were violently awoken by blood-curdling cries and screams. They tried to reassure each other by saying that it was just the calls and screeches of the various birds and animals, but nevertheless, they cuddled in closer as their minds worked overtime, conjuring up thoughts of the devil himself.

They were slowly drifting off when they were once again shocked awake by a mighty clap of thunder. A slow pitter patter of rain on canvas then took over, gradually increasing in tempo until individual droplets could no longer be distinguished from each other, eventually developing into a hard torrent beating down on their tent. The drumming of the persistent downpour was more than welcome, though, as it drowned out the other sinister noises that had been troubling their subconscious. Soon sleep overcame them once more.

The next morning, they were gently roused by the buzzing of a honey bee as it searched for nectar amongst the flowers nearby. Everything appeared drenched in bright sunshine as the morning sun bore down on their temporary home. The rain had stopped, and it seemed as if a thousand songbirds had joined the morning chorus. All thoughts they had harboured during the night of abandoning their trip were soon forgotten as they crawled out of the tent and into the warm morning, blinking like moles as they emerged into the light.

The first task of the morning was to get breakfast started and a cup of tea brewed. As she wandered off into the woods in search of some dry kindling, he started to clean the pots and pans, and fill the kettle. When fifteen minutes had passed, and she still hadn't returned, he began to think she must have been caught up in admiring what Mother Nature had to display. He lay back in the warmth of the sun, and decided to give it five more minutes before he ventured out to join her, when a piercing scream filled the air. He instantly recognised it as his girlfriend. Instinctively, he sprang up, and rushed headlong into the woodland.

As he entered the copse, he looked around blindly, realising he had no idea which way she had gone. However, he slowly tracked towards the sound of her continued screams, leading him deeper and deeper into the woods. Bluebells gave way to brambles, dappled sunshine yielded to shadow. As he ventured further, the screams became louder and louder until, eventually, he saw her in a small clearing, rooted to the spot... both hands held to her face as if trying to block out what she had seen. As he crept closer, moving silently towards his partner, he could now see what she saw: a body lying sprawled on the floor. The corpse was lying on its front, arms and legs twisted awkwardly; most horrifying of all was that it had no head... and no left hand.

The couple had rushed out of the woods, disorientated, stumbling, crashing through the undergrowth, and blundering over the frail flowers. Their camp was forgotten; like the *Marie Celeste*, abandoned in their haste. Frantic, they had ran, floundered and charged over field and beck until they had eventually reached a farmhouse where they had banged and banged on the door, begging to be let in. There, exhausted and frightened, they had breathlessly explained to the startled farmer the horrendous sight they had witnessed before ringing the police to report their macabre discovery.

***

The call had come in while we were in the morning briefing. CID were informed, but, like all incidents, it was up to uniform to attend initially, and assess the situation. Chad and I were tasked with the detail. As we got into our vehicle, Barry kindly thought to enlighten us regarding local rumours that were circulating that I knew wouldn't help us one bit:

"Those woods are supposed to be haunted."

Armed with that additional snippet of information, we began the long drive to the farm where we had arranged to meet the couple. It would take at least forty-five minutes until we got there; ample time for us to think far too deeply on what we would encounter when we finally arrived.

In hindsight, Chad and I probably weren't the best people to assign to the job. We had both been involved in searching a graveyard during the silent hours a few weeks earlier; I say the 'silent hours', but it was some unnatural sounds emanating from the cemetery that had caused us to be sent there in the first place. Nocturnal screams and cries had filled the air, disturbing the sleep of local residents, sending shivers down their spines. We had been called as a result, and sent to investigate. Clearly, as police, we were obviously immune to being scared shitless at the thought of entering a graveyard in the dead of night when spooky noises are coming from it.

I put it down to watching too much *Scooby Doo* when I was young, and I freely admit that I had my heart in my mouth as I walked through the imposing cemetery gates. A damp fog had descended, cloaking the whole of the graveyard in an omnipresent grey mist that swirled around the tombstones, giving everything an eerie soft focus. Chad had confessed that it wasn't so much the thought of a maniac charging towards us – we had our sprays and ASPs after all… and we could run – but rather that he was more terrified of a five-year-old girl appearing out of the mist, wearing a long white nightie, whispering 'help me' over and over again. We made a pact not to hide from each other and jump out, unless Lloyd and Jess showed up, and, then, of course, it would be mandatory. For thirty minutes we searched every inch of the place, wondering what was lurking behind every grave and every tree. I started to whistle to hide my nervousness, until I realised that it would probably help the un-dead locate me more easily. I stopped, and suggested to Chad that he might like to sing instead.

We never did find where the cries were coming from, but Ron informed us later that foxes emit a high pitched, squealing bark if cornered – sounding like a baby crying. "Even hedgehogs make strange noises in the night," added Gwen. I decided to put it down to that, instead of zombies, or the unhappy, tormented spirits of the dead. Well, that's what I wrote in my report.

A week later, I had cause to attend the cemetery again. This time Comms had put a call out, reporting a topless woman lying on one of the toppled gravestones in the grounds. This seemed like an altogether better prospect. I had desperately tried to get on the radio to say I would assist, but was unable, due to all the other units saying they would attend: traffic, dog units, CID, other Kilo units from the town, Ben and George from Kilo 3...

Eventually, I got through and said I would take a look as it was my area, but immediately regretted it as soon as Comms gave me an update on the job; apparently, it was a confused 86-year-old woman who had wandered off from the local nursing home. The image I had in my mind of Linda Lusardi, or Megan Fox, reclining sensually, awaiting the arrival of PC Donoghue, was instantly shattered, and instead I was faced with this terrifying prospect. I shuddered at the thought.

I shook my head to dispel that horrendous memory and looked over to Chad who was driving us to the woods.

"It's going to take us ages," he commented as he glanced back. We were keen to get there, and find out what was going on; it was a bizarre set of circumstances to say the least. It was a fair distance, and the roads gradually got worse the closer we got.

The last time I had blue lighted up to the area it had taken a lot longer than I had anticipated. We race from job to job in and around Sandford, but it's not often that we get called to the outlying villages. The pit villages in Kilo 2 tended to sort their own issues out, and, generally, they didn't involve the police much at all if they could possibly help it.

Last Christmas, we had gone out in the riot bus in case there was trouble in the area's drinking establishments. We had been driving past the working men's club in one of the villages when we had witnessed a disturbance spilling out into the street. We had stopped the van, and four of us had jumped out, donned our gloves in preparation for a fight, and marched into the place. A shout had gone up as we entered, accompanied by the sound of frantic scrabbling. By the time we reached the main lounge everyone was sitting at the tables, pretending to read the paper, quietly drinking or playing snooker, as if nothing had happened.

The only giveaway that something wasn't quite right was the blood splatters up the wall, the broken glass scattered across the floor, the pools of spilt beer, and the snooker players pretending to play with half broken cues and only three red balls. Crimson footprints led to two patrons, holding blood soaked towels to their faces, sitting in the corner. You didn't need to be a detective to get the impression that there was a little incongruity in the situation before us. However, on speaking to the persons present, no one was aware that anything had occurred; no one wanted to make a complaint; apparently, no one had seen anything; no one wanted an ambulance, and, remarkably, the CCTV wasn't recording. We bade them goodnight and carried on our way.

The other call I had attended in the same area just last week, had also been unusual to say the least. True to form, it wasn't the victim who had rung the police; instead, the call had come from a male, pleading to be arrested.

"He has rung in asking to be arrested?" I clarified with Comms.

"He says he'd rather take his chances with us than with the locals," replied Nancy. "He sounds terrified. He says he's in the allotments, up a post, and they are trying to jab him with garden forks."

I lit up the vehicle, and headed in the general direction, first on main roads, then side roads, continuing onto gradually narrower and narrower country roads, until I was on a single track lane flanked by thick hedges on either side. The road signs had now virtually disappeared, and those that remained were peppered with air rifle and shotgun pellets. I kept a wary eye out for anyone playing a banjo.

I eventually arrived to find a welcoming committee that appeared to consist of the entire village, shouting and jeering, all demanding my urgent attention. As I got out of the vehicle, they suddenly parted in front of me, like a human Red Sea, providing a natural walkway leading straight to an old fella wearing a cloth cap, holding his hand out to greet me. As I approached, the seas closed behind me.

As I approached, I got my first sighting of the caller – the man so desperate to be arrested. At the top of a telegraph pole, hanging on for dear life, was an elderly gentleman – clearly terrified, his arms and legs tightly wrapped around the post. As the baying of the melee died down, I could make out the sound of metal gardening implements being secreted away, passed backwards through the crowd, until all evidence of any instant vigilante justice had vanished into thin air. I could see Pole Man mouthing something... it looked like 'help me'. I motioned for him to hang on up there until I could establish what was going on.

"I want him locking up, officer. It's a disgrace. An utter disgrace," voiced the elder. Everyone fell quiet, then murmurs of agreement rippled through the crowd, before impassioned rants about the heinousness of his grave misdemeanour started at the back and quickly spread to the front again. Before long, the air was once again filled with the sound of vitriol and hatred. I was half expecting burning pitch forks, and a wicker man to make an appearance at any second.

"Can someone enlighten me as to what's happened?" I shouted, signalling for the crowd to be silent.

"Look! Just look, lad!" The old chap in the cloth cap furiously exclaimed, pointing towards a couple of pigeon lofts. The crowd had kept a reverential distance from them, as if they were sacred ground. I wasn't sure quite what I was supposed to be outraged at, and sought further clarification.

"What am I supposed to be looking at exactly?"

You could easily been mistaken in thinking that I had put a wet teaspoon in a bowl of sugar, from the disgusted looks I received in return. Women turned away in embarrassment, and the men surveyed me as if to question what kind of idiot they were letting into the constabulary these days.

"The paving slabs! He's moved the bloody paving slabs!" He couldn't have sounded any more exasperated if he had tried.

Sure enough, I could see six empty spaces where paving slabs used to be, which had, clearly, previously formed a neat path over the sacred ground to the loft. The offending slabs were now arranged in a circle a few yards away. When my perplexed expression remained, the village patriarch clearly recognised he was dealing with a first class ignoramus. He grabbed me by the shoulder and took me to one side, addressing me in a hushed whisper, as if he was explaining to the doctor that he had just developed a nasty rash.

My knowledge of *columba livia domestica,* aka the domesticated Rock Pigeon, subsequently increased exponentially. The humble Rock Pigeon, apparently, is also commonly known as the Racing Pigeon, and pigeon racing, it seems, is now an international sport. An international sport that is attracting international gamblers, and, as a result, big money is now involved.

There may be a single starting line, but there are a thousand finishing lines in pigeon lofts in towns and villages all over the land. Apparently, during a race, the time each pigeon returns home is carefully recorded, and then back calculations take place to work out who is the fastest bird: the race winner. Top racers can fetch large sums, one recently selling in Holland for over £200,000. A pigeon that couldn't even fly was sold in Yorkshire for £16,000, purely for breeding purposes; even eggs can change hands for thousands. It has gradually turned from a poor man's hobby to a rich man's sport, and, in this sport, seconds count.

"I still don't see what the problem is," I muttered.

Crash course in pigeon racing part 2 then commenced, delivered by an extremely vexed cloth capped gentleman. It seems that just as we recognise our house from the street, the pigeon recognises his house from the air. Pigeons, it transpires, are also creatures of habit: they like to return to their safe environment. When things change, they become suspicious: is it their house at all? Is there a cat waiting inside? Has Dick Dastardly engineered some Heath Robinson trap for them?

He went on to inform me that moving the slabs would, in his words "confuse the poor little buggers", and make them unhappy birds. Racing pigeons need the same careful nurturing that befits a top class athlete. An athlete can't perform at his best if he's not 'in the zone'. As Mr Cloth Cap explained to me, pigeons are athletes, too – just feathered ones. When he was satisfied that all this had sunk in, he made his demand:

"He's disrupted the harmony of the pigeons. I want him locking up!"

I couldn't actually remember that piece of legislation at training school, but I made the right sort of noises to try and buy me some thinking time. However, it was quickly evident to everyone but me that my ruse wasn't working, and a crumpled piece of paper was quickly thrust into my hand. It transpires that the old timer was the nominated keeper for the village pigeon collective. Pole Man – who also turned out to be Cloth Cap's brother – was the pigeon trainer in the next village. Both brothers, and both villages, it seemed, hated each other.

The piece of paper I had in my hand was a non-molestation order from the court. Clearly, the brothers had previously fallen out. The order consisted of a number of things that Brother X wasn't allowed to do to Brother Y. Breaching the court order would result in the offender being arrested. A finger was jabbed at the section I was meant to take note of. It was clear enough: Brother X was not allowed to 'disturb the harmony of the pigeons'. It may seem like a minor point to some, but to many in these communities this is their life.

I addressed the Pole Man. "I have in my hand a piece of paper..."

He didn't wait to give his version of events. Instead, he just scurried down, and scampered to the safety of my car, letting himself in, accompanied by jeers from the menfolk, and derisive looks from the women. The village elder then came to shake my hand. As a police officer, one minute you can be treated like a pariah, the next moment you can feel like a saviour. In this case, it was definitely the latter, as everyone took turns to come up, slap me on the back, and thank me for my prompt action. I allowed myself a moment of glory, and gave a statesman like wave to the crowd before I got back into my vehicle. I turned to look at my charge, and he met my glance with a condemned man's stare. As church bells sounded in a victory salute, I felt that I had brought peace in our time.

But I digress. I checked my watch, and then gazed out of the window. We were only halfway to our date with destiny, and our mysterious corpse. I looked over at Chad.

"So what do you think about this case? No head, and no left hand? A drug debt settled? A punishment killing? A pigeon related slaying?"

It's always best not to speculate too much before you have all the information... but with a case like this, you can't help it; especially when you have another twenty minutes to dwell on what you will discover when you get there. It wasn't a run of the mill incident. A severed head, for goodness sake!

I remembered Ben telling a tale about a friend of his who had once worked with the notorious serial killer, Dennis Nilsen. She explained to Ben, that after he was caught and exposed, she had invited the girls around one evening to watch a documentary about Nilsen's reign of terror as the Muswell Hill Murderer. His trademark approach was to pick up men and boys in bars, or on the streets, and to take them back to his house, where he would wine and dine them, before strangling or drowning his victims. He would often keep the bodies for several months, admitting later that he also engaged in sexual acts with the corpses. Using the butchering skills that he had acquired during his time as a cook in the army, he would later dismember the corpses. Body parts were boiled to remove the muscle and tissue, whilst entrails were cut into small pieces and flushed down the toilet. He was eventually caught when the drains became blocked, and the cleaning company called out to unblock them raised their suspicions about what they had found with the police.

There were the usual squeals, groans and hiding behind cushions from the women when the gory bits were mentioned, but everyone was slightly bemused when Ben's friend started to violently retch at one particular part in the programme. The presenter had been showing the large metal pot in which Nilsen had boiled the heads, hands and feet of his victims to remove the flesh, when their host had started to heave. There had already been far worse things mentioned and re-enacted prior to this, therefore, her friends couldn't understand her reaction. It was only when Ben's friend explained that every Christmas at the office party Nilsen used to bring his special 'chilli surprise' in that same metal pot that they understood... and began retching violently themselves.

However, there were no current serial killers in the area that we were aware of. Maybe this was the start of a reign of terror? They all have to start somewhere. Maybe the head had been removed to prevent identification? In some Islamic countries, the left hand is cut off to warn people of the consequences of stealing. In this case, however, we could speculate endlessly on what the possible motives might be for removing the head and hand. Chad, it seemed, had other thoughts on his mind.

"Did Barry say the wood was haunted?"

We were both well aware of the phantom black dog that roamed the county – that same black dog that roams every county. The unfortunate creature is often blamed for drivers careering off the road, or crashing into another vehicle, as they swerve to avoid hitting this canine spectre. It's surprising how many drink drivers swear to seeing this black, four-legged menace that has, of course, left the scene before police arrive.

The black dog was something of a joke now amongst officers, and not taken too seriously. It was other unexplained activities that Chad was referring to now. It didn't help that I had told him about a job I had attended recently where a man had complained about ghostly goings on.

He had originally complained that his laptop had been stolen. It was only when I went to investigate this suspected burglary that things became more interesting. There was no sign of any forced entry to the property, and the victim was adamant that he had kept the doors and windows locked. It was when I questioned him further that he opened up to me about the other bizarre goings on that he had experienced lately. Items had been moved around his house, objects had gone missing, only to turn up days later, noises had been heard in the night, footsteps on the stairs, empty glasses placed in the sink, and so on. At first he thought that an intruder had been letting himself in to his house, but he now suspected something more sinister was occurring.

As he relayed this to me, I recalled the case of the man who had hidden in the attic of a house belonging to an unsuspecting woman, for literally months. Every day she would go to work, only to return home eight hours later to discover food missing, the kettle still warm, and the TV changed to a different channel. She had dismissed the notion, telling herself she must be imagining things. Eventually, though, she came home early one day, and saw her unwelcome guest darting behind the sofa. Police were called, and his scam was exposed. He had gained access to an empty property at the end of the terrace, climbed into the loft space, and then made his way from house to house by taking bricks out of the partition wall and climbing through. He had dropped down into each house in turn, looking for the routine that best suited his needs. She was a single woman living on her own, who spent the majority of her time at work – perfect. When he heard her leave the house in the morning, he would drop down, treat the house as his own for the day, and then climb back up before she was due to return from work. I'd like to say that when police arrived, and the whole bizarre situation was exposed, they became close friends and they lived together happily ever after. However, this is reality. He was locked up and eventually sent to a mental institution. She moved into a flat-roofed bungalow.

With this thought uppermost in my mind, I conducted a comprehensive search of Laptop Man's house, with a negative result. On my advice, he got a locksmith in to change the locks and, for added security, attach a bolt to the loft hatch. Finally, once again, he categorically assured me that he hadn't been drinking. This wasn't in his imagination, he stressed to me, this was as real to him as the hand in front of his face. He sounded genuine.

The next day, I received another call from him to say that things had stepped up a level. He had been sitting in the living room, when he was sure he had heard a noise as if someone had farted. He said he didn't know whether to laugh or be terrified. An hour later, he had been doing the washing up in the kitchen, when he had felt first one hand on his right shoulder then another hand planting itself firmly on his left shoulder. He told me that he had frozen in fear. When I arrived at his house, he was as white as a sheet. Something had certainly put the willies up him.

I probed him further as to who had lived in the property before he moved in, and discovered he had inherited the house from his two uncles who had shared the house, and had passed away just a few months earlier.

"I was upset by both their deaths, but it was Uncle Bert who touched me the most," he confided. "Mind you, it was his brother, Ernie, who'd had the original idea of me inheriting the house. I don't know why as I drove him crazy when I visited. I'm a messy fella, and he was a stickler for tidiness."

Despite all my investigations, I failed to find any logical explanation to what was happening, or how the laptop had disappeared. Could it be that this last piece of information held the key? My victim had confessed that he had left the laptop leant up against the sofa; something that his uncle certainly wouldn't have approved of. Could it be Uncle Ernie tidying up? I couldn't crime it as a burglary, as neither of us believed that a human hand was afoot. It was a mystery, and remained unsolved. I hinted that a higher power might be needed.

"Your sergeant?"

"No! Not my sergeant! A priest or something. An exorcist," I replied sharply.

As I was about to go, he looked down, coughed and asked me one final question. "Someone told me, a friend of a friend, he wanted me to ask..."

"Go on," I replied cautiously.

"Well," he continued, averting his gaze, "I was told that a wet dream is a ghost giving you a blow job. Is that true?"

I quickly opened the door, and stepped out, before responding to his query. "To be honest, you're starting to scare me a little bit now. I'm off."

I then beat a hasty exit... although in the circumstances, that probably isn't the most appropriate wording. I decided there and then that if this guy did contact me again, I *would* refer him to my higher authority: Barry.

"Here it is!" exclaimed Chad, thankfully breaking my train of thought.

We had pulled off the road, and were now bouncing along a dirt track towards an isolated farmhouse.

The young couple came running out when they saw us approach, begging us to take them home. When we informed them that we were there to view the corpse, the girl broke down in tears. Her boyfriend reluctantly agreed to show us what area of the woods they had had camped near, but was adamant that he wasn't going to enter the copse again.

"No one ever goes up there," volunteered Alf Geddon, the farmer, who had now joined us. "You'll never get your police car across them fields, either. I'll give you a lift on my machine," he said, pointing to a muddy, single seat, off-road buggy sitting in the yard.

So, with the crying girl waving us off, and Farmer Geddon at the wheel, the rest of us – the frightened boyfriend, Chad and me – all hanging on as best we could, bounced off across the fields towards Todd's Plantation.

It took about another ten minutes to finally reach the copse, but as we got closer, the boyfriend began to hyperventilate. We insisted that he identified which side of the woods we needed to search, before allowing him to jump off, and continue his panic attack in peace. We, meanwhile, bounced along without him. Soon after the farmer, too, got cold feet, and, using the excuse that he had better take the lad back to the farmhouse, he turned back, leaving us to cover the last two hundred yards on foot.

A low morning mist hung over the copse, and as we drew closer I got on the radio to tell Comms that we had eventually arrived at our destination. As the radio crackled, three crows suddenly flew from the trees, cawing loudly and I wondered if we had just disturbed a murder. Their hoarse, raucous calls faded, as we came upon the hastily abandoned camp… it was *Scooby Doo* time all over again.

Were there other bodies in the woods? Was the killer or killers still here? Was the plantation haunted like Barry had suggested? What other secrets did the forest hold for us to uncover?

"Shouldn't we be leaving a trail of something behind to follow out?" I asked Chad anxiously, as we prepared to enter under the dark green canopy of the trees.

"We're not bloody looking for a gingerbread house," came his curt reply.

"Could be a gingerbread crack house," I mumbled back.

I made a mental note of his brusqueness, and hoped that he didn't think he could come running to me if he got himself lost. I guess we were both just a bit on edge. It didn't help when a pheasant suddenly flew out of the undergrowth and flapped right in front of us, causing us both to jump out of our skins.

We exchanged glances, and had a nervous giggle, before we both proclaimed, "Fuck it," and marched determinedly through the soft blue blooms, and into the darkness.

After ten minutes of searching, kicking over dead tree trunks, looking in hollows and clearing a path through the undergrowth with my ASP, a shout went up from Chad. He had found the body in a natural clearing in the woods. I rushed over, and saw my colleague standing over the body. It was clearly a human cadaver, lying awkwardly on its front. This was certainly our man – just as the young couple had described – headless, and without a left hand. We both stood in silence for a few seconds, looking at the sad scene in front of us, before I got on the radio.

I gave a call to Comms to say that cops had confirmed a corpse in the copse, to nobody's amusement but my own. It was my nervousness at the situation that was causing me to say such a stupid thing. It's like giggling at a funeral: you know you shouldn't, but you just can't help yourself; the tension of the situation making you act foolishly to mask your true feelings.

I was informed that the CID Sergeant was on his way. Chad and I then began the unpleasant task of searching for other bodies, or clues, in preparation for our grilling by the Sarge.

Half an hour into our gruesome duty, I heard the rumble of the farmer's buggy once again. Proceeding to the edge of the woods, I could see Barry, Roy Slade – the CID sergeant – and the CSI guy, all holding onto the contraption for dear life as it bumped over the open ground. They, too, had to complete the last couple of hundred yards on foot, as the farmer dropped them off and hastily drove back to the farm to get on with the day's activities. Even with the discovery of a death like this, life goes on.

"So, Donoghue, what's your expert verdict?" asked the besuited Sergeant Slade, as he reached us. I think by his tone it was meant to be a rhetorical question: "We have a headless corpse, with no left hand, lying in the middle of the woods. Give me your qualified assessment of events as they have transpired."

He smirked at the CSI guy, who let loose a little snort, as he nodded back at Slade. Barry just looked a little irritated by Slade's offhand manner.

"Suicide, Sarge," I replied.

"You tit, Donoghue!" exclaimed Slade. Another snort from the white paper suited CSI guy, and this time, a roll of the eyes from my own sergeant.

"John, John, John," sighed Barry, shaking his head, as if he felt that by my flippant reply I had let down the professionalism of E shift, and had finally confirmed that I was losing my marbles.

"No, seriously, Sarge, it is suicide. I can tell you when it happened, too."

Chad nodded in agreement.

Our search of the woodland may have proved fruitless with regard to any further bodies, or for that matter, the missing head and hand. The state of the body, however, indicated that this wasn't a recent death; far from recent. The skin was almost mummified; the remaining clothing looking ragged and dirty.

There is an old expression that says that it's sometimes difficult in life to see the wood for the trees. It can also be difficult to see the hangman's noose for the foliage, too. But there it was; directly over where the crumpled body was found. However, this was no lynching.

Nearby was a small rucksack, which contained the few worldly possessions of our victim: four pounds twenty in change; a key for a door that he'd never open again; an old bus ticket; a docket for a pair of shoes; a ragged jumper to keep him warm, and a couple of old photographs pressed in between the pages of a battered old bible. One was a crumpled over-exposed photograph of two young black children sitting on the floor, whilst the other was a faded image of a young man and his smiling bride. Was this a likeness of you, my friend?

At the bottom of the bag, inside an empty imitation leather wallet, was a suicide note, written in shaky handwriting on a piece of paper ripped out of a cheap notebook. The note told of his depression at losing his family in a civil war in some faraway land, having come to the country as a refugee with hope in his heart, and then the slow decline as he failed to find work, and how he had sunk deeper and deeper into depression. In his desperation, he had decided there was no option other than to end it all. He must have been a missing person that nobody had missed at all because the note was dated eighteen months earlier.

The unhappy male must have hanged himself from the tree, and after several months, as the body started to decay, the neck must have rotted through, sending the body landing in a crumpled heap below. The head had probably rolled off into the undergrowth where a fox or some other animal must have run off with it. I guess that some other woodland rodent had thought that if Mr Fox was having the head, he'd have the hand. As the right hand was folded under the body as it fell, it was saved from a similar fate. Well, that was mine and Chad's considered opinion. We explained it to the trio, who listened intently to our theory.

"It actually sounds very plausible," commented Slade begrudgingly, before asking to see the suicide note.

"I've already checked," I told him as I handed it over, "there's no dog."

Occasionally, tagged onto the end of suicide notes, is a short list of requests such as 'please look after my pet Labrador – I've left him locked in the kitchen'. Usually the suicide victim expects to be found that same day. Luckily, in this case, there was no animal clause. That would just have been too much.

It seems that in life, just as in films, people are often more upset by animals being killed than by human beings. However, in the absence of a deceased pooch, I was feeling sorry for our poor victim. Not only did nobody miss him, but he must have looked down from heaven, or wherever he now was, for month after month at his hanging body. Initially disappointed that no one had found him to lay his body to rest, he must have been devastated when the fox had made off with his cranium. The indignity of it!

There would be no bittersweet remembrance day for our victim: he would just live on in rumours and whispers surrounding the haunted woods. I decided that when I got home tonight I'd have a drink in his memory.

CHAPTER NINE:

The Scorn of the Women

The mini heatwave continued throughout May, and I was in the panda, patrolling the town. It wasn't long before it was sweltering in the vehicle; my body armour sticking uncomfortably to me. The blowers were on full blast, and all the windows were down, as I vainly tried to get something resembling a breeze flowing through the car. As the midday sun bore down on the Sandford shoppers as they headed towards the town centre, it seemed as though even their shadows had decided to stay indoors to avoid the baking heat. I wiped the sweat from my brow, and turned into Shields Way. I yawned widely – the heat conspiring against me. I was feeling listless, and beginning to think that maybe I had been bitten by a radioactive sloth, when I heard those ominous words – words that I'll never forget; words that sent a chill down my spine and snapped me wide awake in an instant:

"Officer! Come quick! The baby's boiling to death!"

Glancing over to where the shout was coming from, I could see a group of people gathered around a small silver hatchback parked near the shops. A few were desperately peering into the vehicle; others were shouting at me and waving, frantically trying to attract my attention. Whatever was going on, it didn't look good.

I gave a series of short yelps with the siren to clear a path across the road. As I jumped out of the police car, I was immediately surrounded by a sea of anxious and concerned faces, all speaking to me at the same time, all wanting to tell me their version of events, their views, comments and opinions.

"She'll die!"

"They should be locked up!"

"It's a disgrace!"

"Her blood will boil!"

"How could they!"

"She'll cook to death!"

"Do something!!"

As I forced my way through the crowd, I could see an infant strapped into a car seat in the back of the vehicle. No-one else was in the car – the child had been left completely on her own. I couldn't believe my eyes: someone had left a baby, who looked only a few months old, in a parked car… and on the hottest day so far this year. I was horrified. Observing her motionless little body, the shouts and rants became white noise to me as I urgently tried the door handle. It was locked. I put my hand on the roof but swiftly removed it – it was scorching hot! Undoubtedly, the car had been parked in the heat of the sun for some considerable time.

"QUIET!" I shouted at the babbling throng. There was no time to listen to people's views and opinions. I needed facts – and I needed them now. "Who can tell me how long the child has been in there?"

"I noticed the baby when I parked next to the car an hour and a half ago," volunteered a woman, moving towards the front. "I thought it was a bit odd, but just assumed that the family were at the ticket machine, or something. When I came back, I saw that she was still there. I'm sorry. I should have done something." She sounded ashamed, as if she felt responsible for not having acted sooner. She had tears in her eyes. I didn't comment.

Over an hour and a half in this heat? It didn't bear thinking about. Babies can't regulate their own body temperature in the same way as adults can. An adult trapped in a metal box in the baking sun would be suffering terribly enough right now, let alone a small child. Babies are particularly vulnerable, and heat stroke can occur within minutes, especially if they are dehydrated. There were posters up all over the town telling people that dogs die in hot cars. Surely, we didn't need to spell it out that babies can perish in the same way?

My noisy arrival on scene had clearly attracted attention, resulting in a gradual swell in the number of bystanders. News of what was going on filtered through the crowd, reigniting general murmurs which grew louder and louder, until they unleashed a crescendo of unsolicited comments into the still, stale air. Any attempt to establish an accurate overview of the situation rapidly diminished, as the mood changed from concern to anger, with gossip and rumour spreading like wildfire amongst the assembled mass; speculation abounded. I understood their anger, but I needed a few seconds to think rationally and logically.

"I blame the parents!" someone shouted, accompanied by a series of derisive jeers. Of course it was the bloody parents! The baby didn't drive here, and then ensconce herself in a car seat in the back!

"I was a nurse. A child can die in a hot car!" a woman shouted in my face.

Speaking as the self-appointed ringleader, she announced her grim prediction for all to hear. She told me that she used to be a matron on a children's ward, before quoting statistics, as if trying to add scientific credence to her initial statement. I knew the statistics. I know babies can die in locked cars left in the midday sun.

"You'll have to do something," she added, with the emphasis on the 'do'. This set off a series of calls for action on my part. The crowd was being whipped up into a frenzy.

I tapped on the window to get the child's attention, but she remained impassive, her eyes still closed. There was no evidence that she was distressed; it wasn't a good sign. At least if she was crying, I'd know that she was alive. Heaven forbid that I'd arrived too late. I drew my ASP, and racked it.

"Kilo 1 mobile, urgent!" Now Comms were getting in on the act.

"If it's about the baby in the town centre, I'm here!" I barked in response. "I'm going to smash the window and get the child out. Call an ambulance."

This was a matter of life or death, and seconds counted. I quickly cupped my hands against the glass and again peered in at the baby. She was sat in the back, so it would be too dangerous to smash a rear window. It would have to be the front. The child hadn't moved a muscle. With her eyes closed she looked eerily still. I couldn't help but think the worst.

"Stop looking and wasting time, and DO SOMETHING!" The stern looking matron broke my train of thought with her demand. The crowd took up her call to arms. There was nothing else for it: I had to get the child out of that car.

"Stand back!" I raised my baton, shielded my eyes, and brought it down forcefully on the passenger window. It bounced off. I didn't realise how hard it was to break car windows – it looks so easy in the movies. I tried a second blow, then a third, before it finally smashed, sending beads of safety glass flying into the vehicle. I quickly used my ASP to clear the rest of the glass out of the frame, and then pulled the lock up, but the central locking system had been activated and the doors wouldn't open. Damn! Undeterred, I leaned in. The heat was overpowering inside: it was like a furnace; the air stuffy and dry. With one hand I managed to unbuckle the central clip of the safety harness on the child seat. I made a grab for the baby, but she was just out of reach. Even with all this commotion, she still hadn't stirred; there wasn't even a flicker. Please God... please let her still be alive!

I wriggled through further, the window frame digging into my stab vest as I stretched. My feet left the roadway as I lunged deeper into the vehicle to grasp the child. Supporting her head as best I could, I lifted her first into the front of the car, and then out of the broken window into safety.

She was limp and motionless. I couldn't see any sign of her breathing. Her eyes were still closed; not scrunched, just gently shut. She looked at peace. Unconsciousness is one of the signs of heat stroke. It didn't look good: all this activity; all this noise; being dragged out of the seat, and then through the window… and still no reaction from her at all. Was she in a coma? Was she already dead? Please don't let me be too late.

I radioed Comms, demanding an update on the ambulance, while I looked for any signs of breathing and desperately felt for a pulse. I couldn't find one. I stood still, just holding her in my arms.

"Here, let me try." The nurse held out her arms, and I placed her gently into them.

I slumped against the car after my exertions. My mind was in turmoil, my head was thumping, my heart beating as though a butterfly was trapped within my ribcage desperately trying to get out. I looked at my hands – they were shaking.

"The baby is out of the vehicle and…" I called through to Comms, my voice betraying my emotion. Only then did I realise how dry my throat was. I looked up at the woman to see how the child was – searching her eyes for the crucial update which would determine how I would end that sentence. My trembling fingers gripped the radio, as I fought the accusations and recriminations swirling in my brain. Had I acted too late? If I had acted seconds earlier, could it have made a difference? Had I failed this child? I couldn't help but fear the worst.

The former nurse cradled the baby in her arms for a few seconds. She stroked the child's forehead and gently raised her eyelids, before feeling for a heartbeat. She then placed her ear next to the baby's tiny mouth and listened intently. Finally, she turned and looked at the crowd behind her, and then with a sombre expression, she offered the motionless child back to me.

I felt sick. I didn't know what to do or what to say. It's funny what you notice at times like this: I noticed that the crowd had fallen silent; I saw a bumble bee land on the remnants of the shattered glass in the window frame; I heard the song of a bird in the distance. Every minute detail of that second was forever burnt into the hard drive of my mind. Above all else, I remember feeling numb. I continued to stare at the nurse and her outstretched arms that held the lifeless infant, and I recall my shame when all I could do was shake my head in disbelief. I had failed her: a life so young had been lost. Inside I was falling apart, but I still had a duty to the public to present the calm, authoritative image that they expected. Looking me directly in the eye, it was the matron that eventually broke the silence.

"Oh, you silly man. It's a doll."

"DOLL!" I exclaimed in astonishment. I think I was in shock.

"A very realistic doll, I'll grant you," she clarified, "but a doll all the same."

"Oh yes," the woman who had been in tears – the one who had felt so guilty – suddenly perked up. "Oh, it's lovely! My seven-year-old niece has one. They're quite expensive, mind you. She treats it like her own baby. She takes it on outings and everything. I wouldn't be surprised to think that's what has happened here."

"You don't say?" I replied in a flat monotone.

"My daughter may be getting one from the school next year," volunteered another. "I think the school loan them out in sex education classes."

"Well, someone will be getting a bloody Fail," I muttered.

"Oh, look at the mess you've made!" came another voice, as if to rub my nose in my grandiose error. "I thought policemen would know these things."

"I thought you were going to pick the lock or something," voiced another, "not just use brute force. Shocking!"

"Honestly," I heard someone else sigh. "everything has to be so dramatic with you lot! The owners won't be at all happy!"

Now that the excitement was over, the crowd started to disperse; to drift off into town, and on with their daily business, but not before they had all tut-tutted at how I'd clearly overreacted at the incident. I was soon all alone. All that remained was the doll, the broken window, the scorn of the women, and my shame. I got my pocket notebook out, propped 'baby' against the wheel, and started to compose the mitigating circumstances to explain why I'd smashed a window of a Saturday shopper's car; there was no more I could do until the owner of the vehicle returned. I was soaked with perspiration, my body armour was ripped where I had reached through the window, and, to top it all off, I was starting to develop a pulsating headache. I was convinced that I would die from dehydration if I stayed there much longer. I was at rock bottom: at my nadir. I leant against the car, and hoped that I would never again encounter that sinking feeling. The only way the day could get any worse was if it involved clowns... or diarrhoea.

I looked down at the doll. Even now – now that I knew it was a doll – it still looked human: the crinkled forehead; the creased eyelids; the intricately crafted appearance. I swore under my breath. Move over Soaper – I'd just found a new arch-nemesis!

I propped Chucky on the bonnet, as I leant against the car, staring blankly, pondering over how I'd be able to explain this one. As I stood there, absorbed in contemplation, a Jack Russell came into my line of vision, diverting me from my thoughts. He ran around and around in little circles for about five minutes, and I was just thinking how easily dogs are entertained, when I realised I had just stood and watched a dog chase its own tail for the last five minutes.

I called him over and introduced him to my nemesis. He had a good sniff as I dangled the baby in front of him. I was beginning to cheer up a bit as he started to bark and jump as I made the baby dance. I was looking over my shoulder to check no-one was watching our illicit antics, when I felt a tug. As I had turned away, the dog had seized the moment and grabbed hold of the doll's leg, jerking it out of my grasp and had started running away. Then I heard a scream... followed by an expletive as a young couple recoiled in horror at the sight of the dog tearing past with a baby clamped in its jaws.

What was I to do? I couldn't abandon the car. I'd already broken the window, and so couldn't leave it unattended. What if some opportunist thief helped themselves to whatever was in the glove compartment when I was gone? On the other hand, how would I explain to their daughter that her precious dolly had been stolen? It was expensive, according to what one woman had said. I was in a dilemma; a quandary; a conundrum. What should I do? Suddenly, my mind was made up for me – I could hear screams coming from the town centre.

Oh dear God! People obviously thought it was a real baby that had been snatched by Sandford's very own dingo. There was nothing else for it: I'd have to go after the doll snatcher. It sounded like it was creating havoc.

As I entered the busy pedestrianised area, children were crying, men were swearing liberally, and women were shrieking. The scene was also punctuated by several others preferring to do silent impressions of Edvard Munch's 'The Scream'; clearly too traumatised to utter a sound. It wasn't hard to locate the baby thief; just follow where the cries were loudest. I raced over towards the furore... and there he was, chewing on the baby's leg, outside the chemist. A red mist descended.

"Got you, you thief."

I sprinted over, but, as he saw me he grabbed the doll again, running off into the crowd. The race was on! He ran into a shop – I ran into the shop after him, knocking over a mannequin, picking it up and apologising to it, only to realise it was a mannequin, and throwing it back down again. The dog ran out of the shop – I ran out of the shop. Then it was back into the melee, accompanied by a bombardment of screams, gasps and disbelieving cries, en route. I was leaving a trail of havoc behind me: onlookers dropping their shopping; some staring at me; others staring at the dog; most tripping over the people in front of them, but all looking on, transfixed. Some men, who clearly didn't quite know what was going on, started humming the Benny Hill theme tune, until they saw the limp baby in the dog's jaws, whereby the tune just trailed off to nothing.

Comms were on the radio again. The council CCTV cameras had picked up a police officer running through the crowd, and had obviously zoomed in to see, to all intents and purposes, a dog running through the town with a baby gripped in its jaws; the child's head bumping violently off the pavement as he went.

"We're sending urgent assistance to you!"

Oh no! I could hear distant sirens: the cavalry was on its way. I needed to catch the bloody dog before any of my colleagues arrived, and before anyone had a seizure. This wouldn't look good; I wouldn't hear the last of it. I had to salvage something from this debacle. There was nothing for it: I had to change my tactics.

I stopped, and shouted a challenge over to my quarry. He stopped and looked around. We were about ten yards apart. The shoppers had parted, and we now had a clear view of one another. He dropped the doll, and cocked his leg for a pee.

I seized the opportunity, and ran towards him, maintaining eye contact throughout. He panicked, and made to grab for his prize, but I stamped on an outstretched baby arm. There was an audible gasp from the crowd. No time to explain – this was war. The dog tried to drag the baby away, but couldn't.

I lunged at the doll, grabbing the head – that would give me most leverage. But I wasn't going to indulge in a crude tug-of-war: he'd have had years of practise with strings of sausages from the butcher. No, in this instance, in this ultimate challenge between man and beast, I would utilise my superior knowledge of the laws of gravity.

I started to swing the doll around, the dog initially scampering in big circles around me; then faster and faster until the dog was airborne, swinging in a great arc, as he hung onto to the baby's leg...

"My God, Donoghue! What are you doing?"

I was snapped out of my haze by the voice of Barry. I stopped spinning, but was still a little dizzy. Sweat was in my eyes, making the image before me fuzzy and distorted. I could just make him out, standing looking at me with incredulity. For some bizarre reason, there was someone dressed as a pirate next to him. They were flanked on one side by Gwen and Jess, and the other by the paramedics, Steve and Lysa. Behind them, peeping around as if for safety, was a good percentage of the town's population. As I stood there facing him, I suddenly realised that I didn't feel at all well.

"Sarge, I can explain...."

Twenty minutes later, and I was in the Sergeant's office at the receiving end of a disheartening tirade. I recall the term 'criminal damage' being liberally bandied about, references to potential public order offences having been committed, and a complaint regarding an officer swinging a Jack Russell around. I listened, open mouthed, horrified at the tale being told. It was only when he mentioned the Jack Russell bit that I realised it was me he was talking about. I now regretted nodding along in agreement to the first half.

Barry was becoming more and more irate as he rattled through the catalogue of errors: how he had entered the town to be met with carnage; how he had witnessed one of his own officers holding a baby by its head and swinging it around, whilst a small dog held onto one of the baby's legs.

"It wasn't a real..."

"I KNOW it wasn't a real baby NOW, Donoghue! We ALL know it wasn't a real baby now. But, at the time, goodness knows what was going through people's minds. I'm surprised the paramedics weren't treating anyone who'd had a stroke!"

"I'm sure he wouldn't have bitten them…"

"I'm not on about anyone stroking the dog, you numbskull!"

He continued on in the same vein for another ten minutes or so. When he eventually paused for breath, I quietly and quickly presented my side of the story. There were mitigating circumstances for my meltdown, I told Barry. I had genuinely thought that I had held a dead baby in my arms only minutes before the dog had ran off with the doll. My head wasn't straight. Perhaps it had been a mistake to have swung the dog around.

"And," added Barry, "the gentleman that you asked where his parrot was… that was the Mayor of Sandford in all his ceremonial regalia. He was less than impressed with the performance of Sandford's finest today! Not in the least! I wouldn't be at all surprised if there was another complaint coming into the office from the town council!"

"Argh!"

"Are you trying to sound like a pirate? Because if you are, it's not appropriate! Not appropriate at all."

"No, Sarge! I was trying to sound concerned. I mean I am concerned. Sorry Sarge."

Barry was the reddest I'd ever seen him. I expected steam to start coming out of his ears at any second.

"Just get out of my sight!"

I deduced from his comment that my presence was no longer required. As I left the office, I looked up the corridor. I could hear the banter coming from the parade room. I couldn't face my colleagues yet. Things were just going from bad to worse. I was at my lowest ebb, and I needed a minute of peace to compose myself. I retreated to the sanctity of the washroom.

I closed the door carefully behind me, went over to the sink, splashed cold water on my face, and looked hard at myself in the mirror. I stood staring at my reflection for a few minutes before I broke my self-imposed silence.

"You idiot!" I muttered. "It's mistake after stupid mistake with you. Call yourself a police officer? You're useless! A disgrace to the uniform!"

It was then that I heard a shuffling coming from trap two. "Who are you?" asked a feeble voice from the cubicle. "And how do you know so much about me?"

It sounded like Soaper. I quickly made my exit.

CHAPTER TEN:

The Last Temptation of Chris

Sometimes I wish I was a morning person... until I actually meet one.

I was on a set of early shifts and as I yawned, I swear I could hear a whale somewhere in the distance answering me back. Shifts are not good for the body at the best of times: the mix of lates, nights and early days ensuring you can never get into a decent routine for sleeping and eating. Apparently, they mess up your circadian rhythm, but, I have to admit, I was never a good dancer even before I joined the police.

It's the early starts on day shift, though, that I really hate, and which make you realise your best friend in the world is coffee, and, by coffee, I mean real caffeine-based coffee. I once had a cup of decaf by mistake, and felt like I was drinking a cup of lies. No, today of all days, I needed some pure hard core Columbian more than ever after the night I'd just had.

I had gone to bed early and fallen into a deep sleep, waking at about one in the morning to the sound of foxes screeching outside; the joys of living in the countryside. I made best use of the disturbance by going for a pee, ricocheting off the walls like a pinball as I walked across the landing. Dirty deed done, I returned to bed, stubbing my toe in the process.

We are the result of ad hoc evolution and outdated software; there must be a better way in the twenty-first century of alerting my brain to the fact that I'd hurt my hallex, rather than a sharp shooting pain followed by a dull ache. Someone ought to look into that.

Fortunately, someone has actually discovered that swearing alleviates pain. According to the boffins, swearing activates activity in the amygdala, a part of the brain associated with the old fight or flight response, making us less sensitive to pain to allow us to get on with our important decision: do I stay or do I go? Apparently, laughing also boosts immunity and lowers pain, too. In this particular case, I elected to take the swearing option. After a sufficient number of profanities had been uttered, I got back into bed, closed my eyes and rolled onto my side for round two of the night's slumber. I had been lying there for about a minute when I heard it:

"Turn around."

I froze. I just lay there, perfectly still. Was there someone in my bedroom telling me to turn around? I didn't move a muscle, just opening my eyes to stare into the darkness. I listened hard, holding my breath to help concentrate on the slightest sound. There was nothing. Just silence... and the noise of my heart beating like a cartoon animal in love. God, that had given me a fright.

"Turn around."

There it was again. It was a woman's voice – a voice I recognised, but couldn't place. Was it someone I had arrested? The partner of a criminal I had sent down? What did she want? Was she alone? Was she intent on revenge? Did she have a weapon levelled at me? I had read about a Chief Inspector who had been followed back to his house by a felon who had just been released from a long stretch inside; a felon who had spent his years of incarceration plotting his revenge.

The second time she gave me the command she sounded just as calm and confident as the first time she had uttered those chilling words. I couldn't lie there and pretend I didn't exist, and just hope she'd go away. I'd have to do something.

My mind raced through my options. It didn't take long: my phone was on the bedside cabinet, but was switched off.

She had sounded like she was standing in the doorway, and before she had time to speak again or move position, I went for it. In one swift move I whipped the pillow from under my head and flung it in her direction, hoping it might buy me a vital second of time. Leaping on the bed, grabbing the alarm clock as I did so, I charged at the door, yelling at the top of my voice in a bid to disorientate my stalker. I raised the clock above my head as a makeshift weapon as I flicked the light switch and looked for my foe.

The lady had vanished. I then heard Barney barking downstairs. I ran across the landing and jumped down the stairs, three at a time, rushing through the lounge and barging into the kitchen. There he was, sat in his bed, barking at nothing. Or, more than likely, barking at me shouting upstairs. I checked the back door and then the front. Both were secure. The windows were all closed and locked, too. Had she a key to get in?

Taking the dog with me, I ventured upstairs again, flicking the light switch on, and edging carefully into each room. Bedroom clear, nothing in my study, and so into the bathroom. I've always wondered what those paranoid people who check behind the shower curtain for murderers would actually do if they ever found one. Now I was that person. My own plan was to shout loudly and threaten them with a digital alarm.

Finally, there was the converted attic – the Anne Frank suite. With trepidation, I crept up the steep stairs. I felt emboldened that I was now protecting my dog from the trespasser, although it should have been the other way around: Barney should have been protecting me, but I knew that if the intruder had the foresight to bring along a biscuit, he would change allegiances like a shot. Still on edge, I poked my head up to scan for the intruder. That room was also empty.

I retraced my steps, and stood on the landing with Barney. The house was empty except for me and my canine companion. As I patted him, and reassured him that it must have been a bad dream, I heard it once again:

"Turn around."

A shiver ran up my spine. Barney froze, rooted to the spot, head cocked and ears pricked in anticipation. Then it dawned on me where I recognised the voice from: it was the voice of a woman who had accompanied me home from Cardiff last weekend. I had spent five hours listening to her before I had got sick of the sound of her voice, and placed her in the boot of my car in my overnight bag, along with my dirty laundry. The really irritating voice belonged to that annoying woman in the satnav. For some reason, the device must have turned itself on again, or maybe I had knocked it when I had stubbed my toe coming back from the toilet. I now felt a bit silly, standing there in just my boxer shorts, and clutching my clock.

I delved into the holdall and turned her off again. I then sent Barney downstairs and returned to bed to desperately try and catch up with some sleep before I needed to be up again for work. It was no good, though, as my head was still buzzing. I had never really taken the threats from the people I'd locked up that seriously before. A fair number had said they would hunt me down, kill me, set fire to my house, and so on, but I had just assumed they were taunts and idle threats. I never actually believed they would be carried out, but this got my mind working overtime. Maybe I really should step up my home security: start switching on the alarm system at night, and change the locks. Perhaps I should get Barney to toughen up.

I tried to banish the thoughts from my head and replace them with nicer ones. What would have happened if it had been a young, attractive female stalker who was obsessed with me? What would I have done if I had woken to find her dressed in just a pair of high heels and one of my clean work shirts? I'd still be mildly irritated, but not quite as angry. They take some ironing to get the creases just right, you know.

But, on the other hand, what would have happened if a man had broken in? All those times I had told an angry thug that I was 'a lover not a fighter' to try and diffuse the situation. What if one of them had broken in to see if I was true to my word? Prison is often referred to as 'a stretch on the inside', and now I dreaded to think of the reason why. I certainly didn't want my insides stretched. Then again, if it had been a male intruder with his mind set on that sort of thing, I guess he wouldn't tell me to turn around.

I decided to banish those thoughts and think again of my potential female stalker, intent on using me as her personal sex toy, and started to drift off to a happy place. I was tired, and as I lay there in the dark, my arms and legs began to feel like lead. As my mind wandered, it was filled with dreamy images of hedonistic abandon – although I hoped that tonight she would be content with just sitting on my knee, being bounced up and down, with me singing 'Horsey, Horsey'. I was tired, and needed to save my energy for the morning when I'd then make it up to her. I must have literally just dozed off to sleep again, a stupid smile on my face, when the alarm sounded and startled me awake; I'm surprised more people don't have heart attacks in the mornings. I must have only had about three hours sleep all night – max!

I padded downstairs, apologised to Barney for scaring him with my shouting in the night, and went to make myself a large cup of coffee. My mind was on a go-slow due to my lack of sleep, and as I left for work I almost forgot to put my bottles out for recycling in next door's green box. Goodness, those people drink a lot!

When I got to the station I found my colleagues in similar early morning zombie like states: sitting quietly, nursing cups of coffee and staring into space. The silence was broken by

Brad from the previous shift, as he bounded through in a characteristically buoyant mood, to update us on the previous night's activities.

Over the past few days we had been searching for a couple of missing persons. The Peacock brothers, Chris and Drew, were local burglars in the town, who had been reported missing by their probation officer. It was more than likely that they were out on a burgling spree, but since they had been officially reported as missing, the system swung into motion, and the process of trying to locate them to see if they were safe and sound, had begun. Even though the general consensus was that they were probably trying to avoid us, we checked with their friends and relations, hospitals and custody suites, searched houses, and generally followed up any lead in an attempt to locate them. You can never get complacent when dealing with people who are missing. Apparently, 70% of murder investigations start out as missing person enquiries. It's the one time when you don't put all your efforts into finding the 'misper' that something bad will have happened to them.

Three days after they had initially been reported missing, a call had come in from the site foreman in charge of renovating some houses on the Yellow Estate. A boarded up house had been broken into and items stolen. He thought that persons unknown were using the property during the silent hours. Brad had been sent to investigate, and that's where he had discovered the Brothers Grim.

It seems the pair had apparently targeted the houses as easy pickings. Building sites are like a honeypot for burglars and thieves. Whether it's workmen's tools or building materials, they're a paradise for the light fingered visitor. The uninvited guests will swarm over the site at night, climbing up the scaffolding and through the half constructed buildings like a troop of marauding apes, stripping them bare of anything that isn't nailed down.

I've been called to numerous construction sites to find blood stains on scaffolding poles, or bloody trails where nocturnal intruders have clearly not adhered to the stringent health and safety requirements – wearing a hard hat probably clashes with their sartorial elegance. Many wouldn't be found dead wearing a bright orange safety helmet – except that one day they actually might be. Found dead that is.

Building sites are dangerous places – even more dangerous in the dark when you can't see what's lying around. It's easy to slip off scaffolding and break a leg, or worse. A crumpled body was found at the bottom of a wall a few years ago, and George told me that he had found a lone finger at a site last year. After finger printing the offending digit, he traced it back to 'Keith the Hat', a well-known burglar in the town. His pinkie had been sliced off as he had been messing around in the compound, converting the 'HATE' tattooed on his hand into the less offensive 'HAT'.

Armed with the above knowledge, Brad was more than a little reticent about climbing through the gap in the perimeter fence to investigate the report. Accompanied by his colleagues, Jacob and Ffion (the girl with the fastest name in the world), he had crept carefully around the planks and bricks, the pools of muddy water, until he reached the house in question. Standing outside he could hear the sound of music emanating from within. Pushing the board quietly to one side, he could make out a couple of figures illuminated by the light from a camping lamp, sitting around a plasterer's table laughing and joking.

Carefully, so as not to disturb the party, the three officers climbed in through the window and hid around the corner. On Brad's command, they strode purposefully into the room, shining their torches on their captives. Chris and Drew looked up, but were clearly too drunk to be bothered about the arrival of the gatecrashers. Cans of lager were strewn about the floor, and adorning the centre of the table was a large stash of white powder.

"Evening, Orifice," slurred a drunken Chris Peacock. "How the devil are you? Pull up a seat and have a can, and partake in some of the finest marching powder that Sandford has to offer."

"And you can't do a thing," mumbled a bleary eyed Drew before falling head first into the pile of powder in front of him, sniffing deeply, and then sitting back up and giggling uncontrollably. "We found the coke!"

"Oh, really?" replied an unimpressed Brad. "And where did you happen to find your cocaine?"

"Here!" shrieked Chris before descending into a fit of giggles and lifting up a half full bag he had by his feet. He then emptied it onto the table, powder spilling in all directions and swirling up and into the air as he did so.

"And was it in these boxes, perchance?" enquired Brad, as he held up an empty white cardboard box.

"Yes!" they chorused, hiccupping and swigging from their cans.

Brad remained poker faced as he turned to his colleagues and showed them the writing on the side of the packet: 'Industrial Polyfilla Powder'. He then cracked a wry smile.

The two brothers exchanged shocked glances, appearing to sober up almost immediately, and at once began jumping on each other, fighting amongst themselves.

Brad and his colleagues waded in, separated the pair and then cuffed them. Two mispers located, who now became two disappointed, bunged-up and hung over prisoners. During questioning, Drew spilled the beans, only too eager to get his own back on Chris who he blamed for the whole miserable fiasco. It transpired that the duo had broken into the site over the last few nights, stealing anything that wasn't nailed down. They had already completed their crime spree, when Chris persuaded a reluctant Drew to return one last time, as he had believed he had found a secret stash of cocaine hidden in the building. The last temptation of Chris proved to be their downfall – and also proved that it's probably worthwhile learning to read properly at school. On the plus side, though, the Peacock brothers now had noses that wouldn't shrink or crack, and came with a three year guarantee.

"I had to enquire," added Brad, "whether they realised that their entire existence on this planet might just be to serve as a warning to others?"

"Maybe they could get a barista to represent them at court?" suggested Barry, who had just poked his head around the corner of the parade room. We all looked at each other with puzzled expressions.

"Come on, people!" he cried, "It's a coffee joke!"

"Oh, barista – barrister," we mumbled. "Too early in the morning, Sarge." He sighed, and disappeared back around the corner.

Of course, the sad part about it is that they would know exactly who would represent them at court. Everyone who is brought into custody for whatever offence is given the right of free, independent legal representation; to see a solicitor either in person, or speak to one on the telephone. I wouldn't have a clue who I would ask for if I was in their situation. In my private life, I only deal with solicitors once in a blue moon; house moves or divorces which are kind of the same thing. However, our 'regulars' always know straight away the name, and even the telephone number of the brief they want. Often when the legal rep turns up, he seems delighted to see his charge; and why shouldn't he? A persistent offender on Legal Aid is a regular little money maker for him.

As Barry slunk back to his office, we resumed the slow process of acclimatising to the early start. Hopefully, there would be a quieter beginning to the shift today; earlies usually were.

Crooks are inherently lazy. Statistically speaking, the vast majority of our customers are unemployed, and seem to live in a different time zone from the rest of us. They live by New York time – about five hours behind us. They don't need to get up for work, so they stay up late... and as a result, they get up late. Most of them don't even possess a watch as time is of no real significance to them.

Instead, they lurk around the industrial estate, hang around back alleys, or have domestics until three or four in the morning. The payoff is that they don't usually bother us with their activities until gone midday, therefore, on early shifts we can just catch up with paperwork and enquiries. There are always the odd calls from the decent members of the public, who have woken to find their sheds broken into or their car damaged, but, generally, it won't be the immediate, crime in progress calls to deal with.

There is another category of call we occasionally get early in the morning, and Iona Rocket fitted into that bracket. To be fair, I just think she was lonely. She had moved to Sandford from Scotland some years ago to make a new start and, as a consequence, had no family in the area. Her new start hadn't quite gone to plan, and she had become an alcoholic who didn't seem to need to sleep. She would use any pretext to get someone round to her house, usually just to chat. Iona didn't care if it was police or paramedics, and at least once a week one of us would get a call from her. The initial 'emergency' would be quickly dealt with, and then out would come the coffee and biscuits in a bid to get us to stay and keep her company for a bit longer.

Last month she had reported taking an overdose. When I arrived, the coffee was already waiting for me along with her explanation: "Sorry, PC Donoghue. I started taking an overdose of paracetemol, but, after two, I started to feel a lot better. Milk and one sugar, wasn't it?"

A couple of weeks ago, Lysa, the paramedic, had informed me that they had been called out by Iona for an altogether different reason: "The cats started to play with my tampon string as I was getting dressed. I may need stitches." Of course, she was absolutely fine, and advised that she might want to invest in a few catnip toys to keep the kittens occupied. Lysa also reported she had been given a KitKat with her brew, which seemed appropriate.

And it was only last week that Iona had reported that she might be involved in human trafficking. It turned out she was just considering getting a job as a lollipop lady. It's not that anyone really minded going out to see her – we'd all far rather sit for half an hour chatting to her if it prevented her from doing something silly.

I had first met Iona last year when she *was* actually doing something silly. In this case, it was attempting to jump from the top of Sandford's multi-storey car park. Usually, we would try and talk a jumper down, get the Force negotiator out, have the ambulance on standby – but she was already starting to climb over the safety railing. As I slid to a halt in my panda car, I had no other option but to sprint over and rugby tackle her, taking us both to the floor. I tried to make light of it as we lay there, our arms and limbs entangled.

"Didn't forget someone's birthday, did you?" Samoa has the highest suicide rate in the world. It's also illegal in Samoa to forget your wife's birthday. I've always wondered if there is any link between those snippets of information.

"Fuck off," she suggested. Clearly, Iona didn't wish to discuss the semantics of such a relationship. I decided not to press the point by drawing a Venn diagram. I am pleased to say that the relationship between us has improved considerably since that initial unsatisfactory exchange.

I sincerely hoped that Iona did get to become a lollipop lady, and I can speak with confidence in saying that my colleagues and I were quite prepared to spend the morning chatting about the virtues of Tufty V the Green Cross Code Man if it meant her doing something positive with her life; anything instead of just sitting in her room, dwelling on her worries and woes. It's a world away from the 999 thrills and spills that many of us joined for, but so much of our role nowadays isn't about crime.

Within any twelve month period, one in four of us will

experience some kind of mental health problem, with anxiety and depression being the most common mental disorders in Britain. Over a quarter of a million people are admitted to psychiatric hospitals each year, but the majority, like Iona, eventually end up back in the community. Added to this, around a million people commit suicide in the world every year. In the UK, on average, someone kills themselves every two hours. When we invest time with people like Iona, it's not just paperwork that's saved.

I had taken Jess to meet Iona back in January when she had first arrived at Sandford. As we had driven over, I had related the unhappy tale of Iona and the high-rise rugby tackle. "Here we are," I announced as we pulled up outside the address. Jessica looked ahead in disbelief: only Sandford social services could house a female with a penchant for attempting suicide by jumping off tall buildings on the top floor of a high-rise block of flats.

"Did I ever tell you about Iona and the massive explosion?" enquired Lloyd, as I finished recounting the story. This was a new one on us and we all scraped our chairs forward to make sure we caught every word of his ripping yarn.

It seems that a call had been received from her, stating she had received an anonymous text. It had read: 'There is going to be a massive explosion in Sandford tomorrow'. Lloyd had duly been dispatched to investigate. This time, however, there was no coffee or biscuits; instead, a worried Iona had paced back and forth in the flat, rubbing her hands together, and muttering anxiously to herself.

Lloyd had tried to put her at ease, explaining that it seemed highly unlikely that some terrorist cell had decided, that of all people to send the warning about a potential impending Armageddon to, they should choose Iona Rocket. His reassurances had fallen on stony ground as she continued to wear out a path in her carpet as she paced nervously back and forth, pausing to sit down only to jump up again and re-start her hand-wringing wanderings.

Lloyd had questioned her intensively, but Iona insisted that she didn't know whose number it was, why anyone would contact her with such a message, or, indeed, when or what it referred to. Enquiries with Comms to trace the number proved negative; no one had answered when it was rang and now time, if this was a genuine warning, was potentially running out fast.

"It won't happen here," or "We're too small to be a target," are regular retorts when the likelihood of terrorist attacks are brought up. The truth is, though, who is to decide what is regarded as 'too small' by a terrorist? No one can be sure that it won't happen here in Sandford... and what if it did? Lloyd had no option but to call Barry who, in turn, had flagged it up to the senior management team. There was no other option but to take the threat with the utmost seriousness.

"I've got to go, I've got to go..." exclaimed Iona, as she pushed past my colleague and ran into the bathroom, leaving Lloyd looking around anxiously. At that very same moment, the phone beeped, indicating another text had come through. Tentatively, he picked up the mobile and opened the message.

"Well, has it happened yet?" it read.

"Has what happened?" Lloyd texted back, feigning ignorance in the hope that it might force the caller to show his hand.

"The toxic waste dump, you nutcase!"

It didn't look like the parlance of a hard line terrorist, Lloyd explained to us, so he took the opportunity to communicate further with our mysterious texter. Soon it all became clear.

Lloyd banged on the toilet door to let Iona know that he was off, and advised her that she might want to check her previous night's conversation on Facebook.

For it turned out that Iona wasn't the unwelcome bearer of bad news after all, and nor was the text a portent of the forthcoming Armageddon. It was all much simpler to explain, although as Lloyd admitted, he was finding it difficult to choose the right words with which to report his findings to the bosses, and yet still retain a degree of decorum.

For us, though, he didn't pull any punches. Iona, it seemed, had been suffering from constipation for several days. She had told her contacts on Facebook as much, and informed them that if nothing had shifted by morning, she was going to take some industrial strength laxatives. In her drunken state, she had forgotten all about her delicate conversation the night before, including giving her number to a new acquaintance on the social media site. Her new friend had then sent what he regarded as a humorous masterpiece: referring to the effect the laxatives might have on the aforementioned Iona as a 'massive explosion in Sandford'.

As he left the address, Lloyd said he could clearly hear what sounded like the Four Horsemen of the Apocalypse galloping around the toilet bowl. He shut the door, and quickly ran down the stairs before the texter's premonition was realised. We all had a little snigger, and pushed our chairs back. As they say, it's all shits and giggles until someone actually giggles and shits. I looked at the clock; it was half seven. Would I have time for another cup of coffee before I ventured out I wondered?

"Immediate response," the radio sprang into life. There was my answer.

Now and again, we'd receive the odd alarm activation from a factory or office on the industrial estate. Usually, it was cleaners arriving for work, and setting the alarms off in error. It would involve a quick blue light run to get the blood going, and then back to the nick. That wasn't so bad.

"Personal attack alarm at the post office... " Hang on, this was different: these alarms were triggered manually. This was a genuine incident!

We donned our body armour, and ran out to our cars, switching on the blue strobes, and waking our sleeping neighbours with our sirens. I'm sure the firemen needed to be up soon, anyway.

The activation had come from a small post office in one of the quiet, sleepy villages on the border of the area that we covered. It was a well-to-do type of place – the type of place where the residents were not usually troubled by crime. I'm sure they were aware that baddies existed, but not in their quiet corner of England; that sort of trouble was reserved for the big towns and cities. You don't pay the house prices that these village properties carry, to have to put up with scoundrels, blaggards and rapscallions. This was supposed to be a haven of tranquillity. However, this morning their tranquillity had been shattered when a gang of armed robbers had kicked in the door of the post office, fired a warning shot into the ceiling, and demanded the money from the safe.

By the time we arrived the robbers were long gone. We radioed through to Comms, the helicopter was scrambled, and every traffic vehicle in the county was dispatched, searching for the getaway car. Meanwhile, we stepped over the debris and entered the shop. The scene was horrendous. Half an hour earlier, this was a quiet, sleepy post office – the local hub where pleasantries were exchanged, recipes swapped and birthday cards posted with love from Grandma. Now the scene was completely different: papers were strewn everywhere, glass from broken windows crunched underfoot, an elderly customer sat traumatised in the corner being treated by paramedics, the smell of cordite hung in the air, and everything was soaked as the fire sprinkler system did its worst. Ten and twenty pound notes were randomly scattered – evidence that the crooks had hastily stashed the takings into their bag. I picked up a couple of twenties and placed them on the damp counter.

The sub postmistress who had been born and bred in this picture postcard village was still shaking, deep in shock. Today, in this this most perfect of places, evil and sin had crept in.

"They came in here with their masks on, shooting in the air, waving their shotguns about, knocking over the Elderberry wine display, pushing old Mrs Porter over and demanding money," she told me. I could see the disbelief in her eyes. If you are a decent, law abiding citizen, who doesn't see the horrors of the world, I guess you expect most other people to be decent, law abiding citizens too. Sadly, real life isn't like that.

We did all we could at the scene, and then finally we just sat with her while she made a pot of tea in the back room, as we waited the arrival of CSI and CID. Despite all that had happened today, when she handed me my cuppa it was evident to me that she hadn't entirely lost all faith in humanity or mankind's inherent goodness:

"I don't know where they could have parked," she mused, "because it's double yellow lines outside."

CHAPTER ELEVEN:

May the Force be with you

Never let the photocopier know you are in a hurry.

I was on my third paper jam, and considering resorting to physical violence, when I was disturbed by the sound of a gentle knock on the door. I looked up to see Samantha, one of the front office clerks, peering around the door frame, smiling at me and twiddling with her hair.

"Hello, Johnny, you're looking particularly handsome today."

Someone being that nice could only mean one thing: they wanted my help. To be honest, anything would be a welcome relief from my battle with modern technology, particularly since I was losing dismally.

"How can I help you, Sam?" I queried. I could sense a potential bargaining chip in the offing. The photocopier seemed to like her.

"There's a gentleman at the front counter..."

She led the way through to reception where I was greeted by the sight of an angry, red faced, bespectacled and balding man. He had a sweat band around his head, and was resplendent in an off white singlet complemented by a pair of unfeasibly short running shorts. He was pacing impatiently up and down the foyer.

"This officer will be able to assist you," she announced to our visitor before turning abruptly on her heels. I'm sure I could detect the beginnings of a grin developing on her face as she quickly shimmied past me, exiting stage left.

"Constable," he began, as soon as he saw me, "I want something doing about those, those…"

He stopped his pacing and approached the counter before taking a deep breath and placing both hands on the desk as if to compose himself. I could see he was shaking with barely concealed rage, beads of sweat forming on his forehead. He pushed his glasses back up the bridge of his nose and started again, this time in barely a whisper. "I want something doing about those…"

I was perched on tiptoes as I leant over, straining to catch his words. I can't say I relished the intimacy of the situation. I could feel the heat from his face, see the veins in his temples pulsating, and hear sweat dripping onto the Formica surface. He paused as he tried to articulate his grievance. As I held my position, cramp forming in my calves, the silence between us was deafening.

After a few seconds, which felt like an eternity, I sensed he had at last found his voice when he stood bolt upright, rose to his full height, took a deep breath and started to slowly jab his right hand systematically in the direction of the open door. He jabbed his finger slowly at first as if to the beat of an invisible metronome gradually building up speed; faster and faster until his hand was a virtual blur. He was like a volcano, steadily building to the point of no return. He began his sentence again, each syllable carefully enunciated, each word getting louder and louder.

"I. Want. Something. Done. About. Those… ," he was shaking now, stuck like a record at that same point in his address. The jabbing continued unabated, until I thought his arm was going to fly off. I stood back: Krakatoa was ready to blow. His sentence climaxed in a punishing crescendo, his voice booming through the corridors and offices. "I want something done… ABOUT THOSE DAMN BLOODY KIDS!"

I peered in the general direction of his extended arm, and saw a group of about seven or eight children over the road, sitting giggling on the library wall. I guessed that they were about ten years old. They must have heard the eruption, too, as they looked over in my direction. When they saw me looking back, they jumped down from the wall and ran off into the town.

Shouty Man had now collapsed back onto the metal bench, clearly exhausted by his performance. I, however, was no further forward. I asked if he could elaborate.

"Mile twenty-one," he sighed, his chin falling onto his chest, his arms flopping down by his side. "I've told the woman."

The woman in question, Samantha, now magically reappeared. She appeared to be struggling to keep a straight face. I enquired as to whether she cared to enlighten me with regard to the gentleman's plight.

It transpired that the male in question was training for the marathon. A splendid ideal, if not somewhat questionable pursuit. Is he aware that the first person who ever ran this distance dropped down dead when he reached his destination?

"Mile twenty-one," Samantha smiled.

I have a brother who runs marathons, and I am aware of the fact that mile twenty-one is the point at which runners often hit 'the wall'. The actual distance can vary, but, in essence, it's the time when you feel that all the energy has been sucked out of your muscles, and you cannot take another step. It's a psychological as well as a physical problem. Some athletes refer to it as 'the inner game' – overcoming self-imposed obstacles that prevent an individual from reaching their full potential. I'm no expert, but I'd say remain focused, and maybe watch it on telly instead. What I couldn't work out was where the 'damn bloody kids' fitted into this.

Samantha kindly let me in on the little secret. Mile twenty-one, it so happened, was also the point at which our long-distance runner looped around, and made his way back through Sandford after a few hours pounding the country roads surrounding the town. Mile twenty-one was where he also happened to pass the Yellow Estate. The Yellow Estate was where...

"Where those bloody kids live," our sportsman interjected.

The children had become familiar with his routine, and, as soon as they saw him coming, they all made their way out into the street, and began running at a steady pace about ten yards in front of our marathon man; running, yet looking back with suitably terrified expressions on their faces and screaming, "Help! The nasty man is trying to get us!"

"Leaving me," added the nasty man in question, "looking like a red-faced, breathless, sweaty paedophile!"

"Or the child catcher from *Chitty Chitty Bang Bang*," suggested Sam. I shot her a glance to indicate she wasn't helping, but she had already turned away, her shoulders shaking.

"I've already had people shouting at me to leave them alone!" he continued, his voice wavering as he re-lived those moments in his head. He pushed his glasses back up the bridge of his nose again, and recommenced his pacing. He looked like he was close to tears. I invited him into an interview room to get some details.

I explained that it was the middle of the long school summer holidays, and the children were obviously bored, and he was their entertainment. They would soon have something better to occupy themselves with. In the meantime, I'd get one of the community support officers to have a word with the children involved. He had calmed down by now, and seemed satisfied with my response. Satisfied, that is, until I led him back through to the foyer.

"That's him!" exclaimed an elderly woman who was sitting in the reception area. "That's the monster! That's the pervert who has been chasing those kids!"

I quickly bundled him out the door before he could respond.

"This lady will explain all," I told the old woman as I turned back to face her, motioning towards a grimacing Samantha who had reappeared at the sound of all the commotion. I let myself through into the station, and back to the photocopier. Maybe I'd just turn it off and back on again.

Anyway, the 'better thing' that the kids would have to occupy themselves required my attention. The 'better thing' was on tomorrow. The 'better thing' was the Summer Fête!

Every year was the same: the quiet and desolate moorlands on the outskirts of the town were gradually transformed as stalls, displays and marquees started to pop up. Groups, teams and clubs would descend on the wilderness, and gather for final rehearsals and last minute practise. The normally deserted Golden Cock public house, that usually only serviced a few tired truckers from the nearby lorry park, suddenly became the busiest pub in town.

Families and friends would plan their day out, make picnics and arrange places to meet. Soldiers, sailors and airmen would arrive, and erect their recruitment tents, PR girls in bunny outfits would be bussed in, complete with bundles of flyers and, just to add to the hustle and bustle, a fun fair would arrive in our fair town of Sandford.

The sights, sounds and smells of the fête began a full twenty-four hours before the grand opening as diesel engines and generators hummed away, powering machinery and rides. Fumes hung in the air. The fields around the site were churned up into muddy furrows by all the wagons, lorries, cars and trucks associated with such a massive operation. No one seemed to mind, though: this was the highlight of the Sandford calendar.

Amongst all this frenetic activity, a quiet, one horse power engine would also arrive. Rusty Rose, the fortune teller, would trundle up in her brightly painted Gypsy caravan, pulled by her trusty steed, Ralph. She would find a spot of land on the main route to the fête, unhitch Ralph, and set up camp.

However, Rusty Rose and Ralph caused more trouble for us than all the other arrivals put together. Every year was the same as Comms were inundated with calls reporting a horse dangerously near the road. Rusty wasn't the problem – it's just a shame about Ralph.

We often get calls concerning livestock on the roads: chickens, sheep, cows, bulls... but mostly horses. The force receives hundreds of calls each year about stray horses on the roads, posing a danger to the animal, pedestrians and motorists alike. The problem is worse in winter as the animals stray on to the roads as the tarmac is warmer to stand on than the freezing cold, damp fields.

Animal husbandry didn't seem to feature on the curriculum at police training school, so it was always a venture into the unknown when I responded to a report of stray livestock. However, a few months ago I had my first real success story, or so I thought.

A report had come in of a stray horse on the winding country road leading to Kilo 3. Picking up Special Constable Emma to assist me, I had made my way to the location. On arrival, I was greeted by the sight of a large piebald cob, standing resolutely in the middle of the Queen's highway. Traffic was building up on either side, too scared to move. As soon as vehicles attempted to manoeuvre past, the cob would take a couple of menacing steps towards them. Discretion, in this case, certainly seemed the better part of valour.

With an audience looking on, I was reluctant to put on a Keystone Cops style show for them by chasing our quarry all over the local countryside. There were fields on either side of the road, and I had noticed, en route, a pile of carrots in the entrance to one of those fields, and, further down a paddock with a playmate for our equine road block.

My genius plan hatched, I sent Emma to collect some of the carrots. She ran off, returning a few minutes later with an armful of orange coloured root vegetables. Then, as Emma trotted behind me holding the supply, I enticed the horse over by laying a trail of tasty food for him. He was certainly getting his five a day as he slowly wandered behind us. We had safely bypassed the waiting cars, and reached the field with the other horse. The gate was locked, but that didn't stop me; I was on a roll. Going to the opposite end of the barrier, I managed to lift it off its hinges and pull it open enough for Emma to squeeze through and lure the stray cob in. Not that he needed much persuading for as soon as he saw the other horse he developed a fifth leg, and happily trotted through the gap.

It was all done and dusted in record time. I'm not a competitive person – I'll be the first to admit it, but I felt pretty proud. Ten minutes from arrival to departure – job well done in my book.

However, as I was to discover the next day, it was job very badly done in the eyes of Lady Peach, wife of the local landowner. Barry had called me into the office, and informed me that she had been most unhappy. In fact, 'unhappy' was not the word. She was livid.

"No," clarified Barry, "make that incandescent with rage." Incandescent with rage because, in her words, "a manky, filthy, flea-ridden neddie," had been put in the field with her champion show jumper. If the pitter patter of tiny hooves were to result from this illicit encounter, the constabulary "had better have deep pockets". I thought it best not to mention the stolen carrots after that.

Incidentally, horses aren't the only potential disaster area for the average police officer: sheep are incredibly fast when they want to be, and can jump pretty high, too. You are guaranteed to look a prize twerp trying to round up a herd of loose lambs on your own.

"You're Welsh, John," Comms would comment as they gave me the job, "this should be second nature to you!" I'm not quite sure about their impression of where I grew up, but flocks of errant sheep weren't really a big feature in the suburbs of Cardiff. It's always the same when people discover I'm from Wales. It's never, "Oh that's interesting. I wonder if he speaks Welsh, or if he could tell me about the country's rich history and culture?" No, it's always about sheep.

Bulls, though, are my worst nightmare. Once a month there is a farmer's livestock market held in the county town, and, occasionally, animals will escape and make a break for freedom down the high street. People laugh when a ram runs past chased by a group of farmers and stewards, but when a bull escapes, it is a different matter altogether. One and a half ton of rampaging animal, complete with horns, charging through the town is a fearsome sight. It's a mobile killing machine, trampling cars and property, sending children and adults fleeing for their very lives. Like the running of the bulls in Pamplona, injuries and death can easily result. Between 200 and 300 people are casualties each year during the Pamplona runs alone. A bull doesn't just randomly charge at a crowd either – it will pick out one person and follow him no matter how he may run, dodge and twist, relentlessly pursuing his target until he gets him. Bulls are left or right horned, just as we are left or right handed, and when their target comes within reach, they will spear their mark with their chosen horn, causing horrendous injuries. They are very clever animals, too, quickly learning from their mistakes, which explains why any bull involved in a bullfight is later killed, regardless of whether it wins or loses; if a bull is victorious once, it's virtually guaranteed it'll be victorious again and a matador will be killed. When a bull escapes, cows are often brought from the market in a bid to calm the bull, but it doesn't always work. Sometimes, death in the afternoon can't be avoided, and if the bull can't be rounded up safely, the only option is to call in the armed response units to shoot it.

Whichever animal is concerned, the one constant is the number of officers it takes to keep the situation under control, and the public safe. With officers on leave, and on courses, we are always strapped for resources. As I drove up to the fête, I was determined that this year I'd put paid to that problem once and for all.

"Rusty," I shouted as I stood outside her caravan. As I waited, I looked over at Ralph. He was stood on the grass verge, happily munching on the grass, oblivious to the cars shooting past.

"Rusty Rose," I called again, and this time I was rewarded with glimpse of a bony hand, adorned with rings, and dripping with large, gold coloured bangles, that appeared from between the folds of dark velvet that hung at the entrance to her caravan. A finger was extended, beckoning me forth into her lair.

"Didn't the crystal ball say that you'd get a visit from a tall dark handsome stranger today?" I quipped as I parted her curtains. I straightened my tie, giving her my best lopsided grin.

"They did, love," she replied. "So why did they send you?"

I could see she wasn't in the mood for small talk, so I got on with the task in hand. As she sat behind a small round table in the dark, I could make out her raven hair framing her sharp features. A bright blue scarf was tightly pulled around her head, and there were more bangles – lots more bangles that jingled and jangled with the slightest move she made.

In front of her, on top of a white lace tablecloth, was the traditional staple of any fortune teller's paraphernalia: the crystal ball. To the left were sprigs of heather, to the right there was an ornate teacup and saucer. An old black kettle sat nearby in case anyone wanted their tea leaves read.

"It's Ralph," I explained to her. "We had this problem last year, too. Why can't you tie him up? Everyone is concerned he's going to wander into the path of an oncoming vehicle."

"He's a free spirit, PC Donoghue. Something you may learn about one day. He's not going to walk off. I'd have seen it coming if he was." She tapped on the top of the ball with a long fingernail.

Would she move him back from the road? This was met

with another negative response. I tried a different tack, and then another, but she wasn't to be swayed. She had every confidence that he would stay put, without the need for a halter or harness. "I don't own Ralph," she informed me. "Nobody owns him. He chooses to remain with me. We are one." I was a defeated man.

"What's the difference between heather and lucky heather?" I asked as I sloped towards the exit.

"Two pounds fifty," she replied flatly.

I just had one last trick up my sleeve. I went back to my panda and rummaged in the boot before returning to see Ralph. He continued to munch on the grass as I approached.

"Sorry about this, fella," I told him before slapping a 'POLICE AWARE' sticker on the horse blanket covering his backside.

I didn't have time to linger – I had real police work to do.

Two high profile persons had been reported missing. Two well renowned figures had disappeared into thin air. Two international film stars had been kidnapped: someone had stolen Yoda and Darth Maul.

On the run up to the fête the different arts and crafts societies in the town entered into the spirit of things with a variety of light-hearted competitions. This year, the different members had been tasked with creating papier mâché figures of stars of the silver screen. The winning entry would be judged at the big event, where its creator would, according to the programme, receive a laurel, and hardy handshake from the mayor.

I turned up at the crime scene, which was a large house in an adjoining village. A bohemian looking woman in her mid-thirties answered. She looked bald, but with hair.

"I believe Yoda and Darth Maul are missing," I announced cheerily. She nodded.

"The police you have called," I continued in my best Yoda before reverting to a serious actor voice for my pay-off line, "So may the force be with you!"

She burst into tears. Her husband suddenly appeared from behind her, and shot me an icy glare.

"Police force, I meant," I mumbled almost inaudibly, realising I had completely misjudged my audience. I shuffled into the front room, and hung my head in shame. I could see the husband straining to note my collar number. I made a mental note not to mention Darth Vader's brother, Taxi Vader, currently under investigation by HM Revenue and Customs, although I didn't think I could sink any lower in their estimation.

"She's distraught," the husband informed me. He was wearing sandals, long shorts, and a t-shirt with the words *All About Eve* emblazoned on the front. "She put a lot of effort into making them."

"You're maudlin and full of self-pity," I pronounced boldly, addressing my comments to the wife, hoping to get her back on-side.

She started to wail. The husband looked at me with incredulity. This wasn't really the reaction I was expecting. I thought she would find it funny. I'd have gambled that at least he'd be pleased; maybe share a little nod of recognition with me, but, no, he just shook his head in disbelief and put his arms around his crying spouse.

"C'mon," I enthused, "You know what I'm on about!"

This just seemed to set her off again. I could see her shoulders rise and fall as she sobbed, releasing an awful sound like a donkey barking.

This sort of thing tends to happen to me on an increasingly frequent basis. I'll make a reference that I think everyone will understand, but instead I'm left with a sea of puzzled expressions.

Last week I thought I'd entertain everyone with a little pub quiz snippet about football legend Emlyn Hughes. It transpired that he had two children, and named his son Emlyn and his daughter Emma Lynn. However, instead of the raised eyebrows and affable comments about sharing such an interesting gem with everyone, I had to fend off question after question from the younger members of the shift as to who this Emlyn Hughes was in the first place. I didn't dare mention after that how George Foreman had named all five of his sons George. I guess not everyone is either as old as me, or shares the same fascination with trivia as I do.

That said, I was sure that if the husband was wearing an *All About Eve* shirt, he'd be aware of perhaps the most famous quote of all from this iconic film. A former girlfriend had been a big fan of the actress Bette Davis. I had happened to mention to her that in the 1980's hit, *Bette Davis Eyes*, it sounds likes Kim Carnes is singing, "All the boys think she's a spaz". As punishment for the slight on her heroine, I was made to sit through all her films – including *All About Eve* from which the quote was taken. "You're maudlin and full of self-pity. You're magnificent" – Addison DeWitt had said. Look, I'm not proud of my knowledge of black and white film miscellanea, but I thought it was better than saying to his wife, "Frankly my dear, I don't give a damn," although from their expressions, I might as well have done.

"It's from the film!" I explained, pointing at his t-shirt as I did so, trying to jog his memory. He continued to look at me as if I was mad before he let out a sigh.

"It's the band," he clarified in a flat monotone, "the rock band, '*All About Eve*'. We don't know what film you're on about." He didn't say it in an angry or irritated way, rather he spoke in an exasperated tone as if he was addressing a stupid child or a stupid step-child; perhaps even a ginger one.

I rapidly appraised the situation: to all intents and purposes, I had entered their home, belittled their loss, and then made fun of how upset they were. Great! Maybe I should just take off his wife's glasses and repeatedly stamp on them and be done with it. Instead, I decided to abandon the small talk and stick to business.

I discovered that both Yoda and Darth Maul were life-sized, made of papier mâché, and had been painted accordingly. Both had been displayed in their front garden overnight, in accordance with the competition rules, and both had gone missing. I was shown numerous photographs of the pair from differing angles. Clearly, they were very proud of their creations.

"Can't you put out an A.P.B.?" queried the wife. Either she had been watching too many cop shows on TV, or not enough. I thought about telling her I'd have a word with the D.A., and if we caught the hoods responsible, we'd book 'em for murder-one. Instead, I got on the radio.

"Comms, can you ask CCTV control if they saw Yoda and Darth Maul on the streets anytime last night?" As soon as the words came out of my mouth, I knew I should have waited until I was out of earshot of the pair before asking the question. I could imagine only too well what response I'd get after saying that. No, Nancy, please not now... but it was too late.

"For you we will look," came back the reply. As the couple glared at me, I just gave them a simpering grin, and pointed to the radio in a 'what are they like!' type way. I put my earpiece in before any other Yoda-isms could be heard over the airways. That part of my scheme to win back their confidence certainly hadn't gone to plan. I excused myself, did some house to house enquiries, and when that proved negative, I set off down to the site of the fête to find out who else had entered the competition.

When I got there, the place was frenetic with the activity that accompanies the preparation for such an event. I toyed with the idea of consulting Rusty Rose over the disappearance of Yoda and Darth Maul, but when I saw a small crowd gathered around Ralph, looking in horror at the sign stuck to his bum, I decided against it, and instead made my way towards the organiser's tent.

"John!"

I heard the cry as I was about to enter. The voice seemed to come from a crowd of children in the distance. I paused and scanned the group for anyone I knew.

"PC Donoghue!" called the voice again, and this time I saw her as she bounced up and down and waved me a salute.

It was Miss Jones, a primary school teacher I had loved and lost over six months earlier. A girl almost half my age, and nearly twice my concentration span; this was the Bette Davis enthusiast. It hadn't ended well between us after she accused me of embarrassing her in front of her class when I had disarmed a rude snowman in the line of duty. However, it seemed like she had let bygones be bygones, and wanted to be friends again.

I waved back and wandered over. She was here with the school's holiday dance club, rehearsing for the big event tomorrow. They were going to perform Michael Jackson's *Thriller* dance as their contribution, and, as Miss Jones looked proudly on, I was treated to my own private showing. Fifteen eight-year-olds proceeded to move awkwardly back and forth to the music, looking more like a group of indecisive T-Rex's, rather than *The Kids from 'Fame'*. I fixed on a smile, and grinned through gritted teeth.

"Magnificent! Fantastic performance, children!" I couldn't be accused of not learning from my mistakes; besides, I had an ulterior motive for my faked sincerity: 'Carpe Scrotum' – grab life by the balls. This was my opportunity, and I grabbed it with both hands. Not literally – you can get arrested for doing that in a public place.

"Would you like to meet up for a drink later?" I asked Miss Jones.

Fifteen hyperactive kids jumping around at her feet, excited by the praise the nice man had just heaped on them ensured that the deal was sealed. I was to give her a ring later to arrange to pick her up. Result!

All I needed now was to sort out the little matter of Yoda and Darth Maul. Equipped with a list of all participants from the competition organisers, I set off to see if my two *Star Wars* friends were the only victim of my mysterious film critic.

Scooby Doo, Shaggy and Velma adorned the garden of the first house I visited. I asked where Fred and Daphne were, curious to find out whether they, too, might have fallen prey to some mild mannered janitor.

"Probably back in the van, making out," came the reply. "I think that's what they did each episode when they sent the other three out to hunt for the ghost." Fair point.

At the next there was a fantastically colourful and realistic depiction of Sooty and Sweep. "Were they actually in a film?" I enquired. There was a pause whilst a horrible look of realisation swept over the face of their creator. The small print on the entry form was frantically looked at. Sooty and Sweep's owner then quickly turned the piece of paper over and over as if he hoped something new would appear when he turned it back again. Eventually, I got my reply: "Oh shit!" he exclaimed loudly, threw the paper on the floor, and then proceeded to kick Sweep around the garden as Sooty looked silently on. I quietly slunk away. I got into my panda car as Sweep's head came bouncing down the pavement past me.

As carefully crafted as the entries were (with the exception of Sweep, who was off his head), so far I was drawing a blank. I visited three other houses with three intact displays, and I still had no leads. I was beginning to think that this might just have been a one-off incident of mindless vandalism, and was ready to call it a day. I had one last house to visit which was just around the corner from the victim's property. I'd expect any self-respecting thief to have stolen their display, too, if he was on a mini crime spree.

I walked up the drive, stopping to admire Mickey Mouse standing resplendent in the middle of the garden in all his big-eared glory. He was about five feet tall, painted immaculately, and clothed in a made to measure red waistcoat. This was clearly a labour of love from some desperate to win the competition.

"Can I help you?"

I was startled by the aggressive nature of the question. I looked up to see an elderly man standing at the side of the property, a shovel in one hand and a tin of black paint in the other.

"I was just admiring your Mickey," I answered.

"Well don't. You'll have plenty of time for that at the fête," he added sharply.

"Touching him up?" I queried.

As he was looking at me as if I was accusing him of sexual impropriety with a papier mâché mouse, I quickly pointed to the tin of paint. "Giving his ears a final going over?"

He grunted in reply.

I thought making figures for a fête was supposed to be a happy and pleasurable activity, but this gentleman seemed to have sucked all the joy out of it. He had put the fun of Disney on ice.

"If that's all, you can go now," he intoned, jerking the shovel in the direction of the road. I was just about to turn on my heel, when I noticed bits of green paper stuck to the shovel blade. Ignoring his guttural rant, I walked past him and around the side of the house following a trail of green flakes, until I discovered a murder scene. There in the back garden lay Yoda, his skull stoved in by some kind of heavy instrument – my guess was a Spear & Jackson rust resistant, wishbone handle, hardwood shafted spade. Darth Maul lay next to him, awaiting his fate. It was an horrific scene of mindless carnage.

I turned to the householder with disgust. "How could you!"

After CSI had attended and taken crime scene photos I went back to see the duo's creators. I wore my cap as a sign of respect for Yoda, and carried Darth Maul in my arms.

"Here's your master of evil," I said as I handed him over, careful not to say anything that could be taken the wrong way. They seemed pleased, if not a little maudlin and filled with self-pity.

I returned to the station and updated Barry. I had solved the mystery of Yoda and Darth Maul, and had arranged for their abductor/killer to come into the office the next day to be interviewed.

"Good work, Donoghue."

As he was in a good mood, I thought I'd push it, and asked for a special favour.

"I met Miss Jones today, Sarge. Any chance I could get off a little early?"

"Only if you make the time up," came Barry's response.

"It's just gone ninety-eight past seventy-two o'clock," I informed him.

He shook his head and let out a sigh. "Just go."

CHAPTER TWELVE:

The Magic Roundabout

Gwen was waiting for me when I arrived at work, grinning broadly and holding the door open for me, causing me to do a little jog of gratitude for the last few yards.

"So," she began, "how was the head this morning?"

She was smiling, and raised her eyebrows expectantly at me, but I was frankly taken aback by her overtly sexual overtones.

"It wasn't like that!" I replied indignantly, "Miss Jones didn't stay overnight."

Gwen suddenly flushed a bright puce as she started to stammer a defence.

"I didn't mean... I meant you were having drinks... Barry said you went off early... I wasn't inferring..." Her voice dropped to a whisper as she looked around to ensure no-one else was within earshot before she continued, "I wasn't inferring fellatio... "

I decided to put her out of her misery, and told her I knew what she had meant, and that we had only had a few beverages as Miss Jones was responsible for the dance troupe today. I was rewarded for my honesty with a sharp slap on the arm.

When I got into the parade room George was already there, today's paper spread out before him, examining his horoscope, reading his daily dose of destiny.

"My friend's star sign was Cancer," I informed him. He

looked up expectantly. "It's quite ironic how she died, really," I continued, "she was attacked by a giant crab."

He shook his head and resumed his reading.

"You're in a mischievous mood today," commented Gwen as she put her body armour on.

"It's shaping up to be a good day," I replied. "First, I'm righting a wrong – Yoda's killer is coming in for interview." I then recounted the whole sorry episode to her, and realised that being raised a Catholic must have affected me more than I had thought. When Gwen interjected with the inevitable "May the Force be with you" line, I couldn't help but mentally reply, "And also with you."

"Next," I told her, "I'm off to the fête. Meeting nice people and seeing Miss Jones in action. Not literally."

"Not literally," repeated Gwen. "Of course not."

I collected the various paperwork from my tray, tapped them on the desk to straighten them up, and headed off towards the custody block. Back in medieval times this would have all been sorted out with a quick trial by ordeal. Anyone accused of a crime would be required to remove a stone from a pot of boiling liquid, their hand would then be bound up and inspected a few weeks later. If the wound had festered they were pronounced guilty, and if their hand had healed they were declared innocent of the crime, and were then set free to live a rich and full life until they died of syphilis at the ripe old age of twenty-three. Apparently, though, medieval justice isn't deemed good enough nowadays, and anyone accused of any offence is allowed to put forward their version of events in interview. Still, as this was an open and shut case, I wasn't expecting it to take long.

As befits a civilised society, I had also arranged for my suspect to come to the station today instead of locking him up last night. He was an elderly gent, and I didn't think he was going to do a runner. I set up the interview room, and sat and waited patiently for my suspect. At bang on two-thirty he arrived, carrying a bulging briefcase in his arms. As I led him through I enquired if he was bringing a solicitor.

"I've decided to represent myself," he informed me in a confident tone, and then proceeded to array his literature over the interview room desk. The custody sergeant raised his eyebrows at me, and tapped his watch as I closed the door. I think he was right: this was going to take longer than I had envisaged.

After turning the tape recorder on, I gave my interviewee his rights and went through the preliminaries.

"For the benefit of the tape, please can you tell me your full name?"

"No reply."

"I beg your pardon?"

"I have the right to remain silent."

"Well, yes, you do... but I was only asking your name."

"Bostock."

"Thank you, Mr Bostock. And can I have your Christian name, please?"

"I'm an atheist. I don't agree with the term 'Christian' name."

"Fair point. Can I have your first name, please, Mr Bostock?"

"Christian."

"Your first name is Christian... and you're an atheist?"

"Can we move on?" Christian Bostock sounded irritated.

I continued onto the main purpose of the whole exercise, and asked for his version of events which led up to the discovery of Yoda in his back garden.

"No comment."

"That's actually a comment," I told him. Two could play at this game.

"In the introduction, you said that I did not have to say anything," and, as if to reinforce the point, he indicated angrily at a highlighted copy of the police caution that he had printed out in front of him.

"Well, yes. I also said '*but it may harm your defence if you do not mention when questioned something that you later rely on in court*' if you recall."

"No comment."

"Basically, Mr Bostock, what that means is that you can stay schtum; it's your right under law. You don't have to say a word, BUT if this whole sorry escapade goes to court, and for the sake of the sanity of the British justice system, let's hope that it doesn't, it also means that if you suddenly come up with a story *there* of what happened, the magistrate may not believe you as you've had your opportunity to give your version of events *here*." I paused for breath, and looked to see if any of this had sunk in.

"No comment," grunted Bostock.

"So, Mr Bostock, I'll say it again, this is your opportunity to give your side of the story before I present my evidence."

"No comment. Prove it!"

"Well, Mr Bostock, I shall. I normally call a spade a spade, but, in this instance I'm calling it Exhibit A." I produced the Spear and Jackson shovel with my evidence label on it. "This is the implement that you were actually holding with bits of Yoda's skull on it."

I then spread out the photographs the CSI had taken. "In the rear of your house we have Yoda's limp and lifeless body. We also have Darth Maul, who has also mysteriously found his way into your garden."

I then produced a letter from the competition organisers. "You are also part of the craft society that…"

"STOP!" yelled Bostock, jumping to his feet. "Just stop." He sat back down, holding both hands to his temple. "I'd like a few minutes alone with my legal representative."

I was perplexed. "But *you* are your legal representative," I reminded him. "You've not got any mental health issue that I should be aware of?"

"Look, PC Donoghue," he clarified, "I've been up all night studying legal document after legal document on the internet. I've been fuelled by drinking copious amounts of coffee, and, to be perfectly honest, I think I've had too much caffeine. I can virtually see sounds. I'd just like some time alone to gather my thoughts." He sounded stressed – a man on the edge.

I wasn't quite sure what to do. If a suspect wants some time with his brief, I usually give them a few minutes together. I guess if he wanted time with his brief, who also happened to be himself, this was no different.

"Would you like a *real* solicitor?" I offered.

His glare back at me said it all. I excused myself, turned off the tapes, and left him alone with his thoughts, his papers and his coffee-induced ability to see noise.

"Finished?" asked the Sarge, looking up from his paper when he saw me emerge.

"He wants a word with his legal representative," I replied.

"Donoghue, Donoghue, Donoghue," muttered the sergeant as he shook his head, and resumed his reading.

Twenty minutes later the interview room door opened, and Bostock indicated he was ready to recommence.

"My client…" he began.

"You?" I clarified.

"I," confirmed Bostock, "have prepared this statement detailing my involvement in the *Star Wars* character debacle." He slid four handwritten pieces of A4 paper towards me.

I took them and read them aloud for the benefit of the tape.

"I, Christian Gerard Bostock, being of sound mind and body…" it sounded more like the opening of his last will and testament, "do admit taking Yoda and his colleague, Darth Maul…"

I skimmed over his rant about the *Star Wars* films in general, and moved onto the juicy part where he confessed that he had smashed up the Jedi Grand Master and, "if the constable hadn't arrived uninvited on the scene," that the same fate would have befallen the Sith Lord. It was all there:

a detailed description of the crime, the reasons why he did it (he wanted Mickey to win, and thought these two were his main competitors), and a plea not to be judged too harshly by his peers, ending with the poetic line: "and I beg make not your anger manifest."

I went out and informed the sergeant.

"So we're dropping the abduction and murder, and going with plain old theft?"

"Correct, Sarge!" Something told me that I was being mocked. I had read somewhere that someone had put forward the idea of scrapping all the existing laws, and replacing them with just two crimes:

1. Out of Order.
2. Bang Out of Order.

It would certainly save memorising all the different acts and legislation. Obviously, it needed some tweaking, but I'm sure the idea had legs.

"Yes, Sarge. He's out of order."

In return I received one of his looks as if to say he thought my only marketable talent was poking things with a stick.

I escorted Mr Bostock out of the interview room, and he was given a basic police caution. I then fingerprinted him, took his DNA and photographed him. I typed up the interview, and quickly put my file together. From start to finish, today had taken up a good two and a half hours. It would only have taken about ten minutes to boil a pot of oil.

I hurried back to the parade room to collect my helmet in preparation for the foot patrol at the fête.

"Don't touch the children's roundabout," Barry casually mentioned as I was about to leave. It was the type of comment that you couldn't just ignore; the type of remark that signalled the prelude to some sort of illicit caper. I checked my watch – I had already missed Miss Jones' children's performance, anyway, thanks to Bostock's stonewalling; it was a bittersweet moment. I put my headwear down, and pulled up a chair.

"It's just that Nina from the other shift had a couple of arrests up there last night: two naked businessmen on the roundabout, celebrating a deal by masturbating each other."

That was some modus operandi. He showed me her report. They weren't just masturbating – they were 'masturbating furiously'. I dread to think of the look on their faces.

"Apparently, she pulled one off," he continued, "the other went for her, but she beat him off. He then ran away, but, after a short chase, she caught him by 'The Golden Cock'".

"Painful," I muttered.

"They both came quietly in the end," continued Barry. "It was a messy business, though." He managed to maintain a straight face throughout.

Things must have changed in business. At my previous job the boss used to give us a bottle of wine at Christmas – if we were lucky. I'm glad I'd got out when I did. I had a thousand questions, the least of which was 'why', but they would have to wait. I thanked him for his warning, and drove to the fairground, and just hoped that the attraction had been wiped down with strong bleach.

When I arrived, I parked up, and began to look for Jess and Andy, who were allegedly already wandering the site, flying the flag for the constabulary. I gave them a call, and agreed to meet them at the organiser's tent in an hour. Meanwhile, I sidled and squeezed through the throngs of happy revellers, nodding greetings, shaking hands with people I'd helped, and telling the bad lads to be good. After sixty minutes of running the gauntlet, I made my way into our rendezvous point for a well-deserved break.

"Pardon the smell," remarked the steward, as she offered me a cup of tea, "it smells as damp as arseholes in here."

I didn't quite know how to react. I wasn't sure what a damp arsehole smelt like, and so was forced to bow to her superior knowledge. Personally, I'd have just called it a musty tent smell. They say the smaller the dog, the crazier the girl; she had a little chihuahua that followed her around, so I think someone was on the right lines there. She also had lovely, platinum blonde hair, although she had unfortunately spoilt the whole effect by dying the roots black. Normally, the teeth to gums ratio are also regarded as quite an important feature, however, she didn't seem bothered by society's norms on that score, either.

Frantically, I began looking for an excuse to slip out before she introduced me to any more of her unique observations. I was about to leave a note, saying I had seen a monkey outside and had gone out to try and catch it, when I received a call on the radio from Jess.

"Tent fourteen. There is going to be some sort of disturbance here soon. The stall holder is complaining that the accordion player has been outside here for two hours already, but he only knows one tune, and has been playing it non-stop. He says he'll be driven to violence soon unless we do something about it."

I politely excused myself, and sidled out of the exit. Tent fourteen was about a hundred yards away, and as I made my way through the thousands of revellers I could hear the familiar wheezing strains, more befitting a French boulevard than a Sandford fête. Suddenly, I heard a noise like a group of cats being simultaneously squeezed hard on their bellies, and then the music abruptly ended. I hurriedly pushed my way through to see Andy talking to the stallholders, and Jess with her notebook out, taking details from our music man.

"It's taken a turn," she informed me. "This gentleman now wants to claim asylum. He says he's been illegally trafficked from Algeria to play the accordion, and a mafia gang take his money off him at the end of each day."

"Surely, they would have brought someone over who could play more than one tune?" I suggested. "Look, there's only fifty pence in his hat. He's not going to be much of a money spinner for them!"

"He also claims he's been fisted," whispered Jess, raising her palms up in front of her as if she was disassociating herself from the remark.

"Fisted?" I questioned. I took the accordion player to one side, and tried to elicit further details from him.

"Where. Were. You. Fisted?" I asked. I received odd glances from some of the passers-by, who put their hands over their children's ears, but strained to hear more themselves. He pointed over to one of the stallholder's trestle tables, and I winced.

"What happened? Were they left or right handed?" Jess enquired, whilst placing a reassuring hand on his shoulder.

The music man looked confused. "They fist me in my face by the table," he explained in broken English.

"Thank God for that!" I exclaimed. He looked at me with horror, as if I was condoning the use of violence towards a musically-challenged, illegally-trafficked alien.

"You mean you've been punched in the face," I clarified. "Don't say you've been fisted over a table because that is a different thing altogether."

He maintained his blank expression. I considered drawing it in my notebook for him, but thought better of it. Instead, I mouthed, "Much worse. Hurty, hurty!" and clenched my fist, bent my arm at the elbow, and mimed jabbing it towards Jess' bottom. She stuck her bum out to illustrate the point. We both quickly stopped when I realised we were attracting undue attention from passers-by.

I was quite relieved when Andy volunteered to take the Algerian down to the station to get further information. We'd probably need a translator, so I guessed he'd be away for some time. A quick word with the crowd of onlookers revealed that the culprit wasn't actually the angry stallholder, but rather a pair of opportunistic teenagers, who were clearly up to no good. I got their descriptions and shared it with my colleague. We'd keep an eye out for them for the rest of the day.

"Fancy a cup of tea?" asked a thirsty Jess as we walked back into the madding crowd. I did, but wasn't up for the strange smell, and even stranger steward, so politely declined.

"You go on," I replied, "I've got some business to attend to in the arts and crafts marquee."

I found the tent at the opposite side of the main arena, pushed back the canvas door, and stepped inside. The whole area seemed to be bathed in a gentle, diffused sunlight, and smelt of a mixture of glue and freshly mown grass; so much better than damp arsehole. It was warm, with a lovely soporific feel to it. I took off my helmet, wiped my brow, and went to look for yesterday's victims to update them regarding Bostock's confession.

I found them chatting and exchanging pleasantries with some of the other competition entrants. Most entrants, it appeared, had entered the competition in the spirit of the fête, and not everyone was a seething mass of jealousy and hatred like Bostock. Perhaps I'd misjudged Bohemian Woman and Rock Band T-shirt Man. I now felt guilty about my faux pas when I had first attended their address, and apologised, telling them I was pleased that I was able to bring things to such a positive conclusion. I wished them good luck with Mr Maul, and bid them adieu.

"I think we all got off on the wrong footing, PC Donoghue," remarked Bohemian Woman after I had said my piece. "My partner and I are really very grateful for what you've done for us." She exchanged a conspiratorial glance with her husband. "Shall we?" she asked excitedly. He beamed back and nodded.

"I hope you don't mind, but we've got a little something for you," she informed me, reaching under the table.

"That's really very kind of you," I replied, "it's all part of the service. I really appreciate the sentiment, but I'm afraid I can't accept anything." I was, of course, flattered. A police officer's role is pretty much perk free: we don't get a Christmas bonus, or extra little something for getting more arrests (despite what some people might think), and so an unsolicited gesture like this by a member of the public was touching. I imagined a bottle of whiskey or box of chocolates was about to be presented to me. I felt churlish turning it down, but the police rules and regulations were clear.

"But we insist," they gushed. "You've put in so much effort."

"It really is very nice, but we aren't actually allowed to receive any gifts. It could be viewed that we were taking bribes."

"Don't be so silly. We want you to have it." I could sense they were beginning to sound a little put out that I was rejecting their kind overture.

"I can't," I reiterated, my voice involuntary raising itself by a few octaves as I tried to make them understand that I didn't want to be put in this situation.

"Look," Mr Rock Band was becoming irritated, "we WANT you to have it. It's a present from us to you. Not a bribe – a simple gift. We don't expect any special treatment from you, and we're not trying to solicit any favours from you. This is just a little something from us to thank you for helping us out. For goodness sake, the job is actually over now. What benefit do you think we're after? Why do you people always think that we're after something?"

'You people'? I could feel myself starting to get a bit hot under the collar. Mrs Bohemia was beginning to get upset now, too. "Satisfied now?" asked Mr Rock Band sarcastically, putting a comforting arm around his wife's shoulders. "You people."

"What is it then?" I asked sharply. I was getting a bit irritated myself now, and I could sense people starting to look over. I felt like I was being pressed into a corner. I really didn't want to be seen walking around the fête with a bottle of whisky under my arm – it just wouldn't look right.

"This!" they both beamed as they ducked under the table and reappeared holding my surprise between them. It took me a few seconds to fully grasp what it was: a marrow. A large green marrow.

"But I don't want it!" I exclaimed. Not a marrow.

"Why not!" They were getting angry again now as the large vegetable was thrust menacingly towards me. "What's your objection now, then?" they added in an aggressive, confrontational tone.

"Because I don't know what to do with it!" I yelled back. There, I had said it. I breathed a sigh of relief.

Suddenly the place went deathly quiet. Mrs Bohemia erupted into floods of tears, and the awful barking donkey was back. The entire marquee seemed to be looking over in my direction to see what all the fuss was about. I also sensed that the crowd was starting to turn ugly.

"Okay, just give it here," I sighed, taking it from them. I had to admit that the latter stages of our conversation had gone past shrouded in a bit of a red mist. I hoped I hadn't sounded too ungrateful. I wiped my brow and felt the warmth radiating from me as my stab vest clung to my body. I tucked my marrow under my arm like a bloated Sergeant Major's baton, donned my helmet, and marched purposefully towards the exit.

I made my way back to the refuge of the organiser's tent; in hindsight, maybe it wasn't so crazy in there after all. Jess and Chihuahua Girl were chatting when I entered. I braced myself for the inevitable questions about why I was carrying the 'thing' around with me.

"That's a big courgette," remarked Chihuahua Girl.

"Actually, I think you'll find it's a marrow," I corrected her. "It was a gift."

"How lovely," commented Jess. "What a fabulous thing to give someone. How thoughtful. I bet they grew it themselves."

"It means so much more than something bought from a shop," added a bystander. Before long the compliments were flooding in about my *curcubita pepo*. Everyone agreed that it was a marvellous deed, born from a desire to show genuine appreciation. The conversation continued, taking in the fact that it was so rare that anyone took the time and effort to make such a heartfelt gesture. I was starting to feel guilty. I'd maybe give it a few days before I went back to see the couple to smooth things over – again.

Jess and I did another patrol of the fête and fairground before meeting back at the tent where I was greeted by the sight of my precious marrow now propped up on the table with a face drawn in Tippex and my collar number on the sides.

"I've made him into Police Constable Marrow," declared a delighted Chihuahua Girl.

Half an hour later I returned to see that he had been promoted to sergeant. Each time I returned, Chihuahua Girl's speech seemed a little more slurred, and she was a little more unsteady on her feet. I suspected that she might have been secretly drinking, and my suspicions were confirmed when I saw two empty bottles of elderflower wine under the table. On my next visit, she was sitting on the floor in the corner of the tent shouting "Speak English!" at her dog.

I decided that would be my last visit for the time being, and set out for the funfair. Sporadic reports had been coming in about two teenagers bullying younger children, and I had an inkling that they may have also been responsible for assaulting the accordion player. Barry, Chad and Lloyd were heading up to the fairground, too. If there was going to be any trouble later, it would be there.

By now the funfair had effectively taken over from the fête, and the music blared from the various rides. The smell of candyfloss and toffee apples filled the air, and children ran excitedly from stall to stall. I soon spotted Jess surrounded by a crowd of distressed kids, giving her the appearance of a cut-price Pied Piper. They had all been victims of the two bullies earlier on. Some had had their popcorn upended, others had been jostled by the duo, whilst the remainder had been verbally abused. It was all minor stuff, but enough to spoil their enjoyment of the fair. This was the children's special day – we had a duty to make sure they enjoyed themselves. Jess passed out the description of the culprits to our colleagues, and we began systematically walking through the crowds, looking for our suspects.

"There they are!" shouted Jess after ten minutes of searching, pointing towards one of the rides.

The two were in the queue for the ironically named 'Long Arm of the Law'. Promising 'the scariest fairground ride outside Alton Towers', ten metal arms extended from a central station painted like a giant policeman. Chairs were suspended on chains from each arm, which spun around violently as the ride gathered speed. True to form, the duo were laughing and jeering at the children and parents queuing for the attraction, drawing disapproving looks from all concerned.

"Shall we nab them now?" she asked.

I suggested that we waited a few minutes, and asked if she would go and gather the children that she had spoken to earlier. Meanwhile, I went and had a word with one of the owners of one of the other rides. We reconvened a few minutes later.

"It's too late," commented Jess. "They're on the ride now."

"Don't worry about that," I told her as I approached the pair. Their seat was hanging from its chains, waiting for the ride to begin. "Excuse me, lads," I said as I got closer, "I've just seen these fall out of the metal arm above you!" I held out my hand, showing them various screws and bolts. "I think we should stop the ride... oh, too late – it's started."

The arm slowly began to move before picking up momentum, and eventually swinging the chair in wide arcs as everyone on board screamed with delight – everyone that is, except for our two suspects. From the looks on their faces, they didn't seem to be enjoying the ride at all. The children standing watching with Jess clearly did, though. As the ride eventually slowed to a stop, two of the palest people I've ever seen staggered off straight into the arms of Chad and Lloyd, who then proceeded to cuff them before taking them down to custody. I can't be absolutely certain, but I think they might also have messed themselves.

I made my way back to the organiser's tent for the final time. Barry was there, chatting to Chihuahua Girl, who, by this time, was only able to stand by propping herself up against the table. To my surprise, Miss Jones was there, too, so I listened patiently to how fantastically well her children had done, nodding and smiling in all the right places. I was just about to ask her out again when Chihuahua Girl staggered over towards me with my marrow.

"Don't forget this!" she slurred, thrusting it into my arms.

"What's that?" enquired Barry, wandering over to get a closer look.

"It was a gift," I explained. "Don't worry, I'll contact Professional Standards tomorrow to run it past them."

"That's charming," he said, smiling as he gave it the once over. "Home grown produce. Better than that supermarket stuff." He took it from me, sniffed it, and turned it around to get a proper look at it. I saw him do a double take when he clocked the face on it... and the sergeant's stripes. I also saw him twitch as he handed my vegetable back to me.

"Donoghue," he whispered menacingly in my ear, "You taking the piss?"

CHAPTER THIRTEEN:

Something in Oil

Picture frames hung at odd angles on the wall, the glass either cracked or missing. Smashed ornaments and wilted flowers littered the floor, and large red stains marred the luxurious cream carpet. I sat in the midst of it, notebook open, trying to work out where to begin.

I knew my side of the story, but had no idea how the woman sat opposite me, with the crimson splatters of blood on her immaculate, bright white summer dress, had arrived at this sorry state.

For me, it had all started at half past one on a warm and sunny Sunday afternoon. I was in the affluent part of town where the people who paid our wages, but rarely called upon our services, lived quietly in a contented state of peaceful law and order.

In contrast to today, the previous Sunday had found me in an altogether different part of the town, and in entirely different circumstances. I had been responding to an emergency call on the Red Estate. The noise of police sirens had filled the air as two patrol cars screeched to a halt outside an address. Three officers had run up the short path, and, as two of them had begun banging and kicking at the front door, demanding to be let in, I had raced around the back. As I turned the corner, a TV had come smashing through the patio doors, closely followed by two males, scarves pulled up around their faces, who had then hopped over the door frame and out onto the broken glass. Taking one look at me, they bolted for the back fence. I had lunged for the nearest male, catching him around the waist, sending us both crashing onto the concrete. His accomplice had hesitated before turning back and raising his foot, preparing to stamp on me as I rolled on the floor, grappling with his friend. At that precise moment, my two colleagues had emerged through the shattered patio doors, and immediately leapt on him, sending them all tumbling to the ground. All five of us had then proceeded to wrestle and roll amongst the empty beer cans and dog turds in the rear yard as we tried to overpower the masked bandits. In the midst of this pandemonium, a female in her early twenties had backed out of the adjoining property, bumping a pram down the steps behind her. She didn't bat an eyelid. Clearly, the spectacle was nothing new to her: she had seen it all many times before.

Conversely, my current location was the type of orderly neighbourhood where the rare sighting of a police car on patrol would set curtains twitching, and provide fuel for coffee morning speculation for weeks to come.

The one similarity that both estates did share, however, was house numbers – or rather a lack of them. I think I'm probably on safe ground to suggest that most police officers would support a law that stated that house numbers MUST be prominently displayed on the front and back of every property in the land. It seems that plenty of homes nowadays like to remain incognito: no identifying numbers on the door, porch or gatepost. It may not sound like much of a big deal to you, but try speeding on blues and twos to an urgent call, only to have to abandon the car in frustration and resort to racing up and down the street on foot, trying to fathom out which order the numbers are going in order to identify in which house the murder is actually being committed. Occasionally, a considerate resident will paint a huge number on the side of their wheelie bin, which is a fantastic help, unless, of course, the bin has been stolen and is sitting outside someone else's house. Maybe I should have taken that diary car job more seriously!

On the affluent development where I now stood, there were names instead of numbers on the gateposts; names, lovingly devised, and displayed on little slate plaques, or on a clean white board hanging between two small picket posts. This, in actual fact, made it even harder to work out where a specific house was in relation to the others, but, luckily enough, our deduction skills were rarely put to the test as so few calls came in from this estate. I've no doubt that here, if we were ever to receive an anti-social behaviour call about graffiti on the side of a house, it would probably just turn out to be Banksy working on a commission.

Here, in Rocking Horse Avenue, there seemed to exist an unwritten rule that cars were to be religiously washed every Sunday, and that front lawns were to be beautifully modelled, manicured and maintained, and any divergence from these stringent stipulations would entail the heinous offender being blackballed by the ladies who lunch, which probably wouldn't be half as much fun as it sounds.

I couldn't be entirely sure, but I was pretty confident that the people here still wore pyjamas with little collars on, just in case they needed to wear a tie in the middle of the night.

The weekend was winding down on this pleasant valley Sunday, and I was stood talking to Charles Fulbright-Brown, the chairman of the local neighbourhood watch committee. There was nothing to report as usual, so instead we were engrossed in an in-depth discussion about his recent prostate examination. He told me he thought it was going to be a little uncomfortable when the doctor gave him a 'safe' word. I had a little chuckle, and looked over at his wife, who looked back at me with eyes deader than a Burger King employee who can no longer bring herself to correct people who order 'McNuggets'. She had clearly heard this story before... many times before.

I decided to change the subject, and pointed over towards the ornamental shrubs that adorned the garden. I knew that topiary was her great joy, and so asked how she kept her living sculptures looking so perfect, all the while fighting my natural instinct to ask her how she kept her bush so neatly trimmed. She beamed and came alive as she animatedly described how she defined the figures with clippers and shears, combined with patience and a steady hand; apparently, shaped wire cages were frowned upon as being the work of the devil. Now it was her husband's turn to glaze over. I, however, was fascinated.

"I must admit, that's a fantastic looking dog," I gushed.

"It's a peacock," she replied. Burger King eyes returned.

I thought she had captured that wagging tail look perfectly. Obviously not. Quite frankly, I was relieved when the sound of a party over the road disturbed our little chat.

"I'll just pop over and ask them to keep it down, and I'll be back in a moment," I promised. Maybe I should have given myself longer. A moment is actually a unit of time from medieval days equal to one fortieth of an hour, or, to put it another way, ninety seconds. That wouldn't be nearly long enough. They should invent another name for the time I needed: the time it takes for the person you've upset to go back inside and forget your gaffe. I'm sure the Germans have a word for it. I'd have to strike up a conversation at the other house until I deemed it safe to return.

There was, however, a glimmer of hope: Mr Fulbright-Brown had confided to me on my last visit that his wife's memory wasn't what it used to be. He said it was getting to the stage where she could almost plan her own surprise party. I smiled inwardly at her sad affliction, thinking how every dark cloud has a silver lining.

I wandered across the road, mulling over what pretext I could use to keep myself there until the coast was clear. It was an imposing property, with two expensive cars parked in the long, gravel driveway. An elaborate six foot wrought iron fence, with matching double gates, defied any unwelcome guest to think better than disturb the residents of this mansion.

I stepped over the small picket fence of the garden to the right, and then hopped over the two foot high dividing wall between the two properties. Obviously, the railings were only effective against polite intruders.

I walked up the drive towards the house, almost feeling embarrassed to disturb their fun. I'm usually loath to bother people when I'm called in my official capacity to a noisy party. It's not really a police matter: more a council or environmental issue. Everybody should be entitled to a party now and again... and how do you keep a party quiet? As long as it's not a regular event, or too over the top, let's all just be a little more considerate and tolerant.

I wondered what they were celebrating. I could hear the music as I approached the house: it was Queen. As I listened to the familiar strains of 'Don't Stop Me Now,' I recalled the scene from Shaun of the Dead where Shaun and his mates are bashing the zombie to death with pool cues to the beat of the music. I smiled.

"I'm a rocket ship on my way to Mars," I sang as I approached. "On a collision course", I knocked at the window. "I'm a satellite, I'm out of control," I continued, as I cupped my hands to the window and peered through. "I'm a sex machine ready to... SHIT!"

In the lounge a woman was lying on the floor, a large male kneeling over her, his hands around her throat, throttling her. I hammered on the window, and then ran to the front door – it opened a few inches and then jerked, caught on the security chain. I got on the radio and called for back-up as I kicked the door open, sending the bracket flying, and ran through to where the drama was unfolding.

I announced my arrival, shouting 'Police!' loudly over the music that was still blaring. I grabbed the male by his shoulders in an attempt to pull him off the woman, but he swung around, using my forward motion to throw me against the mantelpiece, sending ornaments flying as I crashed face first into it. I shook my boots clear of the dried

I dragged the man back on to his knees. He was dazed, but conscious. I wasn't sure if the fight was totally out of him, so I cuffed his hands behind his back just in case. It was the first chance I'd had to get a decent look at him: he was in his fifties, greying hair, and I'd guess about six foot five when stood up. He was also of a substantial build... and he still looked angry. Very angry.

My prisoner knelt in the middle of the lounge, blood tricking down his face, soaking into his shirt, surrounded by the detritus of smashed ornaments and crockery. I was bent over next to him; bloodied face, hands on my knees, desperately trying to get my breath back. The female was sitting on the floor on the other side, hands trembling, mascara running down her face. In the background, the CD selected the next track on the album: 'We are the Champions'.

At that moment, Ron and Geezer barged into the house, batons drawn. In shock, they stopped and looked at the spectacle in front of them.

"What's this all over?" Geezer asked as he surveyed the carnage.

"To be perfectly honest," I replied, "I haven't got a clue."

As I brushed myself down and wiped my face clean, Geezer informed me that I might have to apologise to Fulbright-Brown if I saw him later – not because of the peacock/dog mix-up, but because two of my colleagues had just burst into his house, scaring the bejaysus out of him, demanding to know what he had done with me.

I told Ron and Geezer that I would update them with the full circumstances when I knew them myself, but, in the meantime, that I'd appreciate it if they would take my charge down to custody, and have his injuries looked at. Until now, my prisoner had just knelt quietly, taking it all in, but, as he was helped to his feet, he clearly got a second wind.

"I'll have your job!" he spat at me.

"On an afternoon like this, you're welcome to it," I informed him.

He continued to shout the names of influential people he knew, and how he regularly played golf with them. They wouldn't be happy when he told them what had happened he informed me.

If he meant strangling his wife, and then attacking the police officer who came to her assistance, then I would have to agree with him: they wouldn't be happy at all.

Once in the street, he started to play the crowd that had gathered: "Look what they've done to me! Police brutality!"

A shocked murmur spread through the crowd as he was placed in the back of the van.

"Well, that was embarrassing," I heard Mrs Fulbright-Brown say as the vehicle drove off. "I thought we were all going to wave."

Inside, the female had already brought a bag of frozen mange tout for me to hold over my eye; anywhere else and it would have been just plain old peas.

"The trouble with marriage," she mused, flopping down onto the sofa, "is that it was invented when people lived to the ripe old age of thirty."

I took out my notebook, and decided that this incident would come under the heading of a domestic.

Do you remember that tingly feeling you get when you first meet someone you really like? Well, that's common sense leaving your body. When it eventually returns, you sometimes find that the knight in shining armour is actually a clown wrapped in tin foil, and that girl you called 'The One,' is really a number two. Anyway, calling a girl 'The One' just makes her sound like she has been chosen to lead a rebellion against an evil ruler in a galaxy far, far away.

Potentially, as police, we can become involved in your relationship any time after that first tingly feeling happens – for better or worse. In fact, on average, police are involved in other people's relationships a staggering 1,300 times per day... or about once every minute. Sometimes it's someone in that relationship that calls us, other times it's a concerned other. The one constant, though, is that when one person is unhappy in a relationship it usually means that two people are unhappy, even if the other one doesn't quite realise it yet.

"I can't even remember what it was about," she sighed, brushing the tears from her cheeks. "It was probably over something trivial. It always is." I was quite used to domestics that were over nothing in particular. Flushing the toilet whilst the other is in the shower can be a deal breaker for some couples.

"You don't simply unplug my phone from the charger, and expect things to be ok between us!" is another anguished cry I've heard.

"You don't have chicken on a pizza – it's not natural!" was another reason for a violent argument.

Sex, or lack of it, is often a catalyst.

"She's an old-fashioned girl," one obnoxious male shouted to the whole street of onlookers as I led him out to the police van. "She waited until our wedding night to let me know that she's never going to suck it." She, meanwhile, just raised her eyes heavenwards before she started to tidy up the mess that he had created.

Whatever the reason, all domestics are low points in a relationship, whichever way you look at it.

"What does he do?" I asked, pen poised over the page.

"He's something in oil," she replied. It made him sound like a sardine. "We've been married longer than I care to remember... and just grown apart. In fact, we've been married for so long now that I don't even look both ways when I cross the road anymore. It's like Stockholm Syndrome in reverse."

"Will you make a statement about the assault?" I asked.

She wasn't sure. She had a good job in HR, and, whilst she readily agreed that she would encourage any of her staff to make a stand, she admitted to being a hypocrite when it came to her own situation. At first they had stayed together for the sake of the kids, then for the sake of the grandchildren, and now it was to maintain their lifestyle. It didn't seem like much of a lifestyle to me: life isn't just about money and possessions. It's true that couples need to work at a relationship, but not when it involves violence. I told her that regardless of what she decided, I would be taking positive action, and I hoped that she would, too. After letting her know that there were various agencies and organisations that could support her, I left her to mull things over, and told her I'd get back to her later. I was off to custody to interview her husband.

Once there, the sergeant updated me on my prisoner's medical state. It reminded me of the coroner's report on the body we had found up at Todd's Plantation. In a section about the genitals, the report had stated he was 'circus sized'. This typo had been hastily corrected with a red pen by an embarrassed official to read: 'circumcised'. Apparently, after the knee strikes I had delivered to Mr Sardine's privates during our fracas, 'circus sized' was, however, the right description to use on this occasion.

The angry husband was still as angry as I escorted him to the interview room.

"I've been treated like a criminal!" he protested vehemently, banging his fist down on the table.

I informed him that he was being treated like a criminal because he *was* a criminal. I'm not sure where he had been for the last fifty years, but the Rule of Thumb certainly was no longer on the statute books. The saying, in case you don't know, is said to derive from the belief that English law allowed a man to beat his wife with a stick, so long as it was no thicker than his thumb. Whilst I don't think that this was actually ever the case, it was certainly legal in the past for a man to chastise his wife in moderation (whatever that meant). Thankfully, that too has now been removed from the statute books.

"She won't make a complaint, anyway," he boasted. "She likes her home comforts too much. So all we have left is you breaking into my house and assaulting me."

I returned him to his cell, and journeyed back to Rocking Horse Avenue.

En route, I received a call from George: he had already had a conversation with Rob and Geezer back at the station, and had called to inform me that he'd had dealings with our sardine in the spring.

Last year, it appeared that my man in the cells had put his father into a nursing home. He had discovered, however, that his father's nest-egg, which he clearly hoped to inherit one day, was diminishing faster that he thought it reasonably should be. The police and the nursing home management were called upon to investigate. After some basic calculations the first part of the complaint was proved to be correct: the old man's fortune was, indeed, diminishing at a startling rate. George then had to establish why. This proved to be easier than expected as the old man was only too happy to tell the world.

"It's my money," he had informed everyone. "And how I wish to spend it, is up to me."

How he wished to spend it, however, was by requesting certain female members of the staff to 'perform oral favours' for him, amongst other things. Whilst it was acknowledged that he was paying a significantly higher rate than that charged by Angel Skinner, it was, nevertheless, priced at the industry average, according to George.

"I never wanted to be put in here in the first place," the old man bemoaned, "but, seeing that I am, I may as well enjoy myself."

Since he was compos mentis this wasn't a police matter. It was his money, and he could spend it as he wished. The care home was advised that it may wish to revisit its policies regarding staff conduct, but it was, as the old man had clearly stated, "certainly not a matter for my money-grabbing son".

"The gent you arrested complained about me, too," George relayed. That made me feel a bit better.

When I arrived at the house, Rosalind, my prisoner's long-suffering wife, was on the phone.

"Mum, can I come home for a while?"

I sat and waited to update her. Before I had a chance to speak, she told me that she had thought about what I had said, and wanted to make a comprehensive statement about today and all the other instances where she had been abused. About 20% of all violence per se is domestic related, but, on average, women are assaulted 35 times before they actually report any incident to the authorities. It's not, however, just the physical violence; domestic abuse can also be emotional, psychological or financial.

I went back out to the car to get some more statement paper. After a couple of productive hours, I had the information I needed to build a file to take to the CPS.

"I've tried to make it work," she told me, almost apologetically, after we had finished, "but sometimes some things aren't worth saving." She didn't need to explain that to me. I picked up a dream catcher that had been knocked onto the floor during the fight and handed it to her. "Just throw it away," she gestured, "it clearly doesn't work." I tossed it into the bin.

"He won't miss me," she added, wiping away a tear, "just the money." What an awful thing to realise after so many years together, but, after what George had told me, I had to agree with her.

As I packed up my paperwork, I saw a car pull up outside, with an elderly lady inside. "It's my mum," she informed me with a smile. Before, she had looked beautiful but sad, like a painted fairground carousel put away for the winter. Now, she was transformed as if a burden had finally been lifted off her shoulders.

It's a fact that 40% of marriages end in divorce; the rest end in death. It's not wrong to cry, but it's a waste to weep while your life passes you by. I believe Rosalind had felt she was trapped, but there are always people who can help. Unfortunately, for some victims, it can take an incident as serious as this one to realise that.

As I drove back to the station, I thought: there has got to be a lesson in there somewhere... and it probably goes something like this: love is like a fart; if you need to force it, then it's probably shit.

CHAPTER FOURTEEN:

Wrong On So Many Levels

I've always wanted to turn around in a lift full of people and say: "I expect you are wondering why I've gathered you all here today?". Well, now was my chance.

I was at the hospital with Andy, in the middle of a prisoner watch, which was all related to the recent spate of diesel thefts from vehicles on the industrial estate. Usually under the cover of darkness, whilst the truckers slept peacefully in their cabs, thieves had been sneaking up to the articulated lorries parked up around the business park, taking their fuel caps off, siphoning the diesel, and then making off with it. It had become so rife that the drivers had even started to leave their fuel caps unlocked as they knew the villains would only break them off to get access to the diesel, or, failing that, would drill a hole in the bottom of the tank to drain it out, causing even more damage. Catching the crooks had become our main priority, and every night saw us patrolling the car parks, lay-bys and streets on the industrial estate, searching for the culprits.

On hearing about this lucrative enterprise, Drew and Chris Peacock thought they would get themselves a slice of the action. Armed with a garden hose and a couple of five litre petrol cans, the duo set out on a fateful October night in search of easy pickings. Not being the brightest kids in the cabbage patch, they hadn't brought a pump and instead planned to rely on Drew's innate sucking ability to get the fuel flowing.

Despite the fact that there is safety in numbers, many truckers choose to eschew the official lorry parks in lieu of quiet roads on the industrial estate in a bid to save the parking costs. Consequently, these lone stragglers were more vulnerable than most and, typically, our predators targeted one such lone wagon on a quiet and deserted road, and went in for the kill. Creeping through the darkness, they checked that the driver's curtains were pulled shut before unscrewing the fuel cap and dipping the hose in with a gentle splosh. As Chris kept watch, Drew started sucking. A minute passed, then two. Apart from becoming light-headed, nothing else was happening. A frustrated Chris marched over and snatched the hose out of his brother's hands.

"Fucking useless retard!" he whispered furiously to Drew, "I should have brought Angel Skinner instead. She'd have emptied the whole tank by now!"

A dejected-looking Drew slouched over to the roadside, and reluctantly took over the look-out duties.

"You've got to siphon it below the tank, dummy!" Chris hissed. Then, lying back on the cold tarmac, and forming a tight seal around the end of the hose with his mouth, Chris inhaled for all he was worth, desperate to emphasise the point to his disgruntled sibling. In his angry enthusiasm, however, he neglected to stop sucking when the fuel started flowing. As the liquid hit the back of his throat he gagged as he swallowed a mouthful of cold and oily diesel. The hose slipped from his hands, and he lay retching on the floor, whilst the liquid slowly pooled around him.

Meanwhile, Drew was caught in a dilemma: did he stem the flow of fuel and help his brother, or did he run to get the containers that he had left in the hedge? Never one to take constructive criticism in the spirit in which it was intended, he decided that he didn't like being called a retard, and went home whilst the thought of Angel was still fresh in his mind. But, as a 'concession' to his brother, he did knock on the lorry's cab door before he left and shouted to the driver that he thought someone was trying to nick his fuel. Police were subsequently called, and they arrived at the scene to find the master criminal rolling around, clutching his stomach. He was arrested and promptly taken to hospital for treatment.

When Andy and I had arrived for work in the morning, we had been sent to the hospital to take over the prisoner watch from the night shift. He may well have been lying sad and forlorn in a bed on ward sixteen, but he was still officially in police custody, and we needed to make sure he didn't do a runner.

Criminals know that they have a much better chance of escaping from a hospital rather than a custody block, and will concoct all sorts of reasons to go to Accident and Emergency. I have witnessed Oscar-winning performances where the poor prisoner, demonstrating a range of pained expressions, can barely walk as he shuffles out of custody. Once at hospital, he will then beg the nurses, in a suitably quavering voice, to ask the nasty officers to take off his cuffs while he's being treated. Occasionally, an indignant medical professional will join in and insist, nay demand, that the shackles be removed from his patient, often ordering the police to leave the room to maintain doctor/patient confidentiality. It is then, as the door closes, that their sickly charge will undergo a miraculous recovery: the door will crash open and the prisoner will sprint through the corridors, making a break for freedom, or a cry will go up from the doctor as his patient jumps through the window.

I had seen it all before, and, I, for one, didn't want to undergo the embarrassment of losing a prisoner. As a result, Andy and I sat at the end of his hospital bed as a sickly Peacock alternated between sleeping and telling us how much he hated the police before finally deciding that he actually despised his brother more. After four mind-numbing hours I was heartily fed up. Just as I yawned – nature's way of saying 20% of battery remaining – one of the town officers popped his head around the corner and asked us if we wanted a break. Perfect timing.

As Andy was happy for me to take the first break, I decided to use my window of opportunity to stretch my legs and pop to the hospital canteen for a cup of tea. But first I would disappoint everyone with my lift joke. At the sound of the ping the lift doors opened, and I prepared to deliver my line.

"PC Donoghue, as I live and breathe!" It was the unmistakable voice of Bridget Avery. Bridget was well known to the police; not because of any wrongdoing on her part, I hasten to add, but rather due to the criminal shenanigans of her numerous offspring. That said, her two daughters: Bernadette and Mary, were lovely girls; it was all down to her many sons.

Bridget was a warm, friendly, chatterbox of a woman of Irish extraction, who had a great sense of humour. She was short and plump, with rosy cheeks and wild curly jet black hair that seemed to defy gravity. She was never seen without her trademark blue and white checked apron which reflected the colour of her twinkling blue eyes. She was used to the police arriving at her door at all hours of the day and night looking for Michael, Brendan, Declan or Niall, and always greeted us with a smile.

"They're not big ones for the Ten Suggestions," she would sigh as we searched the property. She neither condemned nor condoned their activities: they were her sons, and so she stood by them. She also knew that we were just doing our job, and didn't hold a grudge against the police for trying to put an end to their nefarious activities. George had called at her house one morning, and had immediately been invited in by the apron-wearing Irish woman.

"I'm just making a cuppa, would you have one?" she enquired of my colleague. He readily accepted her offer.

"I'm just frying the bacon there, officer. Would you like a few rashers?" Never one to refuse an offering of food, George replied that he would love some.

"Sit yourself at the table, officer. Ah sure now the bacon looks a bit lonely on that plate – let me get a couple of eggs on there for you." Half an hour later, and the simple cup of tea had developed into several cups and a full fry-up with sausages, black pudding and tomatoes joining the fray. An hour later, George returned to the police station a very contented bobby, his stab vest straining against his full belly.

"Well, did you serve the summons on Michael Avery?" enquired Barry.

"Oh, shit!" responded George when he realised that, to all intents and purposes, he had just turned up at an address, had a full meal, and then walked off without any word of explanation as to why he had gone there in the first place. Mrs Avery was such a lovely lady that she hadn't questioned his reason for being there either.

"So what brings you to the hospital today, Mrs Avery?" I enquired.

"It's Bernadette," she replied, gently placing her hand on her daughter's forearm. The Avery girls were two of the nicest young ladies that you could ever care to meet – not that many men actually got to meet them. Both girls were in their early twenties, but, to my knowledge, neither of them had ever had a boyfriend. I had heard that their mother was keen for them to go courting, but she knew that it was easier said than done when they were surrounded by four overprotective brothers. Bridget had once confided in me that she had even saved them a piece about birth control from the Catholic Herald if they ever got married. I'm guessing it was a pull-out section.

The two girls were different in their own way: Bernadette was the stereotypical English rose, albeit with a flow of chestnut tresses, whilst Mary was more the thorny stem. Bernadette always wore a dress, whilst Mary preferred the skin tight fashions of the day. Both, however, were kind, and gentle to a fault, if not a little naïve.

"Oh dear," I replied. I wished I hadn't asked now after seeing the embarrassed look on Bernadette's face.

"She's got the myxomatosis, PC Donoghue," Bridget told me. "Absolutely riddled with it she is."

"Mam!" exclaimed a clearly mortified Bernadette. "How many times have I told you! That's what rabbits have! I've got endometriosis!"

"Well, officer, it's..." Bridget broke off, and just mouthed 'down there' as she pointed towards her nether regions. I don't know who was going redder at this stage – me, or poor Bernadette. I desperately tried to change the subject.

"Thirsty?" I enquired of Mary who stood next to her sister, cradling a two litre bottle of cloudy lemonade.

"No, PC Donoghue," she replied, "it's just Bernadette's urine sample."

"I thought they just needed a little cupful?" I remarked, raising my eyebrows.

"Mam!" Bernadette exclaimed again. "I told you!"

"Two whole weeks it took her to fill that," Bridget added. "Sure now we couldn't get the funnel for the first few days. God love her, you should have seen the mess!"

God love her indeed. The poor girl looked like she wanted the ground to open up and swallow her whole. To spare her blushes, I tried again to change the subject.

"You're both looking very nice today." In reality, Bernie looked pretty and demure as she always did, whilst Mary looked like she was ready to go clubbing in her figure hugging leopard skin outfit. Personally, I think there should be a rule that says you shouldn't be allowed to wear animal print if you are bigger than said animal.

"I'm out on a date later," gushed Mary excitedly. That explained the outfit. "My first proper date," she continued, beaming from ear to ear. I could see her brothers frowning as she spoke.

"Anything nice planned?" I enquired as my finger hovered over the lift buttons. "Going down?" The brothers' frowns turned to scowls.

"He's the strong, silent type," she added dreamily. From

the smell, I think there must have been another strong, silent type present, and, judging by the smirk on Niall's face, I think he was responsible. As the lift began its descent, I thought that it was wrong on so many levels.

"Where's your Michael?" I asked Bridget. At twenty-five, he was the eldest of the clan and the ringleader when it came to the brothers' criminal activities. He had started out as a talented cyclist, but had begun taking performance-enhancing steroids to help him compete. Soon he was peddling, too, getting himself deeper and deeper into the drugs scene. One thing led to another, and very quickly he became a drugs runner for Charlie Sellers, transporting his stash around the town. It can't have been comfortable if he hid the drugs where I think he hid them, and especially not on a bike with those saddles.

Sellers introduced him to other opiates, and, before long, Michael was addicted to harder drugs, and was then breaking into outbuildings and shoplifting to fund his ever-increasing habit. Although they didn't take drugs themselves, Brendan and Declan simply got caught up in the whirlwind of it all. None of them were particularly unpleasant characters, and they all viewed their dealings with the police as just a hazard of the job.

Over the last six months I hadn't heard much about the eldest three brothers; it tends to happen a lot: one day a crook whom we've never heard of before will become a regular face on our briefing boards as he thieves and burgles his way around town, and then just as quickly, he'll fall off the radar. There can be a variety of reasons for it: from the love of a good woman, through to the sentencing of an astute judge.

"Michael's dead," came the reply.

Or, they could, indeed, be dead. I shuffled my feet uncomfortably.

"Don't you worry yourself, PC Donoghue," said Bridget, placing a hand on my shoulder. "You weren't to know. What's important is that he died doing what he loved."

"Which was?"

"Heroin."

I didn't quite know what to say.

"It's such a shame. He'd have made a fantastic copper," she added.

I had no idea what aspects of being a smack addict and burglar leant themselves to the office of constable, but I thought it best not to delve deeper. I decided to avoid asking after Brendan and Declan, although I could see they were still with us as they were standing, stony-faced, next to their sisters. Instead, I took the safe option and enquired how Niall was doing. At fifteen, he was the youngest family member and, so far, unlike his brothers, he had avoided getting involved in criminality. However, he wasn't without his own set of problems: to call him socially awkward would be misleading, as it would indicate that there were situations where he wasn't awkward.

By all accounts he had always been a bit of a loner, and had somehow got into thrash metal music: the fast, aggressive subgenre of heavy metal. The shouted lyrics generally revolve around isolation, alienation, addiction, suicide and murder. I only know all this because Niall had told me all about it last summer when I had found him wandering a quiet country road, twenty miles from his home. He had said that he just needed to get away before he did something stupid, and I don't think he meant buying Justin Bieber tickets.

He had been exhausted and hungry, so I had called into a garage as we drove back to his home, and bought him a can of pop and a Mars Bar. Ben had told me I was stupid for doing so as now I'd be his officer of choice if he ever had trouble in the future. To be perfectly honest, I didn't mind. He clearly needed help. When I dropped him off at home, I told Bridget what Niall had told me and she arranged for him to see his doctor.

Ben was proved right when a month later as I left the station to go home, a dejected-looking Niall stood waiting for me in the car park. He informed me that he had just come from the quarry where he had contemplated jumping into the abyss. He believed the music was telling him to do it – willing him to end it all. I drove him home first, and then took him and Bridget down to the hospital to see the crisis team. His mum was at a loss for words. She blamed herself, but it's nobody's fault: an adolescent mind can be a very strange place. I just hoped that the psychiatrists and psychologists would be able to help the young man. Twelve months on, and they had obviously done something right as he was still with us. Bridget must have read my mind, and volunteered the fact that Niall was off the harsh, brutal, hard-core thrash and back to the usual things that fixated most normal teenagers.

"It's not just Spiderman who has the sticky hands after a day on the web now, is it, son?" she laughed.

"Mam!" It was Niall's turn to be embarrassed by his mother. "I told you not to come in if the bedroom door's closed!"

Now that Bridget was smiling again, I felt it was safe to enquire after Brendan and Declan's wellbeing. I started with the usual question: asking them if they had been up to anything silly recently.

"Well, Brendan applied for a job last week," offered Declan.

"And?" I replied, bracing myself for the punch line.

"That's it," he answered, looking perplexed.

"I get paid almost the same anyway," Brendan told me.

"Paid for doing what?"

"Well, nothing," they both answered, looking at me as if I was thick.

I should have known better than to attempt a sensible conversation with those two. It reminded me of the time when Gwen had loaned me an audio CD of one of the Sherlock Holmes books. I had given it a try, but had handed it back to her, saying that I couldn't make any sense of the storyline at all – it was all over the place. It was only when I was driving home that evening that I realised I'd had it on random play.

Apparently, Bridget informed me with a roll of her eyes, 'getting paid' is how a lot of people refer to their benefit money; as if it is their right, rather than a lifeline provided by a caring society.

"You both keeping well, anyway?" I persevered.

"Show PC Donoghue your rashes," interjected Bridget.

I hate it when something like this happens. Silently, I prayed: "Please don't show me your rashes, please don't show me… MOTHER OF GOD!"

Reluctantly, Brendan and Declan had rolled up their sleeves and presented their forearms. I instinctively recoiled, and pulled one of Jess's faces: the cat's bum, combined with a furrowing of the brow. Bridget gave a running commentary on the rash just to make sure I was fully aware of all the symptoms.

"Red, blotchy, angry-looking, blistered, weeping, itchy and irritating." It sounded like the cast of a horror version of *Snow White and the Seven Dwarfs*.

"They won't say how they got them," she added, "but it looks like something chemical has splashed on to their arms." She raised her eyebrows at me and I got the hint.

Last week a metal finishing plant had been broken into, and various items and equipment had been stolen. The building was a Health and Safety nightmare: employees were forced to wear protective clothing and equipment to safeguard them from the splash-back from the open vats of acids as the metals were dipped. In some areas special breathing apparatus had to be worn due to the poisonous fumes created by the dipping process. Why someone would want to enter this hostile environment unless they absolutely had to, I'll never know. Still, enter they did.

Over the course of several nights, intruders had set off the plant's alarm system by kicking the fire doors. Each time it happened, the alarm monitoring company had phoned the plant manager in the middle of the night, who had then duly attended the site only to find nothing awry. After a week of call-outs, he had simply assumed that there was a fault on the system, and so decided not to re-set the alarm: this was exactly what the burglars had hoped for. That night they returned and broke in through the fire-door, going straight to the fuse box and cutting off the power to the whole site. Then, by the light of low-powered torches, so as to not attract the attention of any passing police patrols, they had stolen a very specific list of chemicals and hardware. It looked like the burglars had known exactly what they were after.

As he recounted the tale, the manager added dramatically: "If they had dipped their finger in that vat of acid, and then licked it, they would have been dead before they had taken three paces."

Whilst it had been a chilling thought, I don't know many people who would be inclined to dip their finger in a vat of mysterious liquid and then suck it clean. What had been pointed out to me, however, was evidence of a chemical spill.

"If they get any of that on their skin, it's going to be painful; it'll blister, swell and get very, very red."

"Whoa, too much inflammation," I had told him, but it was a throwaway line that he had failed to catch as he had just continued to tell me more symptoms the intruders could expect following the spill.

Brendan and Declan's injuries seemed to match the description to a T those listed by the manager. I was fairly confident that they didn't have the brains to plan the operation, but I had no doubt that they were involved. I also think that whilst Bridget didn't want to directly turn her sons in, she was well aware of how falling into a life of crime had taken Michael from her. This hint was the signal to me that she wanted her boys brought back onto the straight and narrow again. By the look on their faces, I think the boys realised that, too.

"So, lads, how did you get that?"

"I think mam is using a new washing powder."

"Déjà moo!" interjected their mother angrily. "This officer has heard all that bullshite before!" She sounded livid, and the boys knew better than to try and waffle their way out of it. The game was up.

"Shall we say you'll pop down to the station tomorrow at about midday?" I suggested. They both nodded in agreement. Feeling the need to lighten the mood a little, I enquired as to why Niall was clutching a bunch of carnations that looked like they had recently been liberated from a lamppost.

"Visiting their father, PC Donoghue – the poor soul's not got long," answered Bridget.

My attempt at levity had failed, but I guess there won't be too many upbeat tales in a hospital. I didn't trust myself to ask what was wrong with Bridget's husband. In all my visits to the Avery family, I had never actually met him; he was always either at work, or down the pub.

"I read in Mam's magazine that there is a woman going around killing people in hospital," piped up a concerned Niall. "They call her Mrs A."

I wasn't aware of any recent hospital murders, and looked over at Bridget to see if she could enlighten me. Instead, she just shook her head. "No, son, it's MRSA."

I knew all about MRSA – Methicillin-resistent Staphylococcus Aureus. It is a bacterium that causes infections that are very difficult to treat. It is particularly prevalent in hospitals where there are open wounds and weakened immune systems. Thankfully, however, cases of the superbug have been decreasing year on year, largely due to the use of anti-bacterial hand gel which prevents the spread of infection. Aside from paranoia, the other main effective ingredient in the gel is alcohol – hospital sanitizers contain up to 80% alcohol – but that was proving to be the problem: some desperate alcoholics were now drinking the gel. Initially, they mixed it with orange juice, but some had started to drink it neat. It had become such an issue that some hospitals had even taken to locking the gel away when certain known individuals entered the ward. For the time being, though, I thought I'd keep this fact from young Niall.

"I'm sure he will be fine," I said, trying to reassure him.

"Joseph has asked me to bring in a Bible," Bridget uttered soberly, which seemed to contradict my light-hearted message. "I hope he's not revising for the final exam," she added.

"I told him that whatever happens, Jesus loves you." Comforting words from your wife or daughter as she sits by your bedside – horrendous words to hear if you are an inmate in a Mexican prison.

"He's more religious with each day that passes," added Bernadette. "He never wanted to come to church with us before, but now he says that if he gets out, he'll be coming along so." It made sense: my old commanding officer in the army used to tell me that there are no atheists in foxholes.

This was all becoming a bit too deep and maudlin. There's an old proverb that says just about whatever you want it to. I tried to find one to fit now, but drew a blank. I dared to steer the conversation back to something positive.

"So, have they given you any good news about your husband?" I asked as the lift reached the floor for the canteen and I stepped out, leaving Mrs Avery and her clan, and my many social blunders, behind.

"Well, on the bright side," she shouted after me as the doors started to close, "they say at least he's not a hypochondriac."

CHAPTER FIFTEEN:

Egg Patrol

It was October 31st and sales of Halloween costumes had peaked at an all-time high. Whilst women had opted for sexy devils, naughty witches or slinky cats, for some unknown reason, apart from the usual zombie attire, quite a few male revellers had decided on Superhero outfits. However, because of unfortunate events in previous years, costumes now came with a warning that the ensemble didn't actually endow the wearer with actual super powers, nor did it give the wearer an automatic right to see his children.

Still, the night was young, and so the boisterous party goers would have to wait: for the time being the streets of the town belonged to the bands of happy children dressed as ghosts and skeletons, skipping merrily from house to house to 'trick or treat', collecting their candy plunder in little plastic pots shaped like pumpkins.

Many people regard Trick or Treating as just another Americanism to be lumped with other unsavoury imports such as McDonalds, jazz music and group hugs. However, calling round to houses at this time of year dates back to the centuries old English tradition of 'souling' where children would sing and say prayers for the dead to release them from purgatory, in return for cakes. The 'trick' element – 'making demands with menaces' – was the import.

Usually, 'trick or treat' is an idle threat, but there are always killjoys out to spoil things. 'Egging' was fast becoming popular, where gangs of youths would throw eggs at houses, cars or people. However, it isn't always just an innocent prank: eggs can break windows, dent the bodywork on vehicles and the whites of the eggs can degrade certain types of paint. There have also been a number of incidents where innocent victims have been blinded after being struck hard in the face by such a missile. As a result, at the start of our evening shift, most of my colleagues, including me, were on egg patrol.

I began by visiting Sandford's various stores and supermarkets to monitor who was doing the buying. Fortunately, our preliminary talks with the managers of the shops in the weeks building up to Halloween had yielded positive results, and most of the responsible outlets had made eggs an 'adult only' sales item for the night thus limiting the potential armoury available. Inevitably, there will always be someone out to capitalise on an opportunity, and at the twenty-four hour convenience store on the Yellow Estate the shelves were packed high with tray after tray of large white eggs, all proudly exhibiting their date of produce, country of origin and red lion quality logo.

"There is always a big demand for them at this time of year," explained the owner, Yamoo.

"You do know what they buy them for?" I asked, although it was more of a rhetorical question. "You've had things thrown at your windows before, and you know how much trouble and distress it causes you."

"I know, I know," replied Yamoo smirking, "but business is business – and every little helps." He walked away, patting his back pocket twice.

"I think you'll find that both of those tag lines and the action are patented," I called after him forlornly. I left the shop and got on the radio to Andy to let him know that I'd found our supplier. I suggested that we wouldn't have to look far to catch some of the culprits red-handed. Obviously, most of them wouldn't have heard the old saying, and so would be quite happy to shit on their own doorstep;

criminals tend to be quite parochial. It wasn't long before he called me back to say he had stopped two suspects on Tudor Way. I made my way over.

As I approached, I could see two of the usual suspects standing in the road near Andy's vehicle. If I wasn't mistaken it was Edgar Bergman and Charlie McCarthy. Bergman, from the posh end of town, had found an eager sidekick in McCarthy who lived on the wrong side of the tracks – literally: the train line bisected the rougher estates from the newer, more upmarket developments.

The double act had first come to our attention during the summer. Following a spate of thefts from the allotments on the east side of town we had stepped up patrols in the area. Early one August afternoon, a nearby resident had reported hearing banging, and seeing two figures fleeing from the scene; one was carrying a large black rucksack. Their clothing description was similar to what most of the town's youths were wearing, but what made these two stand out was that they both had mops of bright ginger hair.

All available units had immediately converged on the area, trying to flush out the culprits who had gone to ground on hearing our sirens. Dividing the area up between us, we had paced back and forth through the dense woodland to the rear of the allotments, but to no avail. However, after twenty minutes of fruitless human activity, it had only taken a few excited barks from a tracker dog that had just arrived on scene to yield positive results: the pair broke cover and made a run for it. I hadn't been able to see them, but I had heard the rustle as they had rushed frantically through the undergrowth. I had hidden behind a tree at the edge of the woods and waited.

As the seconds passed, I had heard the barks getting louder, followed by the sound of a couple of desperate fugitives crashing blindly through the trees. Closer and closer they had come, and then, suddenly, they were out in the open. Both had paused for a second as the bright sunlight hit them; instinctively, they had put their arms to their faces to protect their eyes. Before they could pick up their pace again, I was on them. Placing a hand on each of their shoulders, I delivered my line: "You're nicked!"

As they turned around, I realised they were both about fifteen. I handcuffed Ginger #1, the bigger of the two, and took hold of the other tightly by his right arm to prevent him from running off. Ginger #1 had dropped his bag to allow me to attach the cuffs, and, as I did so, Ginger #2 had surreptitiously picked it up and tossed the rucksack into the middle of a patch of nettles nearby.

"Do you think I was born yesterday?" I asked the pair. "I saw you do that."

Ginger #1 had remained silent, but, from the long and involved answer given by Ginger #2, I realised that we had someone on our hands who thought he was a criminal mastermind in the making. Ginger #2, who turned out to be Bergman, informed me that they had no knowledge of the bag; that it was up to me to form some sort of legitimate connection between the said article and the pair of them, and that handcuffing his friend amounted to false imprisonment, and that I had technically assaulted him by grabbing his arm. He further refused to recover the rucksack from the bush as this was 'all part of a wider police conspiracy to plant his DNA on the potential evidence'.

At this point, McCarthy broke his silence and muttered, "What he said," nodding towards his accomplice.

I had escorted them to my vehicle, and informed Lloyd where we were. When he arrived, we separated the pair, placing them in our respective vehicles. I had then gone back and received several nettle stings in pulling 'Exhibit A' from whence it had been discarded. As it happens, it was worth the effort because as well as containing several stolen items and various implements to facilitate entry to the sheds, it also contained a black plastic folder; inside this folder was a folded up sheet of paper from a flip chart.

Bergman had looked out through the bars of the van as Lloyd and I had spread the paper out on the bonnet of the panda. Up until that stage, he had been steadfastly quoting legislation at me, listing the various complaints that he would furnish to the Chief Constable when he was eventually released, and how he would get me sacked for this unlawful arrest. Interestingly, he then changed his tune, shedding his veneer of calm composure, and started to shout angrily to McCarthy who was sitting passively in the back of my car.

"I TOLD you to leave that back at base, you idiot!" He then turned his attention back to us, stating that the contents of the folder were private, therefore, we were forbidden to look at it. We ignored him, much as we had done during his previous rants, and studied the document laid out in front of us. It was then that we realised we had struck gold: this was a map of the entire operation, complete with study notes regarding each of the key points of the job. I had chuckled to myself as I folded it back up. This tied the duo into the crime scene perfectly.

"Hoist by your own petard, my friend," I had joked, waving the paper in the air before putting it back into its case.

"Could you be any more annoying?" Bergman had countered sarcastically.

I made a mental note to ask Miss Jones if I could borrow her tap shoes to wear in the interview.

To call the document an operational plan would be an understatement. It was a detailed, hand-drawn map of the area, with relevant comments regarding the key aspects of the operation. You could be forgiven for thinking that the two had been planning a major bank raid rather than breaking into a few sheds. Clearly, they had carefully surveyed their targets, monitored police response times, and planned the crime meticulously. The allotments, approach roads, footpaths and dumping area for their booty were all there, complete with miscellaneous notes, and the results of their brainstorming session. Every aspect was covered:

1. Council bins against fence will allow us to climb over at point 'X'. Surveillance shows shed 'B' contains step ladder. Break into shed and position ladders at egress at point 'Y'.
2. Combination locks on sheds have a 65% probability of being left on factory setting. If not, all locks are removable by using a hammer on the hinges. Disadvantage – noise.
3. If alerted, police should take 5 mins give or take 30 seconds at an average speed of 60 mph. Add 45 seconds if roadworks in place.
4. Once we hear sirens, we have 3 minutes to exit before their arrival.
5. Disadvantage of breaking in at night – police may use silent approach and we may not know until they arrive. Advantage – less likelihood of being seen by public.
6. 84% chance of police arriving at main entrance.
7. If police approach from town, use exit route 'RED' – there is a 13% chance of being spotted.
8. If police approach from estates, use exit route 'BLUE' – 50% chance of being spotted.

McCarthy was obviously regarded as the mule:

9. Charlie able to carry 50kg – if we share bag, should take 4 mins 18 seconds to reach rendezvous A – if Charlie carries alone, 5 – 6 mins. Figures correct for RED route. Add 2 minutes if BLUE route used.

He did, however, show concern for his partner in crime:

10. Charlie suffers from hay fever. If pollen count high on day – choices – 1. Leave operation until another day or 2. Give him a tablet 30 minutes beforehand.

If the worst came to the worst, the plan also contained some handy advice:

11. If police about, ditch bag in stinging nettles.
12. If police in area, go to ground. Ring in alternative incident on other side of town to draw resources away. Wait until police leave before continuing.
13. If caught, they hold your right arm (tight).
14. Handcuff keys are round – non-pickable.

Bergman also clearly saw himself as the brains:
15. Charlie NOT to talk to police. Leave talking to me.

Unfortunately, the pair had disobeyed their own golden rule which was written in block capitals on the top of the sheet:
16. DO NOT take these plans on the operation.

It hadn't helped that there was no phone reception in the woods, and they hadn't factored in the possibility of the dog section turning up. Both adopted the 'no comment' approach in interview, but, ultimately, their comprehensive plan was their downfall, and our master criminals were eventually charged with twenty shed burglaries on the allotments during the summer period. The dastardly duo duly entered the criminal justice system, although I was sure we hadn't seen the last of them. I was right: less than three months later here they were, illuminated in the headlights of Andy's car; McCarthy even had two trays of eggs in his hands. I got out and joined my colleague who was already in full swing.

"And what are all the eggs for?" he enquired.

"Tell him we're making an omelette," Bergman confidently urged his accomplice.

"We're making an omelette," muttered McCarthy.

Andy told them that he didn't accept their excuse, and informed them that he had reasonable cause to believe that they were involved in criminal activity. On that basis, he would be searching them for Class A materials.

"Drugs?" McCarthy questioned, his voice betraying his shock.

"No, eggs," came the reply. "Class A ones are the ones with the lion logo on – like the convenience store sells."

"Tell him you've got nothing to declare," instructed Bergman.

"I've got nothing to declare," repeated his parrot.

"Well, except for those two trays of chuckies we've just found and were about to bring into the police station," clarified Bergman, immediately conjuring an excuse for their possession of the incriminating items, and pointing towards the eggs that were now sitting on the car bonnet.

As Andy started to vigorously pat McCarthy down, I saw Charlie looking over at Bergman with a worried expression on his face – and then I heard a couple of tell-tale cracks. Andy instinctively sprang back as the area around McCarthy's coat pockets began haemorrhaging a dark, sticky goo.

"Have you got more eggs in your pocket?" asked my colleague incredulously.

Whilst McCarthy looked ready to cry, Bergman started to laugh, and informed us that there was nothing illegal about buying eggs. "You'd better let us go before you embarrass yourselves, officers."

Back in mediaeval times, the question of whether we were embarrassing ourselves or not would have been decided very quickly. The Ordeal of Ingestion came to mind. The law prescribed that the suspect was given dry bread and cheese to eat; if he choked, he was considered guilty. Fast forward to the twenty-first century, and I'm sure swapping cheese for eggs wouldn't be an issue.

As Bergman and McCarthy were juveniles, perhaps some of the simpler trials might be more appropriate; not all the ancient ordeals were as harsh as you might imagine. Take the 'Ordeal of the Cross': the accuser and accused stood either side of a cross with their arms stretched out in front of them; the first one to lower his arms lost. Even Lothar, the Emperor of Rome, thought this was ridiculous and eventually abolished it in the year 879 for being 'a bit silly'.

In Iceland, looking ridiculous didn't seem to be an issue as they had an ordeal that involved the accused walking under a piece of turf; if it fell on his head, he was pronounced guilty. As there were no sods readily available (present company excepted), I decided to opt for searching Bergman, to see if he had anything on him that could possibly link him to a potential crime.

Alas for our criminal mastermind it appeared he had once again broken his golden rule: don't take the paperwork on the job. In his pocket he had a folded sheet listing a number of houses – all located near the allotments. Against each house was a percentage. The legend at the bottom of the page revealed that this represented the probability that the occupant had seen them during their summer spree, and alerted the authorities. According to the key, the higher the percentage, the more eggs were to be thrown at the address. Suffice to say that both boys were locked up for possession of articles with intent to cause criminal damage.

As we booked them into custody, I looked over at Andy. We had managed it all without once saying *'The yolk's on you'*. I didn't know whether to be proud or disappointed. By the time we had finished dealing with them the night shift had taken over the core duties. We trudged upstairs to the canteen to rendezvous with our colleagues. We would be forming a rapid response team on the riot bus, attending the more serious incidents of the night.

"Remember Jack Gough?" asked Gwen as soon as I walked in.

"I do, indeed," I replied, pulling up a seat. It was a sad tale: He had previously worked as a roustabout on an off-shore oil rig, where he had received terrible injuries after he was unexpectedly pounded by a massive derrick. His life was subsequently turned upside-down, and he had resorted to drugs to get him through each day. He had smoked so much cannabis over the years that he now lived in an almost perpetual state of paranoia; living precariously on the edge, certain that someone, or something, was out to get him. More than once he had thrown himself out of a top floor window whilst on a skunk-fuelled high, believing that he was being pursued by ghosts and ghouls. In fact, for Gough, it was always creatures of the night that scared him more than anything else. On the last occasion, he had broken both his ankles after jumping to escape his imaginary pursuers. He wasn't someone you forgot in a hurry.

"Well, he's been at it again," continued Gwen. "He had another episode – swearing blind that he was being chased by spirits and apparitions. He jumped out of the top window, smashing his ankles that were still on the mend. As he lay there, a group of children trick or treating came up his garden path, dressed up in their little horror costumes. When they saw one another, I don't know who screamed the most!"

On the subject of screaming, Jess revealed that she had spent the evening on foot patrol. Maintaining her usual blank expression, she told us that when she was approached by children, she simply pretended to look shocked, murmuring: "so you can see me?" Most quickly ran away, hollering for their mums. I'm sure there is something wrong with that girl!

Meanwhile, Lloyd and Andy were eager to tell the assembled group about an agitated male inside a house on the Red Estate. Reports had come in from concerned trick or treaters regarding a well-built man, pacing back and forth in full view of the lounge window, screaming, "Die! Die! Die!" at the top of his voice. Without knowing who, or what, was in the house, or the exact location of any victims, or if the male intended to harm himself, they had forced entry to the house under Section 17 of PACE: to save life and limb. A tense stand-off had ensued: Lloyd and Andy had stood with pepper drawn and ASP raised, yelling at the male to calm down, whilst he, too, stood with his fists raised in the air, yelling, "Die, Die Die!" with even more gusto than before.

Into the middle of this chaotic scene had then walked a middle-aged hippy-looking gentleman, naked except for a pair of saggy, thousand wash grey underpants, who had seemed only mildly surprised to discover such a potentially explosive confrontation taking place in his lounge. Removing two large wads of cotton wool from his ears, he had politely asked if he could help anyone.

It turned out that he was the carer for Lloyd and Andy's adversary; who was, in actual fact, a male with learning difficulties called Reuben. The 'hippy' apologised, and informed them that he had just got a little exasperated with his charge constantly demanding his attention, and so had gone for a lie down. When asked, he had explained that the cotton wool was to block out the sound of Reuben's shouting. Reuben himself was now sitting quietly on the sofa.

"I'm pretty disappointed in myself, dudes," he drawled, "but I had my hair cut yesterday, and I'm feeling a little drained. And I've not had a smoke for a while as I've run out of wee..." It appeared to have just dawned on him that he was talking to a couple of police officers, and he held the 'e' for some time before he thought to end it with a "weeeeeeeeeee'll be fine, thank you."

As for the "Die! Die! Die!" the hippy added that there was no need to worry as no third party was at risk: no one else was in the house, and the shouts were directed towards him alone. He didn't seem unduly concerned when he was telling them this, leading Lloyd and Andy to take him to one side and express their genuine concerns for his safety. "Don't worry, dudes," came the reply, "he probably just wants some Scott McKenzie on, and we'll be cool."

"The hippy dude was from Wales," Andy commented after he had finished his tale, turning his attention to me. "He was called Dai. Do you know him?"

Before I could answer that I'd left Wales almost thirty years ago, and that even when I lived there I didn't know everyone in the principality, Barry addressed us as a whole:

"You'll be pleased to know that Iona Rocket has finished her hunger strike, so that's one less thing to worry about on our travels tonight."

I had forgotten all about Iona's protest. She had been camped on the main street outside the housing office, in some sort of protest about her flat. She had been interviewed by the press that day, and had vowed to maintain her one woman vigil, refusing any food or sustenance, until the council granted her demands, whatever they happened to be. I was pleased that she was safe; I wouldn't want her on the streets on such a busy night, but wondered why she had stopped her fast so quickly – she had only started it that evening.

"Apparently, she was hungry and went home to make her tea," he explained. Fair point.

"On the bus everyone, time to catch some baddies," Barry added. We all piled on board, George driving, with Barry in the front. In the back were me, Ben, Chad, Gwen, Andy, Lloyd, Jess and Ron. Soon we were patrolling the pubs and clubs, on the lookout for any action. There appeared to be a plethora of witches, devils, cats and not so demure angels, teetering from pub to pub. Superman, the Incredible Hulk and zombies galore, also staggered from hostelry to hostelry. A couple of tours of the town and outlying villages seemed to indicate that we were in for a quiet night. It was busy, but good natured; Halloween normally was. It was Bonfire Night that had the potential to turn nasty.

Barry accordingly dropped us off in pairs, and we proceeded to patrol on foot amongst the revellers. I was paired with Chad for the night, and we donned our helmets and headed into Sandford town centre.

It seems that when people are drunk they either want to tell you how much they love you or how much they hate you; there doesn't seem to be an acceptable middle ground. Luckily, tonight love was in the air. As ordered, we patrolled through the various pubs to show a presence, usually entering to a cheer from the groups of drunken cats and devils. We had to explain several times, shouting over the noise of the music blasting out, that we weren't the strippers. In all honesty, I think they may have asked for their money back if we had been. The various pubs and clubs were packed, and I'm surprised that veal calves weren't writing in on behalf of the patrons, complaining about the cramped conditions. It was like running the gauntlet: women making suggestive comments about our handcuffs and truncheons, and pinching our bums as we squeezed through the crowds (at least I hope it was the angels and witches, and not a rampant zombie). Thankfully, most people were in high spirits, but you can never know when things might turn nasty. We left our last venue and headed back into the town centre.

It was then that we heard a clatter from a side alley: a bin being knocked over, accompanied by a chorus of colourful curses. We froze, listening intently, and then crept up towards where the noise had come from. We heard a series of animalistic grunts, and then a deep female voice eclipsed the sounds with an aggressive cry.

"Harder! Harder!" she demanded.

"What's the capital of Nicaragua?" I whispered to Chad.

"Managua," he replied sniggering. "Something tells me, though, that she's not wanting to practise tougher questions for the pub quiz later."

We both shone our torches up the alley to reveal a rather large cat girl on all fours. Either side of her stood Batman and Robin, each with his trousers around his ankles. Unfortunately, our feline's costume, which clearly would have strained against her ample form at the best of times, appeared to be half off, too. It took her a second to realise why her male colleagues had ceased their activity, but, when she did, she turned her head to face the light. Her hair was all over the place, her mascara smudged, while her lipstick looked like she had applied it in the car whilst going over a speed bump.

"Police," we called out, just in case they thought we wanted to join the queue.

"Oh, ain't I a flirt?" the girl simpered. It sounded like a bit of an understatement to me.

"I'm Anita," she added, giggling.

"You're not wrong there, love," added one of the males rather unkindly.

"Oi!" she shouted, slapping his leg playfully, "I'm not fat, I'm just easy to see. I'm big boned."

"You have been," the other male joked.

Still on all fours, she then stretched her hand out in our direction. I felt a little self-conscious, but took a few tentative steps forward, leant in and gave it a shake. Chad just looked at me, and shook his head.

"I was just being polite," I whispered as I re-joined him.

"Look, fellas," began Chad, addressing the trio.

"And lady," interjected Anita in a high pitched staccato.

"Look, fellas and lady, we appreciate you have taken your celebration to a quiet part of town, but could you take it somewhere quieter?"

"We're all finished here now," replied one of the suitors. "You, Geoff?" he enquired of Robin.

"Holy cow, Batman! Now that we've sorted Cat Woman," replied the Boy Wonder.

"Remember to pull your trousers up first, boys" I suggested, "otherwise they'll think the penguin is back in town." They did so, and sidled past, grinning. Never let it be said that I don't learn from my mistakes, and I refused their kind offer of a high five, although I did feel a bit churlish.

"Who were they?" we enquired over our shoulders, turning away as Anita stood up and rearranged her clothing.

"Bruce Wayne and… well, I don't think anyone knows Robin's name." She then sat back down on the ground, chortling to herself. She told us that she knew her rights, and that we couldn't strip search her without her permission. We informed her that we had no intentions to.

"Can I request one then?" she giggled.

Instead, we offered to call her a taxi, but she insisted on going back to the pub, giving us a cheeky look, and twirling her tail in her hand as she did so.

We had one final wander around the pubs, and then met up with the rest of the crew for a last drive around the villages. When we got back to the station, after listening to our colleagues' tales, we shared our story about how Anita had been taken up the back alley. Whilst the others listened in and laughed, Gwen in particular looked quite shocked, suggesting that we should have sent her packing, with some stern words.

"I hope you gave her a good roasting!" she declared indignantly. As soon as the words left her mouth, she instantly regretted it, putting her hands to her face as if attempting to cram them back in again. "I saw that going better in my head," she conceded. I could feel the heat emanating from her from where I was sitting. The rest of the group just fell about giggling uncontrollably.

Stories all told and laughter dissipated, we sat and waited patiently in the parade room, watching the clock count down the end of our shift. It had been a long day, and we were all ready to go home and just fall into bed. It was almost four o'clock in the morning, and the last nightclub would have closed an hour ago. It would just be the stragglers now, and the night shift could deal with them. As the clock struck the hour we let out a little cheer, put our coats on, and started out the door.

As if on cue, Barry emerged from his office. "Coats off, body armour back on and take your pick. Two immediates have come in, and nightshift are tied up with a domestic in Kilo 2. So, who wants to go to youths throwing eggs at the convenience store on the Yellow Estate, and who wants to go to a fight at the taxi rank between three zombies, a cat and the Incredible Hulk?"

Here we go again …

CHAPTER SIXTEEN:

The Other Side of Summer

"Do you think I should seduce my dog?"

An awkward pause ensued as the woman stared at me and I stared back.

"I think you mean 'sedate'," I corrected. At least I *hope* she meant sedate. I was engaged in a conversation in the front office about the nuisance of noisy fireworks on Bonfire Night, and I certainly didn't want to unwittingly be the advocate of any dodgy practices. The woman was wearing a badge that proclaimed that she was a Pekinese lover. Surely she was aware that that *was* actually illegal? She just looked at me blankly.

"Well, what can I do otherwise?" she implored, breaking the silence.

"I sympathise," I informed her, "I know pets hate loud bangs, but it's not really a police matter. I suggest you visit the vet and ask for something to calm your animal if it's frightened."

"Will my insurance cover it?" she enquired.

"I haven't a clue," I answered with a resigned sigh, "although I do know that when my dog was ill my insurance company wouldn't give me a courtesy dog to take for walks."

"Eh?" The woman's blank look returned. Maybe I shouldn't have told her the old joke, but I was tired of explaining that there was nothing we could really do about fireworks on the fifth of November; it was just one of those things. With all the explosions it was also probably the best day of the year to go and shoot someone, but even with that little snippet of information out in the open, there was still nothing the constabulary could do. Neither would we want to: it was a fun night for millions. Well, I say millions, but I'd probably exclude my old friend, Bernard Hill, from that statement.

The origins of Bonfire Night, as you probably already know, date back to 1605, when Guy Fawkes, as part of the Gunpowder Plot, tried, but ultimately failed, to blow up the Houses of Parliament. Fawkes himself was caught, and tortured horribly for a week, until he eventually revealed his co-conspirators to the authorities. All were then arrested, and each of the condemned was ordered to be executed with the instruction that: *'their genitals would be cut off and burnt before their eyes, and their bowels and hearts removed'*. Not content with that, they were then decapitated and their bodies cut into quarters and sent to the four corners of the country as a warning to others.

There is also the myth that before he was executed, Fawkes was dragged by his accusers to the top of Big Ben's clock tower, stripped naked and strapped to the enormous bell. As the clock struck the hour, the massive hammer fell, pounding his testicles to a pulp, which, I'm guessing, certainly would have smarted. I bet Fawkes himself was relieved that he wasn't the lead story on *News at Ten*. However, whilst it's a colourful addition to the story of Guido Fawkes, this apocryphal tale actually has no basis in truth whatsoever: Big Ben wasn't actually cast until 250 years after Fawkes was executed, so you will only find that sort of historical inaccuracy portrayed as 'fact' if the tale of the Gunpowder Plot is ever made into a Mel Gibson Hollywood blockbuster.

Blissfully unaware of this historical blunder, and, celebrating the fact that he had himself survived, King James I declared the fifth of November an annual public holiday in thanks for the plot's failure. Towards the end of the 18th century, these festivities had expanded to incorporate large bonfires on which images of popular hate figures of the day were burnt. There were strong anti-Catholic sentiments at the time, and the Pope was often one such target. In more enlightened times, people realised that popery wasn't the evil they all thought it was, and that it just smelled nice.

In later years, children began making effigies of Guy Fawkes that they would burn on the pyres and, being nothing if not opportunistic, they would ask passers-by for 'A penny for the Guy' in a bid to earn money for their efforts. Victimless capitalism.

End of history lesson; return to the present day. Well, not exactly the present day: rewind about thirty-odd years or so to be imprecise. My old school friend, Bernard Hill, thought he'd earn some easy money by pretending to be a guy, sitting limp and lifeless on the pavement, with a collection tin for the donations. Things were going swimmingly for him, until someone on a motorbike drove along the foot path and over his legs. Capitalism now had a victim.

However, apart from poor Bernard, who, no doubt, still has nightmares, and probably knees that can predict cold weather, most of the population seemed to look forward to the Bonfire Night celebrations. However, the night wasn't without its own set of problems. These would normally start a few days before the big event when some unlucky town resident would wake to find their entire garden fence had been stolen and stacked on a makeshift pyre five hundred yards away on local scrubland. If the culprits were ever caught and brought to justice, there were usually plenty of other fences to be taken into consideration.

To combat this, as well as trying to limit the inherent dangers of scores of unregulated fires burning out of control all over town, both we and the fire service had been patrolling the area for days, identifying potential rogue bonfire sites. The council would then dismantle them, and, not wishing to be accused of being killjoys, they would then encourage the local youths to attend the official Sandford town firework display instead. It was early days, but it seemed to be paying dividends as more houses seemed to be hanging onto their wooden patio furniture and gates this year than ever before.

The crux of the problem appears to stem from our primeval urge to make fire. This may also be a contributing factor in the explanation of the increase in incidents of general arson on the night. Before John Walker invented the first 'friction match' in 1827, if local yobs wanted to set a 'horseless carriage' alight they had the laborious task of rubbing two sticks together; nowadays, it is a doddle for youths to be arson about.

The other modern phenomenon that was causing problems were Chinese lanterns: those flimsy paper tubes with candles inside, that float prettily into the air, and then land five miles away on some poor farmer's barn, causing a major inferno. The other big problem was having red hot molten lava from the firelighter inside drip all over your jumper as you struggled to light the bugger.

The real danger of the night, though, was fireworks of course. From rockets to sparklers, all had the potential to create mayhem if not controlled correctly. Rockets can be lethal missiles flying up to 250 metres and reaching speeds of 150 mph. Even the simple sparklers that toddlers are given to hold reach temperatures five times hotter than cooking oil; three of them burning all at once generates the same heat as a blowtorch.

Don't get me wrong, in safe hands, bangers can contribute to a fantastic display, but, in the wrong hands, they can cause havoc. I say 'hands', but things can get even worse when other body parts are used. One man suffered severe internal injuries when he attempted to launch a powerful rocket from his anus. I had relayed the story to Gwen, indelicately informing her that he had 'placed the firework in his arse'.

"Rectum," she suggested, rather primly.

"Yes," I confirmed, "blew it to pieces."

On the night, fireworks are also often thrown indiscriminately or used as weapons, and sometimes they just simply malfunction. Sadly, half of all casualties are children under sixteen, with hands being the most common injury, followed by eyes and face... and, of course, following closely behind, bums. We could try and limit the collateral damage on the night by trying to control the sales of fireworks, limit the proliferation of unregulated bonfires, and reinforcing the safety message; regardless, however, it was going to be a busy night for all the emergency services. With this in mind, Inspector Soaper had arranged a tri-service briefing in preparation for the Big Night.

I eventually excused myself from the woman at the front office, and trotted through into the packed parade room. Representatives from fire and ambulance were already there, so I squeezed past them and found a seat near the back next to Jess and Gwen. Both of them raised their eyebrows at me and tapped their watches.

"Nice of you to join us, Donoghue," announced Soaper.

"The Inspector who cried ASAP," I sarcastically whispered to my colleagues. "What's the problem? The briefing hasn't even started yet!"

"Anyway," Soaper continued, addressing the room, "that concludes my assessment of the challenge to the emergency services this Bonfire Night, and my proposed solution to combat it."

"Oh," I looked down, and slumped deeper into my chair. "So what was it all about?" I asked Gwen.

Essentially, it seems that attacks on paramedics and fire fighters have been increasing over the years. Specifically on Bonfire Night, fire crews often found themselves being targeted when they attended fires, particularly if the blaze had been deliberately set. There is always a dark flip side to any event, however celebratory the occasion. There's magic and malice in every season.

Our two busiest and most violent nights are New Year's Eve and the Friday when everybody breaks up for Christmas. It's known as 'Black Eye Friday' because that's what a lot of people end up with as a result of alcohol-fuelled fights.

We also see the other side of summer: on balmy evenings the decent folks of Sandford will be enjoying the sunshine with a glass of wine or cold beer out in their garden; for others it's an excuse to drink all day and spend all night fighting. In late July, I saw an example of just how far things can get out of hand when I attended an incident where someone had been stabbed to death following a drunken argument at an animal rights barbeque.

I also dread hearing that there is going to be a big wedding, funeral or christening in the town, because if violence is going to erupt anywhere, you can guarantee it will be there.

Only last August I had come in early for duty when the radio had announced that two males were fighting inside a church in Kilo 2. The previous shift were still out attending other jobs, so I flung on my body armour, grabbed a set of car keys from the board and blue lighted to the job. En route, Comms had updated me, informing me that the men had moved into the street, and that there were now reports of fifty people fighting. Fifty! I started to regret my keenness. I wasn't even officially on duty yet – I wasn't even being paid for this!

It would have seemed a bit churlish to turn back, so I carried on regardless. A few minutes later I turned into the street to be met by the sight of a mass of people in their Sunday best. I say Sunday best, but, whereas for some that meant a suit and tie or summer dress, for most of those gathered here it just meant their favourite track suit. I had hoped that my sirens would have dispersed them, but instead they parted to allow me to drive in, and then closed in around me. Being a lone copper in the middle of a hostile crowd I felt totally vulnerable, but I could see children crying in the midst of the fray, so there was no way I was going to turn back now. Besides, it would have been humiliating. I had no other option than to get out of the car, keep up the pretence that I was in control, and go and see what I could do.

There was a lot of pushing, shoving, posturing and shouting, but, in the centre of the group was a hard core of about ten males, who looked like they had been seriously engaged in violence. One of them was still stood in a fighting stance, his shirt off, blood running down his face. To me, he looked like the catalyst in this fracas, even if he did appear to have come off worst. I had very quickly learned in this job that it's usually a safe bet that the one with his shirt off is usually the trouble maker. I decided that if I could remove him from the situation, then, hopefully, the rest would start to calm down. It usually worked that way: take out the ringleader and things quickly settle. Well, in theory they do.

I was out of the car like a shot – I thought it best not to linger. I chose to ignore all the voices screeching in at me from every direction, telling me their version of events: who I should lock up; what had started all this; who had assaulted whom. Instead, I ordered the guy with his top off to get into the police car, and pushed him towards the back door. He reluctantly allowed himself to be bundled along as shouts and threats filled the air. I didn't even have time to cuff him in front of his audience; I just opened the door and shoved him in. I slammed the door shut, and locked the vehicle. I was acutely aware of the bellicose crowd around me, and asked Comms for back-up, only to be told that all other crews were already at immediates; there was nobody free.

Despite the fact that I now had the instigator in the car, I couldn't just drive away leaving behind a still volatile crowd. I really didn't want to remain, but there were still distressed children and innocent bystanders present, and the whole place was like a tinderbox: it could all explode at any moment, and I had a duty of care. I knew I wouldn't stand a chance if any further fighting broke out: I was completely surrounded, and I kept catching glimpses of people I had previously locked up, staring over at me. I checked my watch. I still had ten minutes before my actual shift started. I shook my head at myself.

I tried to present a calm, confident image to the gathering, but my heart was pounding inside my chest, my mouth was dry and my palms were clammy. I got back on the radio, and hoped I didn't sound too needy as I asked Comms if there was any other unit – anywhere – that could attend my location as the tension in the air was palpable. One half of the crowd seemed to want to have a go at my prisoner; the other half wanted to release him. Some grabbed at the door handles, some spat at the windows whilst others hurled abuse. Inside the car, my prisoner was now shouting and getting angry, kicking at the windows; playing to the crowd.

The rest of my shift would have arrived for work by now, but I had taken the last set of car keys on the board; no doubt they would be listening to their radios, but powerless to help. I was beginning to feel desperate when I finally got word that a traffic car was en route, and would be with me in ten minutes. I kept a tight grip on my pepper spray and baton on my belt, although, realistically, with the weight of numbers, there would be no hope of releasing them in time if the crowd turned on me. While I waited, I tried to elicit the gist of what had happened as the mob jostled around me.

I established that there had been a christening. The mother was now engaged to another guy, and so the actual father hadn't been invited. The father of the child, however, had turned up with his family en masse, wanting to know why he wasn't on the guest list. Or, this was what I was able to piece together. It's difficult to get a coherent version of events when twenty people are yelling at you all at once. No one starts at the beginning; it's edited highlights from their own perspective, shouted in their own form of colourful language. Either way, whatever had happened, the disagreement that had started in the church had spilled out into the street. At this time, from my perspective, all that mattered was that as long as I was listening, they weren't fighting, yet a tense stand-off prevailed whilst I waited nervously for the promised cavalry. One day I'd look back at this debacle and laugh; one day, but definitely not now. My sense of humour was temporarily missing in action.

I eventually heard my reinforcements before I saw them, and, I can say hand on heart, that I've never been more pleased to hear the sound of a police siren in my life. The crowd again parted to let the car through, and I eagerly waved at the traffic officer, although I don't think he shared the same level of enthusiasm as me when he surveyed the situation. Gradually, more units eventually arrived. I guess my colleagues had detected the subtle variation in my voice when I was on the radio. I had fallen short of pressing the orange emergency button that would have had units dropping everything and coming to my aid, but I think the fact that my voice was a few octaves higher than usual was a giveaway that I wasn't exactly at ease with the situation I had found myself in.

Within half an hour everything was under control. I started to regain my sense of humour and I went into the church to speak to the vicar, who had wisely remained inside throughout.

"It all started with the family fighting over the font," he declared.

"I'm sure they'll all be going to Helvetica," I responded. He didn't laugh.

Christenings aside, a wedding is also a special day for all concerned. It's certainly a day that every bride will remember for the rest of her life. Andy and Lloyd had attended a job a few weeks ago where a woman had been kicked unconscious in a pub. She couldn't describe the offenders' faces, but said that one was wearing a wedding dress and the other two were bridesmaids. Some brides, it seems, remember their wedding day for different reasons: the day they were thrown in the cells.

Incidentally, speaking of married life, research proves that domestic violence peaks during the World Cup, and particularly over Christmas. It's not the season of peace and goodwill for everyone.

It is shocking to realise that the UK actually has the worst record for violent crime in Europe. You are also more likely to be a victim of violence living here than in the US and even South Africa, which is always flagged as *the* crime hotspot. This, however, is nothing new: the British have always been a volatile race. During the Roman occupation, 10% of the entire Roman army was stationed in these islands, putting down rebellions. We had the dubious distinction of needing more occupying forces than any other province of the empire.

Furthermore, although I can understand why some sections of society don't like the police because we are seen to spoil their fun, it still shocks me that our colleagues in the other emergency services are also targeted. I'd seen it first-hand myself, though.

There is something about joggers that makes me suspicious: it's always a jogger who happens to find all those dead bodies. Actually, you can probably point the finger of suspicion at dog walkers, too, and dogs for that matter. Early one morning last week, a runner had contacted both police and ambulance to report that she had found a body down by the river. The paramedics, Lysa and Steve, had arrived before us and were checking for signs of life. The alleged victim, however, wasn't dead; it appeared that the male was simply 'out of it' due to drink and drugs. Lysa was just covering him in a foil blanket to keep him warm, when he woke, swore at her for disturbing his nap and kicked her hard between the legs. It wasn't his best move as it's the paramedics who choose your needle and catheter size. Moreover, as we had just arrived on scene, it meant he spent the rest of his time sobering up on a hard mattress in a cold cell, rather than being cared for by the lovely Lysa. For the firefighters, it tends to be long distance harassment with the chavs and yobs shouting abuse and throwing stones from the safety of a hundred yard start.

Tonight, Gwen informed me, one of us was going to accompany the fire brigade on each job to ascertain if any blaze had a criminal element to it, and also to identify if a hostile crowd was gathering at any of the incidents. If this proved to be the case, a second team would be on standby; to be called in to quickly target and arrest the ringleader, removing him from the scene before things escalated.

The general chatter in the room that had started when Soaper had finished his piece now ceased as Barry cleared his throat and got to his feet.

"John," he announced, barely looking up from his clipboard, "you'll be liaising with the fire crew."

"Jess and Gwen," he continued, "You're the Snatch Squad."

"Just don't say a word," hissed Gwen, directing her comments specifically at me. She then proceeded to turn a now familiar deep crimson.

"You never know," added our sergeant before winding up the briefing, "after the good people of Sandford have enjoyed their display, PC Raine might put in an appearance and help us to clear the stragglers off the streets." There was a general rumble of approval as everyone filed out to resume their duties.

I'd often heard the expression or variations of it: "PC Raine is worth an extra ten officers on shift," or "PC Raine will clear the streets when he turns up". I always thought this PC Raine was some sort of hard case who would come down from the north and make short shrift of any miscreants who happened to be hanging about the town. It was a good few months before I realised it was just a fancy term for plain old precipitation. Criminals don't like getting wet, and a bit of rain is always helpful in persuading them to desist their shenanigans and go home. Yes, PC Raine might certainly be a good help, but his mates, PC Freezing Fog and PC Black Ice, were right bastards.

We made our way out into the car park. It was cold and dry, with a clear night sky: ideal weather for the firework extravaganza. We all got into our respective vehicles, informed Comms which areas we would be covering and then set off to patrol our areas and wait for the calls to come in. However, before I took up my position, I decided to head up to the official display to see if it had attracted many takers. As soon as I arrived, I realised that I should never have doubted the town's fantastic community spirit. Maybe it's because we only see the worst elements of society that we sometimes forget that every town has a lively beating heart, and despite what we may sometimes think, it's the good, honest citizens of this varied collection of bricks and mortar that we call Sandford that really own this place.

There in front of me, as far as the eye could see, the roads and streets leading to the official bonfire site were chock-a-block with cars parked on every available kerb, side street and piece of grass. Weaving between them were the happy families; throngs of excited parents and children, all wearing their thick padded coats, long woollen scarves and warm winter gloves. The older kids were holding hands, the smaller children sitting astride their fathers' shoulders, wearing their little bobble hats and mittens, whilst mums and dads carried bags of toffee apples and flasks of hot soup. Their joyful chatter and laughter filled the air. It was at times like this that I wished I was in amongst them, taking my own daughter to the show; enjoying the spectacle with loved ones instead of sitting on my own in my cold and impersonal panda car.

I got out of my vehicle and stood there, breathing in the beautiful sights, sounds and smells of the place. About twenty yards in front of me, a group of children were swishing their sparklers back and forth, leaving trails of effervescent light hanging in the still air. I smiled and they smiled back. There followed some frantic whispering between them, and then they all formed a line to face me before they each lit a fresh lightning rod. They then arranged themselves into a line of four, and after leaving a little gap, another group of three completed the row. They started swishing their sparklers back and forth again. These weren't just random strokes and twirls: they were spelling something out – their own personal message to me. As the pyrotechnics spat their rich white sparks into the blackness, I started to make out the different letters. I no longer felt like an outsider – I was now part of the night; it was wonderful and exhilarating. I watched the letters form in the darkness with joy in my heart: I was now an accepted and integral part of this community. I felt my heart swell with pride as I made out each letter: 'P… I … S …'

What was it? I could just about see the word forming. Finally, as if by magic, there it was… "PISS OFF".

As their sparklers started to splutter out, the kids turned and ran away, laughing hysterically.

I silently got back in my car. To be honest, I was glad when the first calls started coming in as it took my mind off my disappointment. It appeared that a group of youths were roaming the streets on the Red Estate, throwing bangers into people's gardens. It wasn't just one call: there were numerous calls from concerned residents all along their route. By the time my colleagues got there, the culprits had fled down one of the numerous alleys; calls then came in from another street on the other side of the estate. It was just one big game to the yobs. For us it tied up numerous resources as we tried desperately to track them down.

Meanwhile, as I listened to the chase unfold, I was notified that the first call for the fire service had been received: a garden fence was ablaze. I set off to join the fire fighters across town. A family had a small, backyard bonfire going, so it was hard to tell if this was a malicious act or simply an accident caused by a spark from a rogue cracker. Nevertheless, a small crowd had gathered to view the proceedings. It didn't take long to extinguish, and soon the crew were back in their engine and preparing for their next call.

As the skies erupted with the finale of the display across the other side of town, my colleagues were already tied up with their next job. Bangers were being thrown at traffic from a bridge, and the shift had hurtled to the scene, blue lights flashing, eager to put an end to the gang's fun. I didn't have time to help out as by now another conflagration had been reported.

This time, a couple of wheelie bins, not more than half a mile from the first call, were alight. This was definitely a deliberate fire: they don't just spontaneously combust. There are about 30,000 wheelie bin fires in the UK each year, costing a staggering £50 million in time and resources to put out. These fires can easily spread to houses, cars and hedges, with numerous deaths being reported and scores of people needing to be hospitalised due to smoke inhalation. You just never know what is inside them; aerosols or other accelerants may have been discarded and could cause the bin to explode at any moment. Once again, a group of onlookers had gathered at the scene. I moved them back to a safe distance, but, apart from some grumbling, there was no real trouble.

There were now reports of fireworks being thrown through the doorway of the local convenience store. As it was difficult to determine if the same gang was responsible, or whether it was another lot, units diverted from their current search and headed down to Yamoo's shop.

The fire crew had barely arrived back at their station after tackling the wheelie bins, when another shout came in. This time a car had been torched. Our arsonist (if it was the work of just one individual), had upped his game. The vehicle was a veritable inferno when we arrived on scene. The firefighters rolled out their hoses and got to work on the blaze, dousing the flames.

There are various offender profiles for arsonists depending on their motivation, but I was sure that part of the thrill for the culprit would be in witnessing the aftermath as the fire crew struggled to control the blaze. The inevitable crowd had assembled to see the drama unfurl, and I scanned it from the shadows to see if I recognised anyone. As the flames lit up the onlookers, I was sure I recognised a youth standing on the edge of the group who had been at all the other incidents, too. Once could be understood, twice was unusual, but three times put him on my list of likely suspects. He was dressed in typical chav uniform: hoodie, tracksuit bottoms tucked into his socks, and trainers. He seemed to be particularly enjoying the spectacle, standing as most male chavs do, with his hands down the front of his trackies, fiddling away. I sidled up to one of the older residents who had come to watch, and asked if he recognised the youth. He didn't. I'd normally expect the onlookers to be local to the area. This was enough for me to make the decision that he was worth bringing in.

He was about thirty yards away, but I knew if I advanced towards him he would run. I got on the radio to Jess and Gwen, requesting that they approach the scene from Cooper Lane. They would then be able to sneak up behind our target and block his exit route. They had been assisting the rest of the shift in their search for the firework gang, but now made their way over, adopting a silent approach. I didn't want our suspect spooked.

The inferno roared as the firefighters directed their jets of water into the heart of the blaze. My suspect became excited, constantly looking around, hopping from foot to foot. What his hands were *actually* doing down the front of his trousers remains unclear, but you could easily be forgiven for thinking he was rubbing two sticks together. It wouldn't be long before he was off to set his next blaze. I checked my watch, but there was still no sign of my back-up.

Before long, the firefighters were damping down the last of the embers, until, finally, just the car's skeleton remained. Anything that could burn had burnt, and we were left with the sad spectacle of a mass of twisted metal that once had been someone's pride and joy. My suspect looked like he was

finished with the current show and about to move on to his
next extravaganza. I decided I had to do something to stall
my target until Jess and Gwen were in position.

"Did you see how it happened?" I shouted over to him.
He looked over, startled to see me, but I could see he was too
on edge to be lured into conversation. He stopped his trouser
jive and removed a hand to give me a one-finger salute.

"You'll never catch me, copper!" he shouted and turned
to run, only to see my two colleagues walking up the path
behind him. He seemed to know the game was up as he
turned back to me and raised both his arms in defeat.

"Here comes the posse!" he muttered sarcastically, and
stretched both his arms out as if he were some master criminal
eventually cornered by the forces of law and order. His limbs
were immediately grabbed by my two colleagues. He was led
back to their van, and put in the cage. By the time I joined
them, the male was sitting impassively in the back and Gwen
was sitting quietly in the passenger seat. She didn't look
happy; the windscreen steamed up with her ire.

"What's up with Gwen?" I enquired of Jess. She simply
shrugged.

"I can't understand it," she added. "It's a good arrest, I
thought she'd be pleased, but she just seemed really disgusted
with the guy and told him to wash his mouth out."

I could understand her being annoyed at the damage and
trouble he'd caused, but she seemed to be taking this a little
too personally. She was the consummate professional; this
wasn't like her. Perhaps there was something I was unaware
of. I was concerned about my colleague and wanted to find
out what had upset her. I opened the cage door and asked the
youth what he had said. He simply shrugged, too.

"Look, copper. I set those fires, I'll admit it, but I didn't
do anything to your mate. I just like the buzz. I'm not a nasty
bastard." Now that he had been removed from the action, the
bravado had evaporated. He looked close to tears as he spoke,
and seemed genuinely concerned that he had distressed

Gwen. I got in the driver's side next to her, and just sat in silence. Sometimes, that's all we can do. Eventually, when I sensed some of the tension had dissipated, I tentatively asked what was troubling her.

"Just his language," she confessed. "I'm a police officer just like you. There is just no need to be so demeaning." The anger seemed to have gone, replaced with a deep melancholy.

I was at a loss for words and replayed the whole incident back in my mind. I couldn't put my finger on anything that I thought could have caused offence. We'd been to hundreds of jobs together, and the usual abuse we received was like water off a duck's back to Gwen. This was something different. I asked her what she meant, and she leant over, and, in barely a whisper, she repeated the offensive phrase. I immediately got out of the vehicle and returned to the cage to confront our fire starter. He assured me that he hadn't uttered those words, swearing on the lives of various family members as the villains are oft to do. This time, though, I believed him. Jess looked particularly shocked at the accusation, and backed him up, stating she agreed that our charge hadn't said it either. I replayed the scene in my head again and again until I thought I'd clarified what had actually happened.

I went back and sat next to Gwen again. "You need your ears seeing to, missus," I told her. "He said 'here comes the posse' – like in the cowboy films; the people helping the sheriff out." I waited for it to sink in.

"Oh!" she exclaimed, as the realisation hit her. "So he never referred to me as 'pussy' then?"

She immediately perked up, and started the van. It's surprising what little things can tip a colleague over the edge sometimes. I was pleased it had been sorted out, but before she drove off to custody, I just had one last word of warning for her.

"Now that you're all friends again," I added with a wink, "resist the urge to shake his hand – not after what I saw him doing earlier, anyway."

The fire crew had gone when I returned – off to a barn fire a few miles away. I was pretty sure that this was the result of someone's Chinese lantern, although I'm absolutely certain this wasn't what they would have wished for. I waited for another half an hour, but no other calls about fire came in. Nothing had been heard from our firework gang for the last thirty minutes either; maybe they had run out of crackers, or perhaps they had just called it a day. As I made my way back to the station, I looked at the night sky. The clouds had gathered, but it looked like PC Raine was having the night off. I drove past the site of the official display, but by now all the crowds and cars had gone. That was it for another Bonfire Night, and it appeared we had got off lightly: no attacks had been reported on fire crews or paramedics, and there hadn't been any violence in the town to speak of. Our twisted fire-starter had been caught, and, despite the disruption caused by the firework gang, no-one had been hurt. Not a bad result. All the preparation had been worth it. I was sure that if we hadn't planned for the worst, then the worst may well have happened.

I was just discussing this with Barry back at the station, when the radio crackled into life. Someone had put a firework through the letter box of a house belonging to an elderly woman on the edge of the Black Estate. Before we could react, Lloyd, who was still out on patrol, came over the air with his dramatic update.

"It's blown her flaps off!"

The airwaves went silent. With bated breath, we all patiently waited for his update – a lot hinged on what he said next. I know we all wanted to know the same thing: did she need a paramedic or a carpenter?

CHAPTER SEVENTEEN:

All Roads Lead To Rome

"Report of a boy kicking off with his mother. Any units available to attend?" The urgent radio call shattered the tranquillity of the parade room.

Instantly I had a mental image of an angry teenager shouting obscenities and smashing up the family home as his terrified mother cowered in the corner. I pictured her crouching, hands raised to protect her head as cups and plates crashed all around her, showering her with broken crockery and pieces of china. Whilst angry outbursts are an accepted part of a child's development, I'd seen first-hand how aggressive and abusive some children could be. Worryingly, recent studies have shown that children are also increasingly likely to physically attack their parents, so there was no time to lose. Lloyd obviously shared my thoughts as he ran out with me and jumped into the passenger seat of the police car. We hit the blues, cutting through the morning commuters as we raced to the address.

Five minutes later, and the tyres smoked as we screeched to a halt outside the address and sprinted up the drive, banging on the front door, demanding to be let in. Lloyd peered through the window into the lounge, but all he could see was a ten-year-old, sitting cross-legged on the floor, quietly watching television. The action must have been going on in a different room. This poor lad shouldn't have to hear such things at his age; I was getting even angrier as I thought about it. Eventually, a middle-aged woman opened the door, and we stepped inside.

"Where is he?" I enquired curtly.

"Through there." The mother, hands on hips, nodded towards a door. Lloyd and I opened it, and marched through, only to be met by the sight of the same youngster sitting watching the telly.

"Are you okay, son?" asked a concerned Lloyd. "Where's your brother?"

"I haven't got a brother," came the bemused reply.

I got back on the radio to check that we had the right house. I've almost scared the living daylights out of an innocent family before when I've burst in to confront an intruder. As they looked up from their tea, holding a forkful of spaghetti hoops and their eyes betraying their shock, Comms have updated me. "Sorry John, don't go to that address. It's Regent Terrace – *not* Regent Road." Too late was the cry. I was pretty sure that's what must have happened now.

"Are you at Eugene Street?" asked the dispatcher.

"I am," I confirmed. "At number four."

"That's where the call came from, John. Report from the mother that her son was kicking off with her. She demanded an immediate police response and then hung up. She didn't answer when we rang back."

It must have been a hoax call. Regretfully, malicious calls are made, yet sometimes you only discover they are false when it's too late. Earlier in the summer, a woman had rang in to say she was concerned about her husband. She said he had been depressed, and had rented a remote cottage in the countryside to think things over. That night he had phoned her to say that things had got on top of him; that he'd had enough of life, and had taken an overdose. He had been slurring his words; the phone had gone silent. Fearing the worst, she had asked the police to check on him.

Naturally, with the information given, we treated it with the utmost urgency. Grabbing the enforcer – the big red battering ram – we sped through the night to the address, alerting paramedics en route, who were soon blue lighting behind us. If he had taken the cocktail of pills and alcohol that his wife had told us he had, he'd be virtually in a coma by now – seconds counted. We arrived, sprang out of the vehicle, banged on the door – no response. Geezer had donned his protective gear while travelling, and now rushed forward with the enforcer, smashing the door in. We poured through the opening into the lounge. There were empty wine bottles, but no sign of our potential suicide victim. Into the kitchen; still nothing. Finally, the bedroom, and there he was: not comatose; not depressed; not contemplating taking his own life. Instead he was in bed – with his male lover. It turned out to be a ruse by his wife to embarrass her husband for his infidelity. By the look on everyone's face, she had succeeded. We quickly made our excuses and left.

Back at Eugene Street, I looked up at the mother, ready to apologise for the mix-up, when she astounded me with her reply.

"Yes, I called you. It's him," she shouted, pointing aggressively towards the cross-legged child. "He's watching his DVD, and the little shit said he won't go to school."

Unfortunately, this isn't the first call of a similar nature that I've attended. A few months ago I was called to a house where a nine-year-old was refusing to get into his evening bath. If they knew what the report was actually about, our Comms staff would never send us to such incidents. Callers, however, usually 'jazz things up' on the phone to get a police response. I think I told the child something along the lines of that if he didn't have a wash he'd be stinky. The words of advice that I gave to the parent were a little stronger, although I did also suggest some bubble bath and a rubber duck as I left.

The police may be a public service, but we're not there to offer basic advice on parenting skills. Lloyd instructed the DVD addict in no uncertain terms to get his school bag, whilst I re-educated the mother as to our actual role.

We walked back out to our car shaking our heads, leaving the mother muttering furiously. As I went to hop over the low wall at the front of the property I slipped, and went stumbling into the side of the panda.

"It's slippy!" I exclaimed in mitigation. Although it was only mid-November, a cold snap had hit the area overnight. Most of it had melted away but there was still the odd icy patch left, particularly in the shadows. "I'm surprised we haven't had a spate of rush-hour road accidents reported."

Clearly my brain had switched to 'psychic mode' as the radio sprang into life again. This time it was a report of a collision on Drover's Lane – the back road to Kilo 2. This was a long, winding country road, and the call was no more specific than that the crash had occurred somewhere along that route. The blues were illuminated again as we headed out of town.

It had been a year since I had attended my first fatal road collision, and I hoped I wasn't heading to another. Still, I wasn't holding my breath: motorists race along the twisting country lanes, and, in these conditions, a misjudged turn on a slippery road could spell disaster. You may be confident in your own ability, but you can never be sure of the other driver's capabilities. Only last week, both Lloyd and I had thought our time was up when a car had come flying through the air towards us.

I had been sent to carry out a welfare check on a known female prostitute, who was also a regular self-harmer. She had recently been released from hospital, and there were concerns as no-one had seen her for a few days. However, as she was prone to making sexual overtures to any officer who attended, Lloyd had said he would accompany me. Not relishing the thought of any further false allegations being made against me, I was grateful for his help. There had been delays on our usual route, so we had taken a shortcut, travelling in convoy up the motorway.

As we drove, suddenly, and seemingly out of nowhere, a

thick black cloud had engulfed the opposite carriageway. Emerging from the smoke was a car, flying in mid-air and heading directly towards us. Instinctively, we had both veered into the hard shoulder, and braced ourselves for the impact. Thankfully, the car had fallen short, smashing into the central reservation and had then shot backwards into the traffic on the opposite carriageway. It had been like something out of a movie. As the smoke had cleared, the car had become visible again. It had come to a stop at right angles to the traffic flow, steam now billowing from where the engine had once been. The engine block itself had landed a good ten yards away, straddling the middle and fast lane. It hadn't looked like any other cars were involved and, miraculously, it seemed to have missed the other traffic as it had shot backwards. Fortunately, a lorry driver who had been travelling behind, had had the sense to position his truck across the motorway to prevent any other vehicles from slamming into the wreckage. Both Lloyd and I had lit our emergency lights, and as Lloyd had got on the radio to request back-up, I had looked for an opportunity to cross the road. I had been convinced that someone was dead or seriously injured in the wreckage, and had been desperate to get over to help. I could see that Lloyd had had the same thoughts as he stood poised to cross the busy carriageway twenty yards further up the motorway.

It had been dusk, and, despite our blue lights, cars still flew past, ignoring our pleas for them to slow down. I hadn't relished the prospect of racing across three lanes on a fast motorway, but someone might have been bleeding to death over there. When a break in the traffic did come, I had darted across, climbing over the metal wires dividing the traffic flows, but not before I had checked that the wire hadn't been about to recoil at any moment; I hadn't wanted any assistance in hitting the BeeGees' high notes any time soon. When I had finally reached the vehicle, I had been amazed that the two occupants were uninjured; shocked, but physically unharmed. Modern cars are built for safety, but it can also be a problem as it gives young drivers a false sense of security, allowing some to feel they can drive recklessly at high speeds with little consequence. I had ordered them to get out of the car and climb up the grass verge to safety, whilst I joined my colleague in controlling the traffic.

An ambulance had soon arrived on scene, followed by the highways agency and, finally, the fire service, who made short work of shifting the engine block. Within ten minutes recovery had arrived to tow the offending vehicle away. After a quick sweep of the carriageway, traffic had again flowed smoothly as if nothing had ever happened.

Today I was hoping for a similarly miraculous result; I hoped our luck would hold out, but, statistically, sooner or later I'd come across another fatal accident. There are almost 2,000 deaths on the road each year, with the main causes being speeding, careless driving and drink driving. Sadly, about three hundred of those lives could have been saved if seat belts had been worn.

Dealing with a death is never pleasant, but it's all part and parcel of the job. However, it's not just our roads that are dangerous: only this summer, I had attended an incident following reports that a male had been struck by a train. When I arrived, several officers were already at the scene, the sergeant was on his way and British Transport Police were also en route. Ron was speaking to the driver who was sitting on the locomotive steps, pale and shaking. Andy was on-board the train, talking to the passengers, enquiring if any of them had seen anything. Geezer, George and Ben were walking up the tracks, looking for the body; it actually takes a while for a locomotive to eventually come to a stop, and so the victim could be some considerable distance down the line. It was Geezer who actually spotted the cadaver first, reporting that it looked like the man's face had been turned inside out. Being caught under a train has been likened to falling into a giant mincing machine or being caught in a tumble dryer. It's not a pleasant sight.

It appeared to be a suicide, but what a horrible way to die: there is no guarantee that you'll be killed instantly, or even killed at all. One rail worker told me how he had ended up with a badly injured woman trapped under his engine, screaming in agony. Of course, if a suicide attempt is successful, someone has to collect the body parts from the tracks, and scrape the mess from the train itself. You can't have the engine pulling into the station with blood and gore all over the front of it, frightening the commuters on the platform half to death. Those people tasked with picking up the pieces are usually police officers. Still, I'd far rather do that job than be tasked with delivering the death message to the victim's family: to let them know that their beloved husband or wife, mother or father, son or daughter is dead. That is one aspect of the job that I really dread; that every officer I know dreads.

When the BTP officers finally arrived, I chatted with their sergeant before he began their grim task of investigating in detail what had happened. As I commented that I didn't envy him his job, he was about to tell me that nothing really shocked or surprised him anymore, but he stopped himself mid-sentence.

Now and again, he told me, a job will come in that has the ability to have even the most experienced and hardened of cops shaking their heads in disbelief. On this particular occasion, he continued, a train had been halted a few miles out of the station due to reports of an animal on the track. This wasn't anything unusual, and officers were dispatched to locate it and move it on. Whilst this business was going on, the train was stuck on an elevated section of the line, and the bored passengers looked aimlessly out of the windows on either side down onto bare, open countryside. As a mother was taking in the uninspiring view, she noticed a horse next to a stable block not far from the track. Bringing it to the attention of her family, she smiled at the beauty of mother mature. It was her son, who had considerably better eyesight than her, who first noticed it: something, or someone, crouched down next to the animal. Taking his binoculars out of his backpack, he studied the horse... and then focused on the person crouching down next to the stallion; the person was a young male not more than twenty.

The youth, clearly oblivious to the stationary train, was crouching – not to hide from anyone, but rather to get better access to the horse's large penis, which he then proceeded to administer oral relief to. It's open to conjecture whether the other animal further up the track was trying to escape from a similar fate. Our enthusiastic hippophile was reported and subsequently arrested. The horse, the sergeant believed, was still in therapy.

"Hippophile?" I queried, "Surely not?"

"It's a term for a horse lover," he clarified, placing a hand on my shoulder. I think he could sense the consternation in my voice. "Don't worry," he added as he started to walk off towards the dead body, "he didn't get into the zoo."

Lloyd and I, meanwhile, were now on Drover's Lane, searching for the accident. The road is about twenty miles long, so we balanced our need to cover ground fast with our need not to become the next traffic casualties ourselves. We were about to call Comms to ask for an update, when we turned the corner and there it was: a basic three-vehicle shunt. It looked like one vehicle had slowed, the other had gone into the back of it and then the third car had followed suit. One vehicle remained on the road, whilst the other two cars involved had already pulled onto the verge. I positioned our car so no-one else could join the party, and then we ran from vehicle to vehicle to see if anybody was injured. In this type of rear end collision participants may feel fine at the time, and only realise the effects of whiplash sometime later. Pain or discomfort may gradually set in up to twenty-four hours following the bump, or sometimes, some cynics might say, the full and debilitating effects are only really felt after they've received a phone call from a personal injury lawyer.

Just as we had ascertained that no one was seriously hurt, a driver pulled up to inform us that there was a worse pile up further along the road. Leaving Lloyd to deal with this current situation, I sped off to search for accident number two. I drove around a couple of sharp bends, and then there it was: four vehicles with bodywork damage to both front and rear. Drivers and passengers were already out, exchanging their insurance details. Before I even had a chance to join them, one of the owners ran over and started to wave me on.

"There's an even worse accident further down the road."

I wasn't sure how many calls had come in about the accidents. I didn't know if Comms had assumed it was multiple reports of the same incident, or even whether the other collisions had been rung in at all. I wasn't even certain which collision the initial call had referred to. All I did know was that we needed more units to assist. I asked for back-up and tried to explain the situation as I drove on to accident number three.

This time I knew that there would definitely be serious injuries. I could see the skidmarks where the car had started to lose control, then the gouges in the hedgerow where the vehicle had bounced from the left then on to the right hand side of the lane before finally landing on its roof, blocking the entire road. I slewed my car across the lane to stop any other cars approaching, and then rushed to the wreckage. The contents of the vehicle were strewn all around; the back and side windows of the small red hatchback smashed. There were blood stains everywhere. I squatted down and looked into the driver's window but the car was empty.

Two ambulances were already parked up behind the car, and so I made my way over and knocked on the door. It opened and I was greeted by Steve.

"Lucky they were wearing their seatbelts," he announced, grinning, "otherwise, they'd be goners." Both driver and passenger had freed themselves from the wreckage by sliding out of the rear window. Looking at it, I was surprised that anyone had managed to get out of there at all, although if you are stuck upside down and waiting for another vehicle to slam into the side of you at any moment, I imagine that your motivation levels would be pretty high. It was another miraculous incident, but I could have just as easily been looking at a double fatal.

The paramedics had received the same report as us, but just happened to be coming to it from the opposite direction. Whilst we had been at the first accident, believing it to be the only incident, they had been treating the casualties of accident number three a mere six hundred yards away.

"We could hear your sirens in the distance," he added, "and wondered why they had stopped."

I popped into the back of the ambulance and had a quick word with the male. He was lying on the bed with a big white collar supporting his neck. I didn't want to disturb him too much, but I needed some basic information. According to him, there was no other person or vehicle involved; not even the county dog. He explained that his wife had been driving, and had lost control on the bend. I asked him if she had been doing anything she shouldn't have, but he assured me that she hadn't.

Apart from the obvious distractions like texting or chatting on mobile phones, switching CDs, reading maps and even breastfeeding, I've seen women putting on make-up and men using their electric razors while driving. But on only one occasion have I ever heard of a combination of the last two – a woman driving *and* shaving. In this case, she was reportedly landscaping her bikini area:

Florida, USA and, according to the report from the highway patrol trooper, her ex-husband (!) was in the passenger seat, reaching over and taking the wheel from her so she could concentrate on her topiary; nevertheless, she drove into the back of a truck at 45 mph. However, there was still more to this story.

Apparently, she explained, she was on her way to a hot date and wanted to look her best. Well, surely, that must make it all ok? With such an understanding and thoughtful ex-husband, it makes you wonder why they ever split up in the first place? Still, it could have been a lot worse: you can get a nasty rash when you dry shave!

I bore this case in mind as I climbed into the other ambulance to speak with the driver of the car. As she lay there in her anorak, beige slacks and sensible shoes, I decided that we weren't looking at a case of history repeating itself. Besides, if I remembered it correctly, I think there was some mention of the woman in the original story being Brazilian.

Now that the excitement was over, the second phase of the operation swung into action. The fire service were called as the engine was still smoking and smelt strange. I didn't want their miracle escape to be in vain if we all went up in a massive fireball. The firefighters duly arrived, and were only too happy to chop and saw through anything they could; it was a shame that the vehicle was on its roof as I know that they love nothing better than slicing the lid off a car at any opportunity. The nearby garage was also notified that several vehicles needed to be recovered as soon as possible. Whilst other units were travelling to the other two accident scenes, I had also requested that another panda be sent to my location to help me with traffic control.

Jess soon arrived on site and I immediately dispatched her to block the road off at the next junction. Usually, as cars pass an accident, there is the added problem of rubbernecking. Vehicles slow down to see what's happening, and sometimes there will be another bump as they drive into the vehicle in front of them whilst they are gawping at the wreckage. That, however, wasn't really going to be an issue here as the entire road was still blocked. I was more concerned about the fact that there was a village nearby, and the possibility of having groups of onlookers coming out to see what had happened. It was perfectly understandable: people are curious and it's not every day that you see a car on its roof. It's just that I wanted to spare Jess any embarrassment after what had happened at a collision in the summertime. She didn't linger and quickly drove off. I don't think she knew what I was thinking...

Only a few months ago at the height of the rush hour, a report of a collision on the high street had come in: car versus bicycle. Jess had been first on scene and was comforting the youth as he lay on the tarmac, waiting for paramedics to arrive. A crowd had gathered on the footpath adjacent to the accident. It wasn't your usual rubberneckers, but instead consisted of elderly ladies standing with their tartan shopping trolleys by their sides. She had told them to move along as there was nothing to see, but they just stared back at her with perplexed looks on their faces. When she asked again, some appeared to be reluctantly considering going, but other members of the group told them to stay where they were. Slowly, the crowd began to swell. Jess became increasingly irritated as she was forced to tend the injured cyclist with an audience looking on. Again she told them to move, this time with a little more force in her voice. However, the anarchistic pensioners defied her requests and steadfastly stayed put. It was only when Andy arrived on scene and a clearly vexed Jess asked him if he would move the morbid voyeurs along, that it all became clear.

"What? Move them on? From the bus-stop?" he enquired.

Cue a trademark Jess belly button mouth and bright red embarrassed face.

Back at my crash scene, the fire engine had departed and a police traffic car had long since come and gone, following the paramedics to the hospital to take further details and breathalyse the driver. I hadn't really wanted to do it while she had her neck in a brace. A breath test is mandatory in all accidents that we attend – not that we expect most drivers to have been drinking that early in the morning, but it's the effects of the night before that we sometimes unwittingly discover.

Virtually everyone accepts that drink driving is dangerous and socially unacceptable, but some still do without actually realising they are doing it. It takes a lot longer than most people think for alcohol to pass through our system. A rough guide is that it takes an hour for the alcohol to enter your bloodstream in the first place and then another hour for your system to rid itself of each unit of alcohol. Having said that, there is no hard and fast rule and it varies from person to person. Interestingly, last Christmas more people were arrested for failing the breath test in the morning than in the evening.

As Jess drove off down the lane to divert the traffic, I drove in the opposite direction to re-route any vehicles at the next junction. All that remained at the crash site was the car, sat forlornly on its roof patiently awaiting the arrival of the recovery wagon.

As the heavens opened, I parked my car across the junction, put my blue lights on and stepped out into the wind and the rain. I didn't fancy sitting in the car and becoming a casualty myself if a careless driver ploughed into it. Besides, plenty of cars would be stopping and asking for directions.

Traffic control can be an interesting facet of policing for two reasons: we generally encounter a whole different set of people to those we usually deal with and as soon as some people get behind a steering wheel it seems their character instantly changes. We are all guilty of that to a certain degree.

Imagine walking down the pavement and someone almost bumps into you as they come out of a shop. Normally, you would both smile, apologise and then carry on your merry way. Now, imagine a similar incident when the participants are in their metal boxes on wheels. Then it's swearing, shouting and maybe a gesture suggesting the other party should consider wearing a seatbelt.

Today, however, most drivers were polite, courteous, enquired as to an alternative route, adding that they hoped the parties concerned weren't too badly hurt before finally waving cheerily as they turned around. Some, though, were just downright rude; as they approached my car they threw up their hands in exasperation.

They say: 'All roads lead to Rome'. Originally, the phrase came about because all roads did indeed lead to Rome. With twenty-nine major highways radiating from the city, interconnecting with hundreds of thousands of miles of well-built roads across the Roman Empire, Rome was the centre of the known universe. Nowadays, it has come to mean that there are many different ways to reach the same outcome or destination, but, from the exasperated demands of the drivers trapped at my diversion, you could be forgiven for thinking that only one road actually led to Sandford.

"I'm sorry, Sir, the road ahead is closed due to an accident."

"Well, that's just perfect!" they exclaimed sarcastically, "Now I'll NEVER get to my meeting!"

I received looks as if I had blocked the road on purpose just to spoil their day. Some insisted that their satnav had told them that this was the only way to get to their destination, therefore, I had to let them through. Others angrily informed me that they only needed to get to the next junction, suggesting I was being churlish by preventing them from going any further.

I then reiterated that the road was actually blocked by an upturned car and I wasn't just sending them on their way for the fun of it. I could lip read their curses as they revved their engines aggressively before turning around.

It was frustrated and stressed businessman – the captains of industry, that were so stumped by the road closure. Women on the school run, or heading for a day out didn't seem fazed at all.

In fact, I'm sure Cellophane Man wouldn't have been put out by a blocked road, either. On the contrary, he would have loved such an opportunity to interact with the constabulary.

He should probably have actually been called Cling Film Man due to his propensity for driving around the county wearing nothing but a nappy fashioned out of clear plastic wrap, but someone had given him the cellophane moniker and it stuck. He seemed to revel in being stopped by the police for some minor traffic violation, and then jumping out of his car in all his nappied glory.

"I can see he's nuts," a passing member of the public had shouted on more than one occasion; or it might have been 'his nuts'. Still, it might have been too cold for our flamboyant friend today.

It was certainly getting too cold for me. I stood in the wind and rain for over an hour and a half before the recovery wagon eventually arrived to move the overturned car. I was freezing and miserable. Moreover, I had a very pressing issue that I needed to attend to.

Sometimes, having a hot drink in the police service is akin to playing a special type of Scrabble – one in which 1 T is worth 3 P's. You never know when you will get back to the station toilets and I had taken to rationing my liquid intake accordingly. This morning, I'd had a couple of coffees to help me kick start the day and now I was desperate. It had been over four hours since I had left the station and I think the cold was making it worse. When I couldn't see any further oncoming vehicles, I seized my opportunity to nip behind a barn and unleash hell.

As I emerged, I saw a car trying to squeeze past my roadblock. My roadblock! I ran over and asked him what he thought he was doing. He explained that he wanted to travel to Sandford as he had important business to attend to. I politely enquired what he thought my vehicle was doing, blocking both lanes with my blue lights illuminated. When he shrugged his shoulders in reply, I informed him that I hadn't parked my car inconsiderately, rather I had deliberately positioned my vehicle to block the road as there had been a serious accident which had resulted in a vehicle being on its roof further up the lane.

"Well, you should have been standing next to your vehicle, Constable," he replied indignantly. "How was I supposed to know? Some of us have more important things to do than stand around all day. I'm the regional manager for a large refrigerator company and I NEED to be at a meeting," he continued. Business men appear to go to a lot of important meetings nowadays.

I informed him politely that there was a recovery vehicle in operation a short distance away, and that he would be putting the worker in danger if he continued driving, but I was just met with an angry stare. My suggestion that he might have considered setting off a little earlier to take account of such possible contingencies only served to inflame the situation.

"Don't be so pedantic," he told me, clearly irritated. "We need less pedants like you!"

"Actually, it should be 'fewer pedants'," I corrected.

Unfortunately, this was the red rag to his bull and he began to quote the names of long-gone senior inspectors and superintendents whom he would be contacting in relation to this. Some would have to be via a ouija board as I knew at least one of them had since shuffled off this mortal coil.

"And what are you doing now?" he demanded.

"I'm just writing your comments in my notebook, sir."

He let loose an expletive, over-revved his engine and then stalled. Next he performed an overly dramatic five point turn before wheel-spinning into the distance. If he had only waited a minute, I could have told him that the recovery was almost complete. Sure enough, seconds later the recovery wagon drew up to confirm that the road could now be re-opened. I called up Jess and told her I'd meet her back at the station.

No sooner had I got back into my car and started on the drive back to Sandford than I received a call from Sarah in Comms. This time it was a call to Sugar Rush primary school. I was cold, wet and irritable, and, after my confrontation with my impatient and condescending fridge magnate, I was in no mood for ineffectual parents or disobedient children.

What was it now? A toddler refusing his afternoon nap? After this morning's naughty schoolboy debacle, perhaps my mind was working overtime. If it was, though, I was determined to nip this problem in the bud once and for all. There would be no messing about; no attempts to reason with the kid; no long discussions with the teachers. I'd had enough of all that. No, I'd simply march right in and tell them I'd be locking him up for resisting a rest.

CHAPTER EIGHTEEN:

The Crying Machine

It was three o'clock in the morning on a cold, moonless night and I was on my own in my panda car, travelling on the long, winding, country back road up to Kilo 2. There wasn't another car on the road and the silence of the police radio suggested to me there wasn't a crook on the streets of Sandford either. I didn't blame them in this weather; it was freezing outside.

I was alone with my thoughts as I drove. Police cars don't have stereos or cd players in them, and so my musings weren't even disturbed by the drone of a late night radio chat show or the singing of a love sick troubadour.

I was just reflecting on the fact that it was a fine night for shooting stars when I turned the bend and then, suddenly, the shock of what I saw hit me like a three ton sledgehammer. My body was momentarily sent into spasm. I struggled to control the car as the trauma of the horrendous sight momentarily paralysed my limbs. I stood on the brakes and fought to control the wheel as the car finally slewed to a halt about twenty yards further down the road. My heart was beating so fast I could hear the blood pulsating as it raced around my body; a steady thudding reverberating in my ears. I looked down at my hands – they were shaking. My blood ran cold. I sat there for a second to allow my breathing to stabilise, and then slammed the car into reverse gear. The engine whined as I negotiated backwards at speed to where I had seen the spectre.

As I had rounded the corner my headlights had momentarily illuminated a naked woman, covered in blood, standing at the side of the road.

I shot past where she had stood, and then skidded to a halt so that my lights would shine in the same spot. She was still there; standing stock still, surrounded by the pitch black empty night. Dear God, what could have possibly happened? A thousand thoughts filled my mind as I jumped out of the vehicle and ran over to help, but, before I even reached her, I could see that she wasn't breathing...

In fact, she wasn't even human. As I got closer, I could see it was only a shop mannequin that someone had positioned on the bend so it would be the first thing an oncoming driver would see. The blood looked like it was a mixture of tomato sauce and food colouring. Despite my heart still racing inside my chest, I was thankful that it was me who had first encountered the dummy, and not some poor innocent driver with a weak ticker.

As the adrenalin started to dissipate, I hurriedly got back inside the car and onto the radio, requesting for any other available unit to rendezvous with me at the scene. I couldn't imagine that the dummy had been there long, otherwise we would have had frantic calls by now. The pranksters could still be lurking in the shadows to witness the reaction of drivers. On the other hand, perhaps it wasn't just a sick practical joke. What if there was something more sinister afoot? Were the culprits waiting for a good Samaritan to stop and help so that they could then brutally attack him? Were they after the car, or the driver himself? Would they bundle a hood over his head and manhandle him into the boot of his own vehicle?

As I sat there alone in the darkness my mind began to work overtime. I was half expecting to hear footsteps on the car roof, and then the steady thud as the severed head of the local farmer, skewered on the end of a pitchfork, was bounced off the top of the vehicle. I locked the doors, put the blues on and gave a squawk on the sirens to make me feel better. I even checked to make sure that no-one had slipped into the backseat of the vehicle when I had run out, although I don't really know what I would have done if I had looked into my rear view mirror and seen someone sitting there... silently staring back at me... with a scary clown's mask on. I made a mental note to stop bringing cheese sandwiches to work.

It had been a year since the decree we were to be single crewed on every shift – unless operation requirements dictated otherwise. In that time I had got used to my own company during the long nights. Occasionally, I missed the banter of a crew mate, yet I didn't miss being stuck in a vehicle for ten hours with someone who had no craic whatsoever. Tonight as I sat in my panda car in the pitch black, next to a blood soaked mannequin, on a deserted stretch of country road without a living soul for miles around, I definitely missed having someone with me; anyone.

The ten minutes it took for Ron to eventually arrive seemed like an eternity. I told him what I had seen, and then we carried out a quick check of the area to see if anyone was still lurking before we set about dismantling the thing. I know that both of us could just have easily been attacked by a crazed madman, but with two of us there we seemed more than equal to the sum of individual parts. Striding into the undergrowth to take the dummy apart, Ron began to mock my nervous reaction to the whole incident. Mock me, that is, until a bull snorted from behind the other side of the hedge, and then he jumped in the same way as you do when your foot unexpectedly brushes against a stray piece of seaweed when you're having a paddle. In that moment, I swear that if he was Scooby Doo, he'd have jumped into my arms.

As I recounted my roadside horror story back in the parade room, Ben volunteered his own Christmas tale of woe. Incidentally, I had met Ben's wife, Dorothy, before I joined the shift during my brief involvement with the amateur dramatics society. She had often tried to persuade Ben to join, but he was dismissive of the 'arty-farty, luvvie' types as this keen rugby player referred to them. What I didn't know was that Dorothy was also the HR manager of a large company on the industrial estate. Ben started his tale by telling me that he had been invited to his wife's firm's Christmas party.

The event had been held at the prestigious Sandford Manor Hotel, and no expense had been spared in the organisation of this extravagant black tie affair. Following a lavish champagne reception, the participants had taken their seats in the main dining room. Approximately two hundred of the company's top employees, along with guests, had sat around twenty or so tables in the sumptuous setting of the magnificent Shakespeare Suite. The wine had flowed as the meal was served. Everyone had been in good spirits, and feeling suitably festive as the three course culinary masterpiece had been presented and subsequently devoured. The night was still young as the coffee was served, and the chief executive of the organisation got up to say a few words to the gathering.

As he wished everyone his best wishes for Christmas, and success in the coming year, there had been the sound of raised voices in the adjoining bar. Although he readily admitted that he hadn't really been interested in the speech, Ben conceded that he had been annoyed by the loutish behaviour of these people. It was supposed to be a private function after all. The chief executive had continued his address, only to be nearly drowned out by the shouts that had emanated from next door. His audience, meanwhile, had seemed more interested in what was occurring outside, rather than paying attention to their leader.

After a short pause, the executive had recommenced his delivery, but, at that precise moment, the three men who had been engaged in such a vociferous argument in the next room, had burst through into the suite. Ben had looked around for the serving staff, hoping they would intervene, but they were nowhere to be seen.

Pushing and shoving amongst the trio had then followed. Seemingly oblivious to all around, they had traded accusations regarding something that had happened to a female who had come with them to the hotel. It had all become very heated. The chief executive had since sat down, and the floor now belonged to the warring intruders. Ben told us that he had felt very embarrassed for the boss, Dorothy and the rest of the group at having had their Christmas do spoilt by the arrival of these drunkards. He had considered intervening, he informed us, but it was a company function, and his wife had repeatedly put her hand on his arm, indicating for him to remain seated. He had presumed she must have known that hotel staff had already been alerted as this couldn't be allowed to continue.

Then, out of nowhere, one of the three had suddenly produced a gun; the other two pulling knives out of their jackets. A tense stand-off that lasted no longer than a few seconds had ensued before a shot rang out. One of the males had dropped to his knees, his shirt turning crimson before he keeled over onto his side. The other male shouted, and had raised his knife menacingly.

It was at this moment that Ben knew he could sit idle no longer. Ignoring his wife's pleas not to get involved, he had leapt to his feet. He was only yards away from the gunman, and he covered the ground in a second, punching him in the face, which had sent him staggering into a table of onlookers. Kicking the gun out of harm's way, Ben had then looked for the other combatant. As he met his gaze, the terrified knifeman had thrown down his blade in panic and turned to run. Ben, however, had been too quick for him, and before he could get away, he was taken to the floor by the hefty rugby player. A sudden hush filled the room. Men had risen to their feet, while some women had covered their eyes.

Ben had looked up for support, only to see his wife, the dead man, and the chief executive all standing looking at him with shocked expressions on their faces.

"Didn't you tell him it was a murder mystery themed evening?" the boss had urgently asked Dorothy.

"I thought it would be a surprise for him," she had replied sheepishly. It certainly had been.

"We're all actors, darling. From your wife's am-dram group," the dead man had started to explain to Ben, who by now was holding intruder number two on the floor by the lapels of his jacket. Meanwhile, the 'gunman' was being cared for by two women from the Sales Department.

"I'm sorry," a devastated Ben had muttered to his prisoner. "Are you a friend of Dorothy?"

As two of the main actors were in A&E, the murder mystery event was cancelled, and a free bar had been opened instead. Sadly, Ben wasn't able to enjoy the fruits of his labour as he was gently encouraged to go home. Just as he thought things couldn't get any worse, when their taxi had pulled up and he opened the door for his wife, as she had got in, out of habit he had pushed down on the top of her head. He reported to us that he didn't think he'll be allowed to come on her jollies any time soon.

However, I soon found out that it wasn't just me and Ben who hadn't had the best start to the festive season; soon everyone in the parade room was pulling up their chairs, and adding their own particular story to the pot.

George was up next, reporting his investigations into the human advent calendar. Instead of buying one in the shops, our entrepreneur had been creative, and decided to make his own interactive calendar. He had simply been choosing houses around Kilo 3, with the corresponding door numbers, knocking and demanding a chocolate from them. Our sleuth, George, was trying to keep one step ahead and warn residents, asking them to ring in if Calendar Boy called on them. Instead, a quick thinking Mrs Cadfael of Abbey Way took matters into her own hands and, on the twelfth day of Christmas, delivered her own version of summary justice: she gave her caller her own supply of senna laxative chocolate.

Not only did it put an end to his nefarious activities, but he was unable to fart safely for the rest of the week.

On the subject of wind, Lloyd informed us that he been tasked with visiting a 'bad Santa'. In actual fact, the suspect was a giant inflatable Father Christmas with legs akimbo and arms outstretched, located in the front garden of a house in Tennant's Walk. When there was no wind he just stood there. When the wind blew from the north or south he gently rocked back and forth. When it was from the east he did a bit of breakdancing, but, when the wicked wind of the west blew, his arm kept slamming into his body, making him look like he was masturbating vigorously. The stronger the gust, the more enthusiastic he became in his carnal endeavours. This deeply upset the delicate sensitivities of the woman living opposite. Mr Claus was subsequently given a suitable dressing down, and was left dancing like Salome in the breeze.

Not to be outdone, Geezer informed the gathered throng that he had responded to a call from a concerned member of the public who stated that an Adolf Hitler look alike was in the local park with his two German Shepherd dogs who were fighting. This, apparently, was scaring the children. However, before he even reached the park Comms were back on the radio:

"Just to let you know it sounds like a hoax. They're saying that the dogs are fighting because he's playing fetch with them, but Hitler's only got one ball."

We all agreed that the hoaxer may have been 'Shoe Man', up to his old tricks again. When you get a new pair of shoes you probably throw the old ones in the bin; not so shoe man. He thought it would be amusing to leave them on the river bank with a note saying, 'Goodbye cruel world'. That kept us busy for days.

Andy now chipped in with his own tale about one of our regulars who was intent on ending it all. The male in question had holed himself up in a phone box and then phoned the police, threatening to kill himself by cutting both his own arms off with a penknife. When my colleague had turned up and explained, quite reasonably, that he would probably only be able to cut one of his arms off, the potential suicide victim thought for a second, and then reluctantly agreed with my friend's logic. He gave himself up and was promptly taken to hospital for assessment regarding his mental state.

Chad's contribution to the debate was, perhaps, the saddest of all the tales. It was a story of something that had started out so well and with all the right intentions, but had ended spectacularly in disaster. It was the worst Christmas party that the local care home had ever staged. Staff had arranged a yuletide celebration for the residents – a tea dance, some carols and ending with a few party games. All was going well; everyone loved waltzing to the music and singing the carols, even if the enthusiasm was inversely proportionate to their actual ability. However, it was during the parlour games that things went downhill. For some bizarre reason they had started off with a party piñata – the game that teaches Mexican children that the best way to get sweets is to beat a donkey to death with a stick. In hindsight, this violent entertainment may not have been the ideal activity for a group of infirm pensioners. Still, they had joined in with gusto. It was only during the next game that the exertion caught up with one elderly gentleman, and he had a heart attack in the middle of a game of charades. As a mark of respect, the party was abandoned; everyone was very upset – except for one old guy who had been given 'Bangkok' to mime.

We all had to agree that Chad's story topped the previous bizarre death that we had encountered as a shift. Up until that time, the record had been held by a woman who had literally pooped herself to death. Jess and I had attended the address in late summer after a woman had expressed concerns for her neighbour. When we arrived, we saw flies swarming at the window; it was a bad omen, and neither of us made any jokes about sending in the SWAT team. We feared the worst. I had to push Jess through a bathroom window and hear her tumble into the bath before we discovered the sad truth about what had actually happened. When Jess opened the front door to let me in, the smell in the house was rank. We eventually found the woman dead on her bed; a sea of watery faeces all around: in the bedroom; in the hallway, and all over the toilet. It transpired that she had suffered a terrible case of diarrhoea and, sadly, had died from dehydration. The paramedics had arrived shortly afterwards and they, too, had been gagging on the stench.

"Ah, but did you attach the wristband with her details?" enquired Barry as I retold the tale. Word of my pet hate had spread. Before I could answer, Jess let the cat out of the bag.

"He got Lysa to do it," she piped up, "and promised that he'd give her a cream pie."

"For goodness sake, Jess," I quickly interjected as quizzical stares came from every direction, "It was a cream cake!" I looked at her and just shook my head in despair.

Luckily, I was saved from any further comments by Gwen who was complaining about her lack of sleep after nightshift – at least I think she was complaining.

"I always get knocked up after nights," she commented. "Today it was the postman banging away!"

As she glanced up, she saw that the whole of the parade room had descended into silence. As soon as she realised what she had said, she flushed her usual bright red. "Oh golly gosh. Not like that. I mean he's a perfectly nice man... but no..."

However, her protestations fell on deaf ears as we all dashed out of the office to respond to a call on the radio about another sighting of the Sandford Christmas Burglar.

There are a million burglaries every year in the UK and, although those figures sound horrendous, it's actually one of those crimes where the fear of it vastly outweighs the likelihood of it ever happening to you. Statistically, you are only likely to be burgled once every fifty years. That said, when you are a victim it's a traumatic experience. We normally expect these crimes to rise over the festive period, but the figures this year were abnormally high. After analysis of the incidents, we had put this down to the arrival of a new crook in town. We didn't know his name just yet, so until that could be established, he was dubbed 'The Christmas Burglar'.

December is the ideal month for the opportunistic criminal. They know that you've probably got a stash of newly bought presents, nicely wrapped and conveniently located under the tree. The dark evenings offer protection from prying eyes, and the noise of the arctic winds rushing through the trees blowing dustbins over, provides the perfect cover to mask the noise of their activities.

However, the burglar we were currently after was far more brazen. He would casually walk up the drive to houses in the middle of the day and look through the windows for possible clues and targets. He would knock at a door and if it was answered, he either asked for directions, or consulted his official-looking clipboard before he made his excuses and left. If nobody was home he pushed his luck and tried the handle, or headed around the back of the property. Two times out of ten a crook will simply just walk in to a property. It is surprising how many people leave their doors unlocked. Three times out of ten he'll climb through an open window. It seems picking locks is so passé in the world of the small-time burglar nowadays.

Once he had gained access, he would then be in and out within a few minutes. The first thing he did was to balance a glass bottle on the inside door handles so if the owner returned it would drop off and smash, alerting him that he had better leave. Next, he would go straight to the master bedroom, looking for jewellery and money; with a chest of drawers he saved valuable time by working from the bottom drawer up. He would then proceed to the living room, dining room and kitchen, grabbing en route anything that was relatively small and of high value. He never ventured into a basement or attic, for fear of being trapped should the police arrive, and it seems that children's bedrooms were rarely entered.

Last week I had been sat in the front room of one of his victim's houses, taking details of what had been stolen, when the owner's three-year-old son had ran into the room:

"And they stole mummy's crying machine!"

Sometimes a child's face says it all. In this case, his shocked and anxious little face was accompanied by his shrill, quivering voice. I looked up at his mother expectantly.

I had noted a copy of *Fifty Shades of Grey* on the woman's bedside cabinet when I'd had a tentative look around prior to the arrival of CSI. I was now curious as to what this 'crying machine' actually was. The mother blushed. After a moment spent composing herself she revealed that it was actually her bathroom scales – a new set that she had just bought.

It seemed a little out of character for our burglar, but I suppose even he had to get presents for his own wife this Christmas. In fact, the last couple of burglaries had revealed some interesting choices. At the previous incident, the house owner couldn't be sure exactly what had been taken until she'd had a chance to clean up after CSI had dusted for prints. Her husband had rung in the list of items later as his wife was so upset.

"… and finally, he's taken … a snake? I didn't even realise we had a snake."

I could hear him shouting through to his wife for clarification. He was back within a minute. "I'm sorry, officer, my mistake. It's not a snake at all. He's stolen my wife's Amazon Kindle."

A few days before, Jess had attended another of the burglar's casualties. She told me she had thought she was noting the back stage props for a blue movie, rather than a list of stolen items: a silver ball washer; long shafted wood; gap wedge; brassie; niblick and a jigger. After raising her eyebrows once too many times, she was enlightened that some of these were antique golf clubs. In addition, a rare Sabbath Stick had gone missing. This was the golf enthusiast's answer to the Church of Scotland's discouragement of playing golf on Sundays. Apparently, the club was disguised as a walking stick, with the club head comfortably fitting into the walker's hand. Once the walker was well out of sight, the stick was reversed, the ball was dropped and the game began.

Again, it seemed a bizarre choice for a crook who I expected would only be looking for items that he could easily sell: these were more specialist items. Was he stealing to order, or was he picking up stuff for himself, too? If it was the latter, hopefully, these items would be in his house when we eventually did track him down thus linking him to the crimes.

We had notified the public about the burglar and his M.O. through any and every means possible, and appealed for any information they could give us. Householders were encouraged to lock doors and close windows, keep valuables hidden from view and advised not to put the packaging for any new electrical items out for the bin men: it just advertised to any burglar that there were goodies to steal. It was also suggested to occupants that they might wish to leave costume jewellery out on their dressing tables, and hide the valuable trinkets elsewhere. Hopefully, if he was in a hurry, our burglar would just grab the cheap stuff and look no further.

Hopefully, we were hampering his activities, but it also meant that we were dashing to every report of a genuinely lost delivery driver and door-to-door canvasser. We were frequent visitors to the Black, Red and Yellow Estates – delivery men may as well have shown up with maps saying 'Here Be Dragons' as they tried to make sense of the streets with their lack of house numbers. Still, I'd rather attend a false alarm, than miss an opportunity to catch our thief.

Soon it seemed as though everybody in the town was on edge due to our criminal's activities. One call came in from a woman in Endean Way who said that an anonymous male had knocked on her door and then left a strange package on the doorstep. She was scared to leave her house as she didn't know what was in it. Jess was duly called. When she arrived, she asked the householder if she had ordered anything from Amazon.

"Well, yes, I have. How did you know that?"

"Because the box has the Amazon logo on it. I suggest your parcel has arrived."

"Oh, that was quick!"

I took to plotting all the calls on a map, trying to work out if there was any pattern to his movements. It was difficult to weed out the genuine calls from the bogus ones, and I was even starting to run out of coloured pins. Scores of incident reports were spread out on the desk in front of me, I was clutching a list of stolen items in one hand and had the phone tucked under my chin as I waited for another victim of the burglar to answer, when Gwen casually walked into the room.

"Oh, John!" she exclaimed sympathetically, "I hate to see you with so much on."

I only had time to fire back, "Dirty girl!" to my colleague before the phone connected through and I was talking to my victim of crime. Gwen, meanwhile, coloured up and quickly left.

Barry wandered in next to see why she had hurried off down the corridor and so I quickly grabbed a pen as I took hold of the mouse. I find the pen and mouse combo makes it look like you are working 25% harder than just holding the mouse on its own.

"Good work, Donoghue," he muttered before returning to his office.

Over the next couple of weeks more calls came in, more pins went on the map and more reports were checked out. Meanwhile, our burglar was becoming bolder – and cheeky, leaving a message in peanuts on the kitchen work surface of one house which read: 'Wot no crisps?'

It was late December before we got the break that we so desperately needed. A man had been challenged by a neighbour leaving a house armed with two full suitcases. His suspicions were aroused as this was the same house that had been burgled just three weeks before. Lightning does strike twice and, once you've been a victim of a break-in your chances of being a victim again, increase exponentially. The intruder knows the layout of your property, what sort of valuables you have and he'll reasonably expect for you to replace the goods he's already stolen within a couple of weeks. Unbeknownst to you, he may have taken a key to your front door, and he may well have checked your calendar and noted when you planned to be away from home next. It seems our crook took things even further and looked at opened letters in the house to find out who actually lived there.

His bravado was put to the test when the neighbour asked him what he was up to. He then confidently told him that Alison and Dave (the actual occupants) were splitting up. Alison had been having an affair, he said, and had asked him if he would come round and pick up her things as she couldn't face seeing her ex-partner. The neighbour had been too engrossed in the gossip to become suspicious and our criminal almost got away with it. Luckily though, his wife was not so easily fooled and had phoned us whilst her husband chatted.

As any police officer will tell you, the Holy Grail in policing is catching a burglar red-handed. Units couldn't get round to the house quick enough and soon our smooth talking felon was trying on his smooth talking routine with the officers who had arrived at the scene.

His story was checked out and David, the house owner, was telephoned at work. Unfortunately, he wasn't much help.

"Alison's been having an affair? Is this why she's been obsessed about her weight? How long has this been going on? My God, just before Christmas. The children will be devastated."

It was explained to him again that Alison wasn't having any extra-marital trysts – at least as far as we were aware, and that we thought this was just a ruse used by our burglar in an attempt to avoid arrest. To be completely sure, we rang his wife and asked her to confirm that she hadn't given the guy a key; she hadn't and he was arrested. We then went and searched the suspect's house and, sure enough, amongst the booty were the golf clubs, kindle and a crying machine. The case was solved.

The whole town seemed to breathe a collective sigh of relief. Calls were made to all the victims to let them know the offender had been arrested and we spent the next couple of days laboriously trying to marry up items at his house to each individual burglary. It was the early hours of Christmas Eve by the time we had finished the task. I ceremoniously took the pins out of my map, rolled it up and put it away. Now I felt I could finally relax. As I was going crossed-eyed from all the paperwork, I asked Andy if he wanted to go on a final drive around the town before we went off duty.

As we drove from the station, a gentle blanket of snow had descended on the town as if in celebration. It might mean a dog poo minefield to some, but, to me, this was the start of the festive period. I hadn't really been able to get into the Christmas spirit with the concerns over a burglar loose on the streets of our town; none of the shift could. This wasn't just any town: this was our town. We had taken it personally that an outsider had tried to ruin Christmas for the inhabitants of Sandford. Now that our Grinch was under lock and key, I finally felt I was getting that festive feeling. Tomorrow was Christmas Day: a time for mince pies, hot mulled wine and chestnuts roasting on an open… FIRE!

Suddenly, as we drove along Florian Way, we could see the whole side of a house glowing bright orange in the darkness. The massive outbuilding that ran the entire length of the gable end of the property was ablaze, sending huge flames licking up the side of the house and licking at the

271

fascia boards on the roof. The inferno was roaring, spreading rapidly, reaching around the sides of the house, teasing at the windows and doors. Black smoke was already disappearing into the loft.

As we sprang out of our vehicle, Andy immediately got on the radio, requesting the fire service. As we ran towards the building, the fire spat at us as if it didn't want us interfering in its hellish business; the burning heat conspiring against us. I ran and began hammering at the front door, retreating as the flames leapt around the corner and then advancing again to boot the door to wake the sleeping occupants. The front garden had abandoned bikes on the lawn along with a football and goalposts: there were children in there. We had to get them out!

Andy tried the back door, but it was already starting to warp from the heat generated by the blaze. I continued to kick at the front door as Andy began dragging the wheelie bins away from the inferno. We didn't know what they contained and the last thing we needed was the fumes of melting plastic and exploding aerosol cans to fill the air. Retreating again, I grabbed a bin and pulled it away from the flames, the melting plastic burning my hands. We both then ran back to the front door and kicked again and again with all our might. Finally, the door came flying open, the frame splintering, to reveal a petrified house owner standing in his pyjamas.

He was still in a daze and it took him a few seconds before he realised we were the police and not violent intruders, or an angry Santa Claus.

"Who is in the house?" I demanded. There was no time for formalities.

"My wife, my kids…"

"Get them out NOW!" I didn't need to explain that the house was on fire as this was illustrated to dramatic effect when the flames curled around the door frame, sending him reeling back with shock.

I could feel the heat on the side of my face as I got back onto Comms asking for an update on the fire service. The first of the children came languidly down the stairs; it was three in the morning, and they were still half asleep. They slowly walked to the front door, only to be unceremoniously grabbed by Andy and me, and raced up the garden path and onto the pavement to safety; whilst we shouted at them to chivvy them along.

"Two adults, five children... is that it?" I asked as they all stood shivering at the roadway in their night attire.

"The dog and the cat," replied the wife.

We ran back into the property. Andy seized the cat and I hoisted the frightened dog out of the hallway and into the night. As soon as he was outside he bounded to his family, eager to be away from the human who was so roughly handling him. Just then, an explosion rang out as something in the outbuilding ignited. The terrified family stood watching the flames, their faces bathed in a curious mix of orange from the fire and blue strobes from the police car.

I could now see the lights in the distance as the fire engine made its quiet journey along Florian Way. I went to flag them down, but then felt a bit stupid with a burning inferno just behind me. I'm sure that was enough of a clue for them.

Soon the crew were unravelling their hoses and getting into action. Within half an hour they were damping down the last of the dying embers. It appeared that the outbuilding had been crammed full of firewood and coal, hence the reason why the fire had taken hold so quickly. They would have to send in their fire investigation team the next day, but their initial thoughts were that the fire had been deliberately set.

"If you had given it five more minutes, the whole house would have been ablaze," the family were informed by the leading fire fighter. "As soon as the flames got into the loft, the house would have gone up in no time."

"The smoke would have got them before that, though," he informed us. "Good job lads, looks like you saved their lives."

The parents looked nonplussed. Obviously, they were still in shock from having their door kicked-in in the middle of the night, being shaken from their slumber and violently dragged from their property. To be then told that they were minutes away from death; themselves and their five young children... Clearly, this was not something that you can process quickly when you are still half asleep – and in shock. One of the children, however, had been listening intently and was overly effusive in his praise for us:

"You saved us. You're our saviour."

I've never been described as a saviour before. I can't speak for Andy, but, to me, it held all sorts of religious connotations that I couldn't even begin to live up to. I've forgotten most of what I learnt in Religious Studies at school – I can't even remember which of the seven dwarves betrayed Jesus. I only did what any other police officer, or member of the public would have done in those circumstances.

That said, later that morning whilst out walking my dog, I found a dead rabbit on the path. I was going to move it into the hedge so Barney wouldn't begin playing with it, but, as soon as I picked it up, it kicked its hind legs and quickly scampered away. Maybe I am a saviour after all.

P.S. Saviour almost shit himself.